Amazing Facts
V
Trivia Treats

Thomas F. Shubnell, Ph.D.

ISBN 13- 978-1983972140

ISBN-10: 1983972142

Cover and interior design by TFS

Please ask your local library to carry my books.

We live in an interconnected world. Many are used to reading quickly, then going back and reading more background information later. I have included some links within the text of this book.

Links are easy enough to overlook while reading, but available for further in depth reading online. For eBook readers, the links are live for easy clicking.

Autohagiography

If you enjoy this, you will also love, Amazing Facts and Bite Sized Brain Food, Amazing Facts II Tons of Trivia, Amazing Facts III Trivia Treasures, and Amazing Facts IV Tantalizing Trivia. They are collections of thousands of amazing facts about the things you don't know, but want to know, and facts you think you know, but don't. Nestled in among the facts are bite sized tidbits of knowledge you can use to spice up any conversation.

"Bacon Orgazmia" a pandect of porcineology and a homage to the goodness and gallimaufry of all things bacon, including history, types, recipes, events, and more.

"Gracious Me . . . Is Nothing Sacred" is a non-sectarian and hilarious look at all religions from the beginning of time. From Atheism to Zen it truly proves that laughter is good for the soul.

Medical humor abounds in the best selling "Medical Humor - medical nonsense to tickle your funny bone. A great collection of medical funny stuff, including stories, jokes, and hilarious pictures and cartoons.

"Unelectum All" is a reader's digest of politics. It makes the case for change using politicians own words. It begins with early campaign promises and follows with political absurdities that unfold after elections.

A wacky book, "Men vs. Women, a Book of Lists" examines life from a different perspective and tells it all - the differences between the sexes are real and funny.

Even more fun can be found in "The Best of Terrible Tommy and Yucky Chucky," a collection of the best Terrible Tommy and Yucky Chucky jokes of all time.

More hilarious reading can be found in "Giggles, Gags, and Quips, Special Picks" a collection of the best jokes, pictures, billboards, stories, and cartoons.

Relationships can be funny, as shown in "Flowers, Foreplay, Facelifts, and Flatulence" a humorous romp through the four stages of relationships.

Also collect all the "Greatest Jokes of the Century" series of books. 25 wildly funny and hilarious compendiums of the greatest jokes, tidbits, stories, and trivia that are all sure to induce uncontrollable laughter.

"The Art of Installation and the Science of Implementation" is a serious project management primer, including tools and techniques for successful software implementation projects.

Don't forget to collect my Profound Thoughts, a five book series of great wisdom, aphorisms, and quotes from great minds.

All written by Thomas F. Shubnell and available online, your favorite bookstore, or as eBooks.

Table of Contents

Technology

INTERNET

The following Technology sections contain live links that can be used if you are reading an electronic version of this book. If you are reading a paper copy, enjoy the information and ignore the links. The information is interesting and informative on its own, whether you use it now or remember the next time you visit the web.

Internet Users - Here is a chart that shows the increasing number of internet users for the past few years.

Year	Internet Users**	Penetration (% of Pop)	World Population
2016*	3,424,971,237	46.1 %	7,432,663,275
2015*	3,185,996,155	43.4 %	7,349,472,099
2014	2,956,385,569	40.7 %	7,265,785,946
2013	2,728,428,107	38 %	7,181,715,139
2012	2,494,736,248	35.1 %	7,097,500,453
2011	2,231,957,359	31.8 %	7,013,427,052
2010	2,023,202,974	29.2 %	6,929,725,043

Internet and Web - The Associated Press announced that the next edition of its stylebook will endorse 'internet' over 'Internet' and 'web' over 'Web'.

The change is the latest in a long-running debate over whether 'the internet' is a proper noun, no different than a television or a hair roller. AP Standards Editor Thomas Kent said, "The changes reflect a growing trend toward lowercasing both words, which have become generic terms." *Hopefully the automated spell checkers will be updated by then.*

"

What is IoT - We see these letters more and more, but many folks do not know what they mean. They mean the "Internet of Things." The IoT is a network of objects connected to the internet that can collect and exchange data.

The new car loaded with apps, the smart home devices that let you control the thermostat and lights with voice commands, the fitness tracker that lets you share your exercise progress with friends and health data with your doctor are all part of IoT. Think about GPS-guided agricultural equipment that can plant, fertilize, and harvest crops.

Business Insider Intelligence estimates that there will be 24 billion IoT devices installed globally by 2020, along with an additional 10 billion PCs, and other devices. It is estimated that $6 trillion will be invested in IoT solutions during the next five years.

Browser Tip - Have you ever closed a tab in your browser and then wish you didn't?

Hold down Ctrl and Shift and hit the letter T, the tab will reappear. (This works in at least Chrome, IE, and Firefox.)

Dial-up Internet - According to a study from the Pew Foundation, only 3% of US households went online via a dial-up connection in 2013. Thirteen years before that, only 3% had broadband.

Phone and Internet Use - The International Telecommunication Union reports that Earth has as many phone subscriptions as people (7 billion), even if it does not translate to a phone for each person.

It also finds internet usage is not evenly distributed. Broadband networks are available to 84 percent of the world's population, but just 47 percent actually use the internet.

Hamburger Menu - The three horizontal lines icon on the upper right or left of browsers and on many apps is commonly called 'the hamburger menu'.

In Chrome on the upper-right corner, click on it and under "More Tools" is 'Extensions'. In Firefox it is called add-ons. Click either and you will see a list of all the extensions or add-ons you have installed.

At the bottom of the list is 'Get more'. Clicking that will take you to Google Play or Mozilla and show thousands of free extensions and add-ons you can install.

Internet Growing - The first website (info.cern.ch) was published on August 6, 1991 by British physicist Tim Berners-Lee while at CERN, in Switzerland. On April 30, 1993 CERN made World Wide Web technology available on a royalty-free basis to the public domain.

The number of Google indexed pages has grown from 1 trillion to 30 trillion during the last 7 years. The number of net additional pages indexed by Google each year is also increasing. There were 3 trillion additional pages added during 2010, 5 trillion during 2012, and 8 trillion during 2014.

There are now 3.74 billion Internet users in the world as of March 2017, compared to 3.26 billion Internet users during 2016. China has the most Internet users of all countries, over 731 million users. China currently accounts for more than 25 percent of Internet users worldwide.

> ### Scrolling Tip
> If you tap the space bar while on a web page you will scroll down, but if you hold down the shift key and hit the space bar you will scroll up.

Dark Web vs. Deep Web - Many people use the terms Dark Web and Deep Web interchangeably, but they are two very different things. Dark Web is basically just a part of the internet that is not completely public and you need special software to access. The Deep Web is designed for extra security and privacy that the regular Internet does not have. The Deep Web cannot be accessed by a search engine, and consists mostly of data stored on private networks of corporations.

The Dark Web is an encrypted network of darknets that makes up a portion of the Deep Web. Accessing this hidden section of the web requires a special encryption software called Tor. There is nothing wrong with the Dark Web, nor is it actually Dark. Originally it was designed with privacy, security, and anonymity in mind. It is not illegal, in fact, legitimate sites such as Facebook have sites on the Dark Web. Many people use it to browse the web without being tracked by an internet service provider or the government. There is a dark side to the Dark Web, including graphic content, evidence of kidnappings, hit-men for hire, prostitution, child pornography, drugs, guns, and more. Due to the anonymity the Dark Web provides, it is more difficult for law enforcement officials to track down and stop illegal activities.

The regular web, or Internet you use every day to search for your daily news, shop, Tweet, and watch viral animal videos can be just as bad. Many criminals and other predators hide in plain sight. Almost everything you can find on the Dark Web can also be found on the regular Internet. This includes drugs, solicitation, stolen data, terrorism groups, and various types of pornographic material.

> For most options, icons, hamburger menus, other menus, Start Button, or shortcuts in Windows, left click the mouse to take action, right click the mouse for information. If you are not sure, right click.

The Deep Web is estimated to be around 500 times larger than the regular Internet and the Dark Web is estimated at 7,000 to 30,000 sites hidden from everyday access. *Bottom line, the Dark Web is not so dark, the Internet is not so innocent, and the Deep Web is owned by corporations and governments.*

Catfishing, Ghosting, Phishing, and Spoofing - New threatening online practices are showing up almost monthly. As old threats are stopped, the bad guys dream up new ones. Below are a few current schemes by bad actors to gain personal information to steal from your bank account, abruptly end a relationship, or damage your reputation.

Catfishing is being used more and more often and refers to the act of luring someone into a perceived or real relationship via an online persona that does not actually exist. It occurs in many forms, such as individuals may steal others' photos and use them as their own, claim to have a job they do not actually have, or build an entire fictional personality from scratch in order to appear attractive to the person they are interested in.

Ghosting is a new term for breaking up with someone by completely cutting off contact with them, ignoring their attempts to get in touch, and not providing an explanation for why they ended the relationship. It is often used by people who meet online or by using social media apps. Ghosting is also used as a way to not take responsibility for a relationship and is confusing and hurtful to the person being ghosted.

Phishing is committing fraud by posing as a legitimate and often widely-known company or brand. People who are doing this, buying up domains that are closely related in spelling to a real domain, duplicating the actual brand's website, and capturing information for the purpose of identity or other theft. Some will take payments for products and services that do not exist, and others will infect computers with bots, spyware, and malware. Many internet service providers recommend antivirus programs that contain real-time phishing filters. These filters can block internet pages and websites that are characteristic of phishing.

Spoofing is the act of forging an email so that it appears the email came from someone other than the actual sender. This is common among crooks, who want to install programs that record and transmit keystrokes on victims' computers in hopes of obtaining bank account information and passwords. Most email service providers have become adept at flagging these attempts. Running and maintaining antivirus and anti-malware protection is crucial to staying safe while using the internet.

Piracy - Gizmodo recently reported, the European Union suppressed a 300-page study (2017 Situation Report on Counterfeiting and Privacy in the European Union). The study covered all manner of foods, drugs, goods, and services, from labels to products. Concerning digital piracy, it concluded that piracy did not harm sales of copyrighted material, including books, music, video games, and movies.

The sole area where illegal downloading was found to have a negative impact is with blockbuster films.

From a prosecution standpoint, one problem it found is no funds are generated when a digital game is downloaded. This shortcoming is often overcome by the sale of advertising space on illegal file-sharing sites and this process is facilitated by advertising intermediaries. This no funds process makes it difficult to follow a money stream.

Television and video broadcasts are digital and are available on a variety of platforms such as mobile phones, tablets, smart TVs, and set-top boxes. In recent years, the use of set-top boxes to access large numbers of television channels, films and other protected content has increased due to low prices, improving quality of services, reliability, and user friendliness.

In many cases the media itself is not copied or kept on servers, just the small code needed to play it. "The number of operators providing illegal IPTV (Internet Protocol TV) appears to be on the rise and this trend is expected to continue at an accelerated rate in the future... It is known that some European internet users continue to mistakenly take the fact that a digital content service is freely available online without the authorities having taken action as a sign that the service provides legal access to digital content."

The study concluded that the impact of piracy failed to provide stats which suggested a "...displacement of sales by online copyright infringements." Essentially, piracy does not harm legitimate sales. The report posited that illicit downloads may even bolster legal sales of games and neutral for books and music.

Google

New Endeavors - When starting something new, like a project or hobby, Google "things I wish I knew when starting x" and you will find tons of tips and tricks to keep you from making mistakes and help you get going quickly.

Google Games - Did you know you can play some games with Google? If you want to play Solitaire, search for "solitaire" on Google. You can search for "tic-tac-toe" and more.

To settle an argument, search for "flip a coin". To hear animal sounds, ask Google something like, "what sound does a cow make?" It will play the sound, and you can choose from a selection of other animals, including pig, horse, owl. zebra, dog, cat, and duck. *Caveat Emptor, it can be addicting.*

Google Search Tip - When searching for solutions to a problem, add the word 'solved' at the end and more practical results should show up high on the list.

Another Search Tip - If you are looking up someone's name, it helps to either type in the "at" sign, as in @tomshubnell or use quote marks, as in "tom shubnell". This narrows down your results, because with no qualifier, your search will yield everything that has either tom or shubnell in it. Either of these qualifiers force it to look for specifically those two names together.

Google Energy Use - In 2011, Google's data centers reportedly used 0.01% of the world's electricity, even though it uses low-power servers and high-efficiency data centers. Its networks use 900,000 servers across the world to power the search engine and other services. It uses artificial intelligence to monitor and make best use of electricity.

More Google Tips - Use an asterisk within quotes to specify unknown or variable words. Searching a phrase in quotes with an asterisk replacing a word will search all variations of that phrase. It is helpful if you cannot remember an entire phrase "imagine all the * living for today", or if you are trying to find all forms of an expression "* is thicker than water".

Compare foods using "vs." Type in "rice vs. quinoa," for example, and you will receive side-by-side comparisons of the nutritional facts.

Use "DEFINE:" to learn the meaning of words. Try "DEFINE: mortgage." For words that appear in the dictionary, you will be able to see etymology, a graph of its use over time, and the definition. It may also define slang words or acronyms.

Type "give me a love quote" or whatever topic you need a quote for.

Use "lyrics" in your search to have Google deliver lyrics of songs for you.

TECHNOLOGY

Buying Bulbs - We typically have been buying light bulbs based on how much energy they consume (Watts), regardless of light emitted (Lumens). All that began to change with the advent of different types of light bulbs, such as CFL, halogen, LED, etc., since they consume different amounts of energy to produce the same amount of light.

Lumens measure how much light you are getting from a bulb, regardless of type and regardless of energy consumed. This equalizes all bulbs and types for comparison. More lumens means brighter light.

Another measurement that is not well understood is Kelvin. It is a scale of measurement for the color a light produces. The higher the Kelvin (K) number, the cooler the light appears. Most bulbs will be in the 2,500K to 6,500K range, with 2,500 being the warmest and 6,500 the coolest. Kelvin is usually ignored except for specific lighting circumstances. The 2,700K to 3,000K range is warm and inviting, 3,500K casts a neutral light, 4,100K casts a cool and bright light, 5,500K to 6,500K range is closest to daylight.

To compare brightness of typical old style bulbs, here are a few examples:

- Replace a 100-watt incandescent bulb with a bulb that gives you about 1600 lumens,
- Replace a 75W bulb with a bulb that gives you about 1100 lumens,
- Replace a 60W bulb with a bulb that gives you about 800 lumens,
- Replace a 40W bulb with a bulb that gives you about 450 lumens.

Sixty watt bulbs used to be the standard as they offered the best compromise of minimum required light and cheaper cost. Now that energy cost has been so greatly reduced, 1100 lumen lights are becoming the standard minimum. Brighter lights make it easier to see and make everything look better, especially when trying to sell your house.

Chip Credit Cards - My ever curious friend, Jeff asked if I thought the new chip cards were more secure than the magnetic stripe cards, so I went hunting to find out the latest info.

More than three-quarters of a billion credit and debit cards are in use in the US. By the end of 2016, over 90 percent were converted to EMV (which stands for Europay, Mastercard, Visa) cards with a chip. The US is one of the last markets to go to EMV, on a short list with Papua New Guinea and Mongolia.

About half of all credit card fraud happens in the United States even though the country only makes up about 25% of all credit card transactions, according to a Barclays report. Financial institutions had been required to pay for credit and debit card fraud until Oct. 1, 2015. Now whoever has the oldest technology when the fraud occurs, the bank or the merchant, determines who covers the cost for the crime.

Current US chip cards are vulnerable, because they still employ the old magnetic stripes so that businesses that have not yet made the transition to EMV technology can still access users' credit data.

The new cards do not work quite the same way they do in Europe, but they are a step closer. The type of card being rolled out in the US still requires a signature when you pay. Eventually, what will be used in the US is what is used in the rest of the world, known as "chip and PIN." It would work similar to an ATM card now. You insert your card and enter a four-digit password to approve the transaction. Security experts believe this is much safer than card and signature to pay for things.

The biggest difference between the old card and new one is the metal 'smart' chip embedded on the front, making personal data much safer (once they eliminate the stripe on the back). The chip assigns a unique code for every transaction made on the card. Even if a thief acquired that code, it could not be used to make another purchase. Chip cards are also harder to duplicate although it is not unheard of.

These new EMV cards do not contain the older radio frequency (RFID) technology from a few years ago as some older ones did. No need to worry about covering with foil, etc., as they cannot be scanned within your wallet.

The new EMV chip cards were designed to help curtail credit card fraud. However, there are still vulnerabilities with these cards. *Nothing is perfect, so caveat emptor.*

Practical Artificial Intelligence - Researchers tout the potentials of artificial intelligence (AI) as a game changer in a range of industries, but AI appears to have application in the world of gambling as well.

You may not have thought about using artificial intelligence for your Kentucky Derby bets, but those who did, turned their $20 to $11,000. The artificial intelligence, which had earlier predicted the winners of the Super Bowl and the Oscars, made a prediction of the winners in a recent Kentucky Derby.

The odds for predicting the top four horses in the right order was 540 to one, but this was made possible with swarm intelligence, which amplifies, instead of replaces human intelligence. Swarm uses large groups as they are better at predicting the outcome of an event compared with any one person.

"Research shows that when animals in nature come together in swarms, they can enhance their intelligence to levels they could not have as individuals. UNU asked 20 people who claimed to be knowledgeable about the Kentucky Derby to winnow the horses to the top four and then had the human swarm choose the winning order. The group eventually guessed the winners of the game. Just as the swarm picked, Nyquist took the first place and was followed by Exaggerator, Gun Runner, and Mohaymen. It took about 20 minutes for the AI swarm to pick out the bets. Relying on the swarm's prediction, Unanimous made a $20 bet and won $10,800. Not one in the human group individually predicted the correct order of the horses.

A swarm tends to be more accurate compared with a poll, because a poll merely gives the most popular answer and not the answer the optimizes the group's preference.

Lithium-ion Batteries - The global market for lithium-ion batteries was $11.7 billion in 2012 and is expected to reach to reach $30.6 billion by 2024, according to Navigant Research.

Commercial energy storage system manufacturing is currently consolidated in just a handful of regions, but falling system costs will be a major factor enabling broader global market growth.

South Korea, Japan, and the United States account for 59% of global installations in 2016, with commercial deployments also expected to increase in other regions during the next five years, according to a report from IHS.

The average price for lithium-ion batteries fell 53% between 2012 and 2015, and by 2019 are forecast to again decline by half again.

World's Fastest Computer - The Sunway TaihuLight takes the top spot from previous record-holder Tianhe-2, also located in China, and more than triples the latter's speed. It is capable of performing 93 quadrillion calculations (petaflops) per second and is five times more powerful than the fastest US system, which is now ranked third worldwide. The TaihuLight is comprised of some 41,000 chips, each with 260 processor cores for a total of 10.65 million cores.

Robot Persons - Some lawmakers in Europe want to declare robots 'electronic persons' as part of an effort to anticipate a future legal framework and to be able to tax them as people.

PC Mouse Trick - If you use a mouse with a scroll button, press it toward the right when you are on a page that is too wide to fit on a screen. Now you can scroll left and right without using the scroll bar on the bottom of the screen. Left click and it turns off. Also, you can hold the shift key and use the scroll wheel. Works great with large pictures and articles that are too wide to fit on one screen.

TVs and Nits - Many new TVs come with a nit rating, such as the Samsung HDR (High Dynamic Range) TV, which has 1,000 nits. Computer LCD screens emit up to around 300 nits. The term nit is believed to come from the Latin word nitere, to shine.

A nit is defined as a unit of light intensity and one nit is equal to one candela per square meter. A candela is the amount of light produced by one candle. *Bottom line for TV watching, more nits equals brighter brights and darker blacks.*

X-rays - X-rays were discovered during 1895. The first use of X-rays under clinical conditions was by John Hall-Edwards in Birmingham, England on 11 January 1896.

Up until 2010, over five billion medical imaging studies have been conducted worldwide. Radiation exposure from medical imaging in

2006 made up about 50% of total ionizing radiation exposure in the United States.

The use of X-rays as a treatment is known as radiation therapy and is largely used for the management of cancer. It requires higher radiation doses than those received for imaging alone. X-rays

> X-rays both cause and kill cancer.

beams are used for treating skin cancers using lower energy X-ray beams while higher energy beams are used for treating cancers within the body such as brain, lung, prostate, and breast.

A Computed Tomography (CT scan) and computerized axial tomography (CAT scan) make use of computer-processed combinations of many X-ray images taken from different angles to produce cross-sectional (tomographic) images of specific areas of a scanned person or object, allowing a user to see inside without cutting.

Diagnostic X-rays, primarily from CT scans due to the large dose used increase the risk of developmental problems and cancer in those exposed. X-rays are classified as a carcinogen by both the World Health Organization's International Agency for Research on Cancer and the US government. The radiation doses received from CT scans are 100 to 1,000 times higher than conventional X-rays. Cancers in the United States caused by CT scans performed in the past have been estimated to be as high as two percent.

According to the National Council on Radiation Protection and Measurements, between the 1980s and 2006, the use of CT scans increased six hundred percent. A study by a New York hospital found that nearly a third of its patients who underwent multiple scans received the equivalent of five thousand chest X-rays.

Bottom line, if your doc or dentist cannot convince you that you really need the X-ray do not get it. Consider the X-ray factor of your future health vs. their wallet.

Smartphone Camera Hack - Have you ever been somewhere when you needed to scan a document, but no scanner was available. Use your phone camera to take a picture of the document. It is quick and easy. You can send the picture as a PDF file or as a JPG picture file to your home computer or directly to whomever you choose. It is also handy to use for snapping pictures of bills for itemizing expenses.

TV Types - High Dynamic Range (HDR) is now entering the market and traditional light emitting diode (LED) TVs are benefiting from the extra performance. If you watch movies with the lights off HDR is fine, but the best HDR-equipped full back lit LED TVs can also look good in a bright room.

Among LED TVs, there are two backlight types: Direct LED (full-array) where a large back-light shines through the whole screen, and edge-lit where lights emit from the edges.

Organic light emitting diode (OLED) TVs tend to shine, especially when the lights are off. This is because every pixel emits its own light. OLED is still the best, but if you want a TV above 65 inches you likely will be choosing an LED TV, unless you have a spare $30,000, which is the current cost of large OLED TVs.

Windows 10 Quick Tips - To quickly get at your settings menu, hold down the Windows key and touch the letter i.

Hold down the Windows key and touch the letter x to open a system context menu, where you can use the arrow keys to highlight any of the entries, then press enter to launch the activity without using your mouse or trackpad.

Another Windows 10 Quick Tip - If you have many windows open and want to focus on one in particular, while holding down the left mouse key, grab the title bar with your mouse pointer, then shake back and forth to minimize all other windows. If you want to bring the other windows back, just shake the first window again and all will be right back to normal. *Using the Alt and Tab keys together still works to switch windows.*

Microsoft Word Tip - Did you open up your Microsoft Word document after having worked on it all day and have trouble finding where you ended typing?

As soon as you open up your document, press SHIFT and F5. This will take you back to your last edit. In fact, if you press Shift-F5 repeatedly, it will take you through your last four edits. This feature disappeared briefly in version 2007, but is back in version 2010.

Super Storage - Computers are getting smaller and so is storage, but not data. Businesses are being forced to store huge amounts of data. A recent product is the 60TerraByte SAS solid state device from Seagate, the world's largest capacity solid state drive and it fits into a standard 3.5 inch standard hard disk drive slot.

Windows 10 Tip

If you cannot get into Windows, hold down Shift key when restarting, then go to Troubleshooting options.

The drive is aimed at data centers. It has twice the density and four times the storage of its nearest competitor. The capacity shows room for 400 million photos or 12,000 DVDs.

"Given the demands on today's data centers, optimal technologies are those that can accommodate an immense amount of data as needed - and without taking up too much space. As such, we are constantly seeking new ways to provide the highest density possible in our all-flash data center configurations," says Mike Vildibill, vice president of Advanced Technologies and Big Data at HP Enterprise.

Barometers and Smartphones - Weather predictions rely on sensors on the ground that report data, such as barometric pressure, which can help scientists determine when the weather is about to change. These sensors are also used to help local forecasters predict the weather.

During the last five years, the number of pressure sensors in the world has exploded, because Smartphone manufacturers have started putting them in Smartphones. The purpose is to help determine a device's altitude for location tracking. Samsung's Galaxy Smartphones have barometers built-in since 2011, and the feature came to Apple's iPhone during 2014.

Now, many of the almost three billion Smartphones in the world have one. Developers and weather forecasters have been talking about using Smartphone sensors for years, but the phone operating systems do not make available the pressure readings taken by their Smartphones.

Recently, a popular weather app called Dark Sky introduced an opt-in feature that automatically takes barometric pressure readings. It gets more than a million pressure sensor reports a day.

Dark Sky has several different ways to inform about important weather conditions in the exact spot you are standing with your phone. Precise down-to-the-minute notifications alerts when rain or snow is about to start. Severe weather alerts inform of dangerous conditions, and more. It even has detailed maps.

Another opt-in app, WeatherSignal, takes automatic readings and sends data to a number of academic partners for processing. Organizers are hoping for a commercial piece in the near future.

It may be time we begin to help the weathermen, rather than curse their ignorance.

Windows 10 Touchpad Tips - Windows 10 has some awesome new Touchpad gestures that should make navigating the OS much easier. There is pinch-to-zoom, two-finger scroll, three-finger multitasking, and more. *Gestures for zoom in and zoom out - squeeze fingers together or apart follows.*

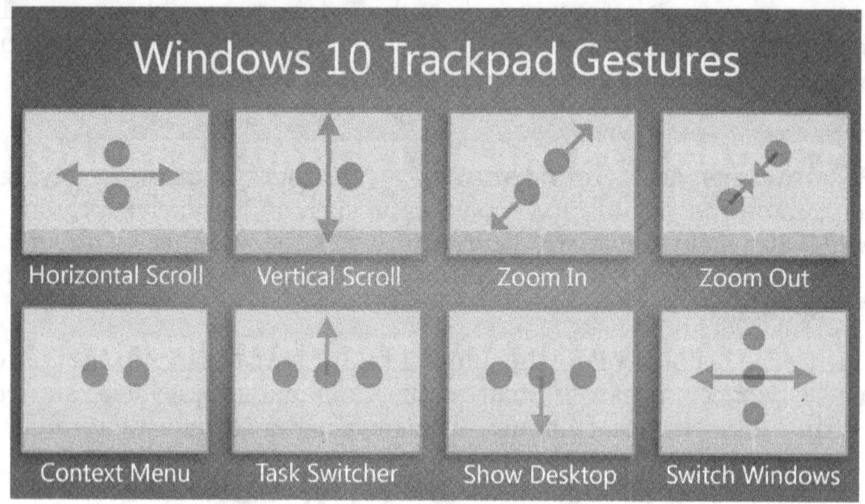

Some of these gestures are customizable as well, go to Settings > Devices > Mouse and Touchpad. You can change the actions of finger taps, adjust scrolling, right click, and more.

Robotics is Growing - An analysis of 752 of The Robot Report's global database of robotics-related startup companies shows that 25% of the startups were focused on industrial robotics and 75% address new areas of robotics such as: unmanned aerial, land, and underwater devices for filming, marketing, delivery, surveillance, security, surveying, and for the military, science, and oil and gas industries (25%); robotics for the agriculture industry (6%); mobile robots as platforms for various uses (7%); personal service bots (3%); professional service bots (7%); medical, surgical and rehabilitation robots (7%); consumer products such as for home cleaning, security, remote presence and entertainment (9%); educational and the hobby market (5%); etc.

Support businesses such as AI and software, engineering and design, component manufacturing, 3D printing, vision systems and integrators make up the remainder. More than half of the startups are predominantly software based and indicative of the new metric that the hardware component represent less than 1/3 of the overall cost of the product.

The industrial robotics sector, whose revenues have represented 75% of the industry's overall sales for the past few years, is forecast by various sources to have double-digit compounded annual growth for the remainder of this decade.

However, when one studies the figures for the biggest five user-countries, all except China are projecting CAGRs of 6% to 9% while China is expected to exceed 25%. Service robots are also expecting double-digit growth with over 80% of those new companies located in Europe and North America. This explosive growth shows that the next 5-10 years will all be double-digit years for the industry as a whole.

Incidentally, Oxford Martin School researchers estimate that robotics and artificial intelligence are on track to take over 40% of the US workforce within 15-20 years.

Apple iOS Failures Going Up - Apple lost its leading position in smartphone performance and reliability to Android during the second quarter of 2016.

iOS has been plagued by crashing apps, WiFi connectivity, and other performance issues. The iOS failure rate more than doubled to 58 percent, compared to a 25 percent failure rate in the previous quarter.

Robots are Coming - Many industries are feeling the influx of robots. Changes are coming faster than in the past. There were only 1,000 robot-assisted surgeries performed in 2000. By 2014, that number was 570,000.

Only 10% of worldwide manufacturing tasks are automated right now. That is expected to increase to 25% to 45% during the next 10 years as robots get much cheaper, smarter, faster, and easier to use.

Some companies, like China's Foxconn are investing in robots that can put together the tiny parts in Apple's iPhone.

Mail Hack - If you seem to be receiving more advertisements than you like, add an email filter. Use the filter to look for the word 'unsubscribe' then move that email to trash. Most ads have a spot on the bottom to unsubscribe, but it is a pain to keep going to the web pages to opt out. This little filter is easier.

Social Media Facts - A surge of new technologies and social media innovations is altering the media landscape and changing the way people behave.

Over one million books are published worldwide every year. A Google Book Search scanner can digitize 1,000 pages every hour. Americans have access to: 1,000,000,000,000 web pages, 10,500 radio stations, 5,500 magazines, and well over 200 cable TV networks.

There are 240,000,000 TVs in the US. More than 2,000,000 of them are in bathrooms.

Runpee - This phone app tells you the best time during a movie to go relieve yourself.

Newspaper circulation is down 7 million over the last twenty five years, but in the last five years, unique readers of online newspapers are up over 30 million.

Traditional advertising is in steep decline while digital advertising is growing rapidly. More video was uploaded to YouTube in the last 2 months than if ABC, NBC, CBS had been airing new content 24/7/365 since 1948 (when ABC started broadcasting).

The number of unique visitors Myspace, YouTube, and Facebook receive every month, collectively is over 250 million. Wikipedia launched in 2001 and now features over 43 million articles in more than 200 languages.

DoS and DDoS - These letters mean Denial of Service and Distributed Denial of Service. They are important, because not too long ago people were not happy trying to get into Amazon, Twitter, GitHub, Heroku, Paypal, Etsy, Spotify, Soundcloud, Reddit, Crunchbase, Netflix, BBC, CNN, The New York Times, HBO Now,

Elder Scrolls online, Yelp, Freshbooks, various Squarespace sites, Pinterest, Twilio, NHL.com, Quora, Business Insider, Zillow, Box, tableau, GrubHub, Overstock, Walgreens, Ruby Lane, Pixlr, PicMonkey, Ticketfly, and ironically, outageanalyzer - plus more.

DDoS originate when multiple compromised devices or systems are used to target a single computer system. Victims of a DDoS attack are both the end targeted system and all systems maliciously controlled by hackers in the distributed attack. The incoming traffic flooding the victim originates from potentially hundreds of thousands to many millions of devices, including PCs, cameras, DVRs, and many smart devices, such as thermostats, etc. The wave of outages moved from the East coast of the US to the West coast as the day progressed. It was reported that 145 thousand security cameras among other devices were part of the attackers causing the outages.

Incidentally, a way you can prevent your devices from being part of the problem is easily solved by changing the default password. Unfortunately many connected devices, such as thermostats, refrigerators, etc. do not provide a means to change the default password. Caveat Emptor.

Windows 10 Sign-in - Are you required to sign in to your computer each time you turn it on? Do you hate that? If you are not worried that someone will use your computer without your permission, there is a way to turn this 'feature' off.

Click Start > Settings > Accounts. On the left choose "Sign-in options." Up at the top, under "Require sign-in" set the drop-down box to say Never.

Now you can turn on your PC, go get a cup of coffee, and when you return it will be ready for you to use.

Picture-in-Picture Redo - Microsoft Windows 10 has a feature called Compact Overlay window. You can keep watching a movie or video chat on one corner of your screen, even when switching apps to check email or browse the web.

The compact overlay mode will be shown above other windows so it will not get blocked. Another way to be unproductive by watching and listening to YouTube videos or Skypeing while trying to get something accomplished.

Windows Ads - Have you noticed those annoying ads for Windows products while you look for files? They might just be small pop-ups for things like Office 365 subscriptions or Skype credits, but they annoy the heck out of me.

You can turn them off by following these steps:
Launch File Explorer and the click View > Options > Change folder and search options.
In the Folder Options dialog that pops up, select the View tab.
In the Advanced Settings box, scroll down and uncheck the option labeled "Show sync provider notifications." Hit OK.
Done, ads are gone.

There are also ads on the Start Screen. Some of these can be turned off by opening Windows 10 Settings app, go to Personalization, and click the Start tab. From there, switch off "Occasionally Show Suggestions in Start". *You are welcome.*

Snapping Windows - Windows 10 supports four window snap positions, one for each corner of your screen. You can use this feature to see two equal size windows at the same time. Useful if you want to compare things. If you have Windows snap activated (It is usually default on), snapping a window into one of these quadrants with keyboard shortcuts takes a double move: Windows key plus left/right arrow, followed by Windows key + up/down arrow.

To snap a window into the upper-left quadrant for example, press Windows key + left arrow and then, while continuing to hold down the Windows key, press the up arrow.

Windows no Longer King - The technology world passed a potentially huge marker during March, 2017 as Google developed Android, with 37.93% overtook Microsoft's Windows at 37.91% software in terms of worldwide users. Apple IOS is at 13%

Google's mobile software tops Windows after almost 30 years as number one. The news comes from online research company StatCounter, which continually monitors the number of users worldwide.

Windows still dominates the worldwide desktop market, at 84%. Android had just 2.4% of all internet usage five years ago.

Hacking Browsers - Google Chrome is the least hackable web browser, the results of the 10th annual Pwn2Own event shows. The computer hacking contest is held each year at the Vancouver, Canada CanSecWest security conference and sees contestants desperately try to exploit popular software and hardware with previously unknown vulnerabilities.

Those who manage to successfully find an exploit win a cash prize, a jacket emblazoned with the year of their win, and, the device they broke into. During the three days of Pwn2Own, Microsoft Edge was successfully attacked five times – racking up $300,000 in bounties. Safari was exploited three times, Firefox was attacked twice, but only once successfully. Google Chrome had no attacks completed in time.

Drive C - Early PCs did not come with internal storage devices due to the expense. Instead, they generally had some form of a floppy disk reader, such as those used to read 5 1/4" floppy disks, initially labeled as "A" in MS-DOS and certain other operating systems.

Some systems came with two such floppy disk drives necessitating the need for a "B". When the 3.5" floppy disk was commonly added, using both "A" and "B" for floppy drives was firmly entrenched.

Browser Tip
You can scroll down a web page by holding down the spacebar. By holding the shift key and pressing the spacebar you can scroll back up.

When hard disk drives became standard in most PCs during the 1980s, since the first two letters were already commonly used for these floppy drives, they logically labeled the third storage device "C", even though it now tended to be the main storage for the computer.

Even though no longer used, the drive designation remains, with A and B not used. Now you can easily change, remove or add drive letters for both physical and logical drives.

Clear Cookies, Cache - Does your web surfing seem to slow down? Are the pages loading a bit slower lately? Maybe it is time to clear the clutter. Every so often we need to remove the crap that browsers and web sites deposit onto our computers. There are programs, like 'CCleaner' to do this for your entire computer, but below is an easy and quick way to clean up just your browser.

Cookies and cache are supposed to help make web surfing and streaming experience better, but as they accumulate, they also bog things down. A quick way to freshen up your browser is by clearing the browsing data, such as cookies, cache, history, etc. If you save passwords, be careful to uncheck that box, or you will be doing a bunch of typing as you get back into those sites.

Here is how to clean up:
    Launch your Web browser (Firefox, Chrome, Edge, Internet Explorer, etc),
    Press Ctrl+Shift+Delete at the same time,
    Select the items you would like to clear (at least cache and cookies),
    Select the Delete or Clear button, depending on your browser type,
    Close and re-start your browser and try streaming again.

Facebook and Artificial Intelligence - Facebook is trying to use artificial intelligence to help prevent suicide. It recently introduced AI to be used a suicide-prevention feature to identify posts indicating suicidal or harmful thoughts. The AI scans posts and their associated comments, compares them to others that merited intervention, and, in some cases, passes them along to its community team for review.

Blockchain - Blockchain is the world's leading software platform for digital assets, offering the largest production block chain platform in the world. The first blockchain was conceptualized by Satoshi Nakamoto during 2008 and implemented the following year as a core component of the digital currency bitcoin, where it serves as the public ledger for all transactions. A blockchain database is managed autonomously and registered transactions cannot be altered retroactively.

Automated voting systems may prove to be the ultimate blockchain-based technology beyond bitcoin.

It is a distributed database that maintains a continuously growing list of ordered records called blocks. Each block contains a timestamp and a link to a previous block. By design, blockchains are inherently resistant to modification of the recorded data. Once recorded, the data in a block cannot be altered retroactively.

Blockchains are "an open, distributed ledger that can record transactions between two parties efficiently and in a verifiable and permanent way.

Blockchains are suitable for the recording of events, medical records, other records management activities, identity management, and transaction processing. Various regulatory bodies in the music industry have started testing models that use blockchain technology for royalty collection and management of copyrights around the world. Previously unimagined applications, from digitally recorded property assets to regulatory compliance and trading are now actively being developed and deployed.

Blockchain is a large electronic system, on top of which you can build applications. Currency, like bitcoin is one of those applications. Millions of users and hundreds of thousands of merchants currently use bitcoin digital currency. You can buy and sell bitcoins on PayPal and buy with your credit card or cash. Bitcoin is the decentralized, global, democratized, highly secure cryptocurrency. It use has grown immensely since it began and this global currency is completely separate from any government and its price is not subject to political manipulation. *Last time I looked, one bitcoin was worth over four thousand US dollars.*

Robot Growth - The International Federation of Robotics forecast that unit shipments for the global market for vacuum cleaning robots, lawn-mowing robots, and other household cleaning robots will grow at a compound annual growth rate (CAGR) of 33% through 2019.

Global medical robotics market is forecast to grow at a CAGR of 21.43% during 2016 - 2021.

Agricultural robots forecast to increase from 32,000 units in 2016 to 594,000 units annually in 2024 and that the market is expected to reach $74.1 billion in annual revenue by 2024.

The Internet of Robotic Things market is expected to be $21.44 billion by 2022, growing at a CAGR of 29.7% between 2016 and 2022.

Video watching - It is estimated that around ten billion videos are watched online annually. Of those ten billion videos, user created videos are most viewed, followed by news and movie trailers.

3d Printed Shoes - Adidas announced it is partnering with a 3D printing company to mass-produce a line of shoes with 3D printed mid-sole cushions. It plans to make 5,000 pairs by the end of the 2017, and up to 100,000 pairs during 2018. Adidas plans a single design to test the tech, but wants to eventually customize each shoe to fit the unique contours of a person's foot.

Incidentally, Nike, Under Armour, and New Balance also have their own 3D printed shoe projects.

International Space Station Facts - The International Space Station, if reduced to two dimensions is roughly the size of a soccer pitch, at about 73 meters (239 feet) in length and 109 meters (356 feet) in width. It orbits the Earth at an altitude of 330 to 435 km (205 to 270 miles).

Incidentally, In 2001, Pizza Hut paid the Russian space agency $1 million to send a pizza to the ISS, Including a Pizza Hut logo on a Soyuz rocket and a video of a cosmonaut Yuri Usachov giving a thumbs up after eating some of the pizza. The space pizza, per the BBC, "spending a long time in space has the effect of deadening the taste buds, so extra salt and spices were added to the pizza and salami had to be used as pepperoni lacked the necessary shelf life, growing moldy."

WiFi vs. Plugged In Speeds - Each Wi-Fi standard is rated according to its maximum theoretical network bandwidth. The newest, 802.11ac offers up to 1 Gbps (1,000 Mbps). However, the performance of Wi-Fi networks practically never approach these theoretical maximums, usually performing at about half of peak speed. If you compare 300 Mbps WiFi to wired Fast Ethernet at 100 Mbps, the Ethernet connection most often outperforms in real world usage.

> No matter how fast your WiFi is within your house, it does not increase the speed of the connection between your house and the Internet.

Wi-Fi networks have a range that is limited by the transmission power, antenna type, the location, physical obstacles, such as walls, number of other devices sharing the signal, and the environment. A typical indoor wireless router might have a solid range of about 32 meters (105 ft). Distance from the source also degrades performance. The fastest theoretical WiFi 802.11 ac is maximum speed of 866.7 Mb/s.

Plugged in (Ethernet) offers advantages, such as faster speeds, lower latency, and no wireless interference problems. A wired Ethernet connection can theoretically offer up to 10 Gb/s.

Bottom line, when it comes to speed necessary for streaming movies and TV WiFi may be more convenient, but is much slower and may cause delays and hesitations. Also, when looking at your speed, consider 15Mbs as the absolute minimum for streaming - and more is better.

Routers and Modems - Routers and modems perform different functions. Modems connect to the Internet and (MOdulate and DEModulate) the incoming signals and routers send/route wired (Ethernet) and wireless traffic around the house. Most home boxes contain both a modem and router and, because of this the terms are often used interchangeably.

Internet Speed - Here is a look as the average internet speed for selected countries. Interesting stuff.

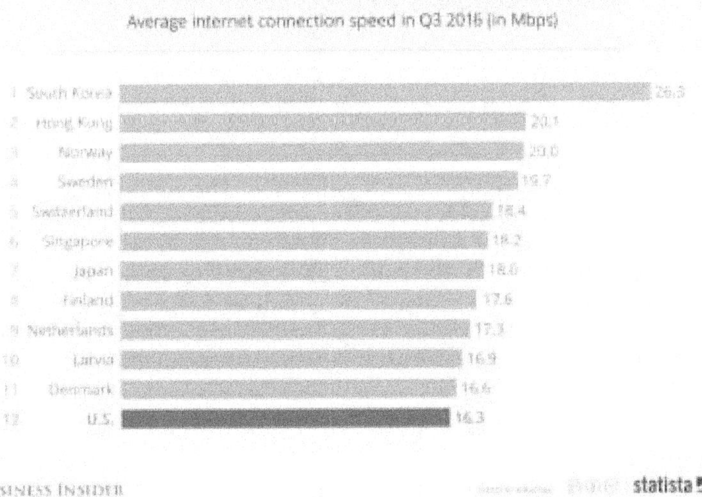

Night Vision - The first practical night vision devices were developed in Germany in the mid-1930s. Night vision goggles are usually green, because people can see more shades of green than other colors. Because the eye is most sensitive to light wavelengths nearer green, the display can be a little dimmer, which conserves battery power.

Photons that hit the lens at the front of night vision goggles are carrying light of all colors, but when they are converted to electrons, there is no way to preserve that information. Effectively, the incoming, colored light is turned into black and white. It is also easier to look at green screens for long periods than to look at black and white ones. That is also why early computer screens were mostly green.

YouTube Facts - During 2012, YouTube was watched 700 billion times, and 99% of the views were of only 30% of the videos.

During 2017 - Amount of content YouTube users watch annually:
46,000 years worth of content are watched annually,
One billion hours are watched per day,
400 hours of video are loaded each minute.

YouTube Tips - Here are a few YouTube keyboard shortcuts to increase your viewing pleasure.

K = pause or play
J = rewind 10 seconds
L = fast forward 10 seconds
M = turn off the sound
Number 0 = jump to the start of the video
Numbers 1 to 9 = jump to between 10% and 90% of the way through the video.

Find your favorite artist's page - type # + the artist's name (without spaces) in the search bar.

To use theater or full screen mode, click on the small rectangle or the open box next to it in the lower right corner of the video.

To change the speed of a video, click on the gear symbol in the lower right corner of any video.

Thomas Edison Phonograph - This was written during 1877 about his phonograph. The same might be said about social apps and smart phones today.

"He has been addicted to electricity for many years," the phonograph, with its ability to record speech, "will eventually destroy all confidence between man and man."

Another paper of the time outlined ways phonographic technology might go wrong: greedy thieves might trick elderly millionaires into vocally amending their wills; sketchy neighbors might use opera recordings to lure women out of their homes; and wives might frighten their husbands out of sleep by playing a tape that yells "POLICE! FIRE!" over and over again. *Editorial fear-mongering has not changed much during the past 140 years.*

What is DLNA - TVs and many devices usually include DLNA as one of the features. For most of us, it is unimportant and we do not even know what it means. Since it is a standard, manufacturers and stores do not use it as a selling point, because almost all devices have the feature.

DLNA stands for Digital Living Network Alliance, the trade group founded by Sony in 2003 to define interoperability guidelines.

It separates multimedia devices into 10 certified classes subdivided into three broad categories: Home Network Devices (PCs, TVs, AV receivers, game consoles), Mobile Handheld Devices (smartphones, tablets, digital cameras), and Home Infrastructure Devices (routers and hubs). All DLNA-certified devices use Universal Plug and Play (UPnP) to discover and talk to each other on the network.

Electronic Spam — Spam is shoulder pork and ham and is also unsolicited junk email. Eighty six percent of the world's email traffic is spam. According to Radicati Group from February 2017 estimates the number of email users worldwide was 3.7 billion, and the amount of emails sent per day during 2017 to be around 269 billion. About 49.7%% of these are spam and viruses.

One way to eliminate spam might be for all of us to reply to the spammer with a copy of the email. When they get a hundred billion messages back, they may just understand what we deal with every day. Oh, delete your signature line, but do not worry that they will get your email address. Obviously they already have it.

Netflix - Netflix can take up almost half of US bandwidth during peak hours. Sandvine reports that Netflix accounts for over 35% of web traffic in North America, followed by YouTube at 17.5%, and Amazon Video at 4.3%. On average, Netflix customers consume 125 million hours a day. On a big day, single-day viewership hours have approached 250 million hours. Netflix, during 2017 has 50 million US customers and over 104 million subscribers in 190 countries worldwide.

> Almost 79% of Americans check their phone for email and messages within 15 minutes of waking up.

3D Pancake Printer - Now I have seen it all. Amazon is selling "PancakeBot PNKB01BK 3D Food Printer." It is a 3D printer, with computer smarts that includes a grill and makes pancakes in any shape you can design. Oh, it costs $299. That is a bunch of dough to spend.

According to the description - There is a proprietary batter dispensing system to draw a perfect customized pancake every time. Software is included to trace any image on the computer. Non-stick electric griddle with removable probe is included and a BPA-free batter dispenser. Quick start Guide and Recipe Book are also included. *Disclaimer - I have no financial interest in this, nor do I have any interest in buying one. However, I do think it is a fun and innovative use of technology.*

Hoopla - Hoopla is a service that works with libraries to offer patrons an enormous selection of digital products, such as TV, Movies, Music, Comics, Ebooks, and Audio books for free and with no ads or commercials. You can download an app from Amazon, Apple, Google, etc. It has a free sign up, but you must also have a valid library card. Nice way to add to your entertainment without breaking the bank.

These days libraries have grown up and offer much more than dusty books. Last time I visited my local branch, I picked up a free prescription card that covers prescriptions not covered by insurance.

Saved over $30 vs. using my insurance on one script a few weeks ago. You do know where your local library is don't you? It is likely the place where you go vote.

Robot Flipper - A robot burger flipper 'Flippy' was installed at CaliBurger in California. Cali Group partnered with Miso Robotics to develop the burger robot. Flippy uses the latest machine learning software to locate and identify what is in front of it and learn from experience.

It has one arm with six axes to give it a wide range of motion and allow it to perform multiple functions. There is an assortment of detachable tools the bot can use to help it cook, including tongs, scrapers, and spatulas, and a pneumatic pump lets it swap one tool for another, rather than a human having to change it out. The plan is to install a Flippy in each of its 50 restaurants.

New Scam - Yesterday I received a "thank you for your purchase" email supposedly from Apple iTunes for $99. There was no credit card info and when I hovered on the link, it was for a bit.ly web site. Other things I hovered on were also not From Apple. *Bottom line, if there is no credit card info, delete the email after you mark it spam.*

Function Keys - Keyboard function keys really do have functions and some are quite handy. Function keys are usually on the top row and have an F followed by a number, such as F1, F2, etc.

The most universal is F1, press it and you get help for almost every program you happen to be using.

F3 is handy for doing searches. For instance, if you are on a long web page, just press F3 and a search bar appears on the bottom of your screen. (You can also open a search box by holding down the CTRL key and hitting the letter f.)

F6 is handy if you are using a browser. It jumps the cursor to the address bar so you can type a new address in it.

Obviously there are more, but some are used by specific programs, such as F7 while in Microsoft Word checks for spelling. Try them, you may be surprised at how much time you can save.

Wireless Charging - To fully understand how wireless charging works takes understanding the concept of an electromagnetic field and electromagnetic induction. Electromagnetic induction is an energy transfer system, meaning that it can be stored or used.

Think of a person making waves with a rope, the other person will receive the waves as they travel down the rope. This is like electromagnetic induction: a force sends energy from one point to another. The base unit (electricity powered) transmits energy to the smartphone via electromagnetic fields. The sensors on the smartphone recover the energy and channel it to the battery for storage.

Qi is the most popular wireless charging technology. It is not restricted to a particular manufacturer. Qi uses electromagnetic induction charging and magnetic resonance technology.

Light Me Up - We have all read the light fixture warning not to use anything higher than a 60-watt bulb, or 75, etc. The newer LED bulbs still fall under that fixture rating, however since the equivalent LED bulbs use much less wattage, you can choose a watt equivalency that is higher than that of the old bulbs. As an example, a 60 watt bulb equivalent is a 9 watt LED. They both put out 800 lumens.

You can replace an old 60 watt bulb with a 100-watt equivalent LED bulb (or higher), which is about 17 watts and therefore well under the safety limit of a 60-watt maximum fixture. You get lower energy bills and almost twice the light. One limiting factor might be bulb size, so be sure to check the physical size of new bulbs to make sure they fit the socket. *Every now and then I come up with a bright idea.*

TELEVISION

Olympic Camera 1936 - Nazi Olympics in Berlin in 1936 were the first to be televised. The six feet long zoom cameras were called "Fernsehkanonen" (television canon). Three of these cameras were used at that Olympics.

AVOD, SVOD, TVOD - These days there is much talk about 'cutting the cord', or eliminating the increasingly high cable TV costs. People are looking for decreased costs and instant gratification. The irony is, while people are installing ever larger TV screens in the home, many people are opting to choose their entertainment on miniscule phone screens and tablets. There are common terms for this instant gratification.

VOD is Video On Demand. Wherever there is a screen, in your pocket, in your car, etc., you can watch the latest episode of your favorite show or watch a movie.

AVOD is Advertising or Ad-based VOD. It is a model that is free of monthly or on demand cost, but you pay by letting yourself be subjected to commercials. Think YouTube as an example or commercial, non-cable TV.

SVOD is Subscription VOD, a type of service that requires a paid subscription agreement, which grants access to movies, shows, or other content. The fees are typically charged monthly.

TVOD is Transactional VOD. It is a service that is paid for as you watch. TVOD is typically free sign up, then pay for any content you watch. This is like an electronic version of the old Blockbuster model, watch a movie, pay a fee, watch another movie, pay another fee.

There are examples of services that operate with mixed models, where the customer will pay a monthly fee, which will grant access to certain types of content, but there are extra fees applied to watch particular pieces of content, such as a live sports event. Cable TV, Rabbittv, Selecttv, and VRV are mixed models.

The Internet, with its Over-The-Top (OTT), or Over-The-Air (OTA) watch anything, anywhere, anytime for free is disrupting most of the paid schemes and forcing cable operators to rethink their business models and outrageous fees.

AppleTV - If you have a 4th generation Apple TV box and want to reduce the loud sounds to equalize volume during some parts of shows, press the microphone on your Apple remote and say to Siri, "Reduce loud sounds." It will change the internal settings until you change it again.

4k UHD, HDR-10, Dolby Vision, OLED, Smart TV - Since the last time I wrote about TVs some new acronyms have popped up. If you are buying a TV for the future these are important, but if you are buying a TV for short term, (the next few years) almost all of these are not important. The reason they are not important is because few are broadcasting to take advantage of 4K and HDR, except some Amazon, Netflix, and Bluray DVDs.

Smart TV - These sets are good to have now and the majority of new TVs are smart TVs. They allow access to the internet from your home WiFi or Ethernet and provide access to Netflix, YouTube, Hulu, and more without the need for a separate box. Many Smart TVs give you a full web browser, so you can use a search engine or visit websites. Some let you play interactive online games.

Over 750,000 American households ditched pay TV during the first quarter of 2017.

4K UHD - these ultra-high-definition televisions offer four times the resolution of a standard 1080p HDTV. Instead of a screen that has about 2 million pixels, these televisions show about 8 million pixels. Some 4K TVs also have HDR and some do not.

HDR-10, Dolby Vision - I lump these two, High Dynamic Range 10 and Dolby together, because they are competing technologies, kind of like the old Betamax / VHS argument. Some manufactures are using one vs. the other and some have both. HDR-10 is currently winning, because it is open source while manufacturers must pay royalties to Dolby for its technology.

The first of the two major differences between Dolby Vision and HDR-10 is that Dolby Vision uses 12 bits per color (red, green, and blue), where HDR-10 uses 10 bits per color. The second, Dolby Vision uses dynamic, or continuous metadata so that color and brightness levels can be adjusted per scene, or even frame-by-frame basis. HDR-10 uses static metadata that is sent just once at the beginning of the video. Both reproduce a wider range of brightness levels, higher contrast ratio, and richer colors. Contrast ratio is the measurement of the difference in brightness between the whitest white and the darkest black. When seen side by side with non-HDR content, HDR-enhanced video is incredibly bright and with vibrant colors. Samples show a very positive marked difference.

> 4K counts number of pixels on the screen and HDR defines color and contrast.
> HDR is more noticeable than 4K.

Some TVs use *OLED* (Organic Light Emitting Diode) screens for a superior image and other benefits. Televisions packed with organic light-emitting diodes are incredibly thin, because each pixel is its own light source, so backlighting is not required. These televisions are more energy efficient than other TV panel types. Some LG TVs are as thin as four credit cards. *Quantum dot* TVs can match the contrast ratio of OLED. Quantum dots are microscopic dots about a fraction of the width of a human hair.

Bottom line, you can get 4K, UHD, HDR (HDR-10/Dolby), OLED on one TV. Every 4K is UHD by definition. Almost all TVs are LED, but very few are OLED or Quantum dot. Most newer TVs are now Smart TVs.

Incidentally, Dolby Vision is for pictures and Dolby Atmos is for sound.

TV No Tuner - For those of you who may wish to get an antenna and ditch cable, check the TV you have and the next one you buy. Some manufacturers have begun to eliminate the tuner in order to save costs.

A TV tuner is a device that converts digital over-the-air channels for viewing on compatible displays and TVs. If you get a TV without a tuner, you will need some kind of converter box, such as an HDTV Digital TV Converter box with HDMI output. You can also get a DVR that will convert an antenna output into HDMI cable. This way not only do you get OTA but a DVR to record your shows.

External TV tuners cost from fifteen US dollars up to multiple hundreds of dollars and can be as small as a USB stick up to the size of a cigar box. You can also buy a TV tuner card for a PC and turn it into a television.

HDMI Cable Facts - So, you bought a new 4k TV and the salesperson is trying to sell you new whizbang goochi goochi 4K, or Ultra HDMI, or HDMI-2 cables to handle the new high speeds. Do not listen. It is a scam to increase store profit.

It is important to understand that HDMI cables are pipes, just like water pipes. Liquid goes in liquid comes out. The pipe does not care whether it is water or soda or rum. In HDMI cables, data goes in and data comes out. No decisions are made, nothing is done to the data, it simply passes through the cable. The cable does not care what type of data it is.

A quote from HDMI.org: "Version 2.0 of the HDMI Specification does not define new cables or new connectors. Current High Speed cables (category 2 cables) are capable of carrying the increased bandwidth."

By definition, HDMI supports standard, enhanced, or high-definition video, plus multi-channel digital audio on a single cable. There have been two HDMI cable standards, standard and high speed. Standard HDMI cables have been out of date since about 2010, but still support devices up to 1080. High speed cables support everything, including 4K, etc. They do not care whether the signal is standard, HDR, 4K, ULTRA, HDMI1, or HDMI2. HDMI cables are marked on the package and on the cable, so just avoid cables marked "standard" and you will be fine for 4K.

Gold ends, fancy cord wrapping, etc., are pretty, but not important for delivering signals to the TV. Manufacturing quality may have some slight affect and might not last long if abused. Of course, when was the last time you abused your cables. You plug them in, hide them behind the TV and forget about them.

The difference in cable quality does matter when you buy longer lengths. Usually HDMI cables are less than about 9 feet in length. If you want to string a 50 foot HDMI cable to a different part of the house, then quality is important, so the signal is not lost along the length. It still has nothing to do HDR, 4K, etc., it is simply manufacturing quality and potential signal loss.

Incidentally, there is a new standard coming out toward the end of 2017 called HDBaseT. The HDBaseT cable combines audio and video signals, USB, network, and even power into one single cable and is set to replace HDMI in the long run. It will be in the next generation devices, but that will likely take years.

TV Watching - Nielsen's fourth-quarter Comparable Metrics Report says that adults spent 509 billion minutes viewing on TVs during the quarter and another 63.6 billion minutes viewing on TV-connected devices. Viewing video on PCs accounted for 31.7 billion minutes, smartphone video 10.9 billion, and 4.4 billion minutes on tablets.

TV Antenna Facts - If you decide to cut the cord and use an antenna to get local TV, you do not need to worry about a special 4K antenna, because there is no broadcast 4K content - and there may never be. Just as with cables, an antenna does not know and does not care what kind of signal it receives as long as it is within the designated frequency (channel) range.

Any digital antenna will work fine for digital TV, HD, and 4K. There is nothing that would make an antenna better or worse for digital, HD, or 4K. However, broadcasters are not required to put out a 4K signal and that means that they probably will not. Current 4K content comes from cable channels and other digital operators, such as Sling TV, DirectTV Now, HULU, etc. None of them require an antenna.

Amplified vs. non-amplified antenna - If you are running a very long length of coax cable or more than one TV, an amplifier might improve your TV reception. It should be placed at the end closest to the antenna, not at the end closest to the TV. For most situations, a non-amplified antenna is equal and sometimes better than an amplified antenna. An amplified antenna may overpower some signals and you actually lose channels, because they amplify noise as well as channel signals.

Bottom line, if you want a digital antenna, buy one, but do not give in to hype about being 4K ready or any other mumbo jumbo from the salesperson. Also, using an antenna will produce a noticeably better picture on your TV, because antennas do not compress the signal as cable companies do.

OTA vs. OTT - The often used abbreviations can be confusing. Think of OTA (Over The Air) as using a TV antenna, where the signal comes into your antenna, literally over the air from satellite or huge broadcast antenna at a TV or radio station vs. on a cable.

> OTA uses the air outside of your house to receive signals.
> OTT uses cables outside of your house to receive signals.
> They both use cables from the wall or antenna to devices inside the house.

Think of OTT (Over The Top) as directly accessing the internet via a physical cable (such as the one that goes into your modem/router.

WiFi also gets its input from that cable. It refers to audio, video, and other media transmitted via the Internet without cable or direct-broadcast satellite television systems controlling content. No TV tuner or receiver is necessary.

OTT devices which support streaming include Chromecast, Apple TV, Roku, and FireTV, etc. OTT services include video on demand services like YouTube, Netflix, Amazon, Hulu, Sky Go, BBC iPlayer, etc.

OTA vs. Cable - Satellite and cable TV companies have massive networks, carrying hundreds of channels to millions of customers. To effectively service these customers, they use digital compression technologies to shrink the size of the signal, allowing more channels to fit on the cable. When compressing the signal, some of the original data is lost. The result is the picture on your TV loses sharpness and detail.

We have been accustomed to cable and with no comparison, the picture we see is presumed to be the best that can be put out by our TV screen. Many channels are not even delivered in 1080p as we presume. They are still delivered as 720p. The only reason pictures look better is that the new flat screen TVs are adept at up-scaling the signal to make it look better (even though it is not as good as it could be).

OTA means Over The Air. It is difficult to compare the new TV antennas with the old rabbit ears, because the rabbit ears were analog and the new antennas are digital. Using an antenna to pick up a signal over the air provides an uncompressed signal directly to your TV. The results are significantly noticeable and better than cable. A few friends and I have recently added antennas and comparing the picture is as easy as clicking on the input to go from cable to OTA. In every case on each TV the resulting picture is remarkably better with an antenna.

Incidentally, if your cable package blacks out some sports, pick up an antenna, just for game day. They are cheap and can be easily hung on a wall or in a window with a pin or sticky tape. Also great if you want to watch TV out by the patio or pool, no extra wiring, just drag out your TV and attach an antenna.

Streaming vs. Casting - These terms are used when discussing getting information from devices to your TV. Streaming is video-delivery sent over the internet to your computer or smart TV. It also may refer to Internet Protocol television (IPTV) also called just Internet TV. It includes Live TV, time shifted replays of live TV, and video on demand, such as movies. IPTV is delivered over a closed, proprietary network, accessed via a specific internet service provider. It is different from OTT (see below), which is open and delivered by providers over the top of any internet service.

Casting refers to the delivery of audio, video, or other media types from a users mobile device or PC to a Television or connected TV device. For mobile devices, such as smartphones, mirroring means casting uses your bandwidth allocation and costs money each time you use it. Video uses an extremely high amount of bandwidth and if you do not have unlimited use, your monthly phone bill could be enormous. Mirroring takes the display from a sender devices and replicates that on a receiving device. Casting without mirroring means that after you cast the video to your TV, you can use the phone as normal, because it hands off the original signal to the TV.

Streaming Movies and TV - 2016 was the first year more movies were streamed than played on DVDs. Amazing, since DVDs were first invented in 1995 by Panasonic, Philips, Sony and Toshiba. Of course, other formats had been around for a number of years before that. Hmm, over the hill at the tender young age of 22.

The first basic cable network, launched via satellite in 1976, was Ted Turner's superstation WTCG. A May 2017 study from Fluent LLC asked internet users about their cable and TV habits. Across age groups, 67 percent of people reported using a video streaming service, such as Hulu, Netflix, or Amazon Prime video. Cable subscriptions, which peaked during 2000, was reported by 61 percent of responders.

Incidentally, during 2008, cable subscribers had 129 channels to choose from, and they watched an average of 17 channels in a given week. Five years later, they had 189 channels, and were still watching only 17.5. Their bills have doubled or more since 2000.

Theater 4K HDR TV - Wow, 4K HDR just grew up. The same TV technology that is in living rooms just began in theaters. Recently, Samsung introduced its immense 34 foot Cinema TV LED Screen, an alternative to projectors.

This cinema display TV features digital cinema 4K resolution and about twice the pixels than what you will find in a normal consumer 4K TV.

Typical projectors will lose color quality as brightness is increased, but the Cinema TV Screen maintains perfect color accuracy at peak brightness levels regardless of the ambient illumination, similar to those found in the QLED 4K TVs, which also achieve strong color volume at high brightness levels. The most remarkable aspect of Samsung's screen is its brightness that is ten times more than that offered by standard projector technologies. *Makes me want to raise the ceiling in the living room to fit a larger screen.*

4K vs. 8K TV - 4K, or 3840×2160, is about 2 million pixels and it contains almost four times the number of pixels on a screen compared with 1080P (current) technology.

As of September 2017 an 85 inch 8K TV costs $133,000 and is only available in Japan.

8K resolution is 7680×4320 pixels. It might look like 8K is about twice as good as 4K, but it is 16 times more dense than 4K. The numbers show 4K at 2 million pixels is compared to 8K at 33 million pixels. Today's TV technology is not yet capable of handling this kind of raw power.

Other comparisons show current HD is 24 frames per second, 4K ultra HD is 60 frames per second, while 8K super Hi Vision is 120 frames per second.

For human eyes to actually differentiate between 4K and 8K resolutions, 8K televisions need to be at least 70 and 80 inches in size. To truly enjoy 8K, the television sets need to be even larger than that. Panasonic has developed a plasma television that is 145 inches.

2020 Olympics will all be broadcast in 8K - Samsung, LG, Sony, and Panasonic have all announced plans to have 8K TVs ready for the 2020 Tokyo Olympics.

Demise of CRTs - CRTs were once synonymous with television. By 1960, nearly 90 percent of American households had one. By 2000, their popularity eroded as LCD panels emerged. Even though CRTs comprised an estimated 85 percent of US television sales during 2003, analysts were already predicting the technology's demise. During 2008, LCD panels outsold CRTs worldwide for the first time. Sony shut down its last manufacturing plants that same year. By 2014, even stronghold markets like India were fading, with local manufacturers switching to flat-panel displays.

Electronic CRT TVs flourished in the years after World War II, and for the rest of its lifespan, manufacturers looked for more uses. The most obvious advance was color television, which took off in the 1960s. Once standards were set, individual companies built loyalty with technological tweaks. Sony's Trinitron abandoned the perforated metal "shadow mask" that most color TVs used to keep their electron streams separate and used vertical wires that produced bright, clean colors and a flatter screen.

Toward the end of the CRT era, manufacturers began directly competing with the plasma and liquid-crystal displays that were threatening to overtake the market.

Sony's 40-inch Trinitron from 2002, one of the largest consumer CRTs ever produced, weighed over 300 pounds. A modern 40-inch Sony TV, the second-smallest option in its current lineup, weighs less than 20 pounds.

PHONES

Three Smartphone Photo Tips - Use a flashlight from a different phone to light your subject from an angle will result in a better image than relying on your smartphone camera's flash. You will achieve a more crisp picture.

You can optimize your smartphone camera's ability to focus and meter light by tapping on the screen before you shoot. Tap a dark spot in the shot to make the image brighter or tap a bright spot on the screen to darken it a bit.

Shoot in landscape mode and your photos will look better on the Web or your PC screen.

Self Destructing Phone - From noses to ears to phones. Researchers in Saudi Arabia have developed a mechanism that, when triggered, can destroy a Smartphone or other electronic device. The self-destruct mechanism consists of a polymer layer that rapidly expands when subjected to temperatures above 80 degrees Celsius, effectively bursting the phone open from the inside. The mechanism can be adapted to be triggered in various ways, including remotely through a Smartphone app or when it is subjected to pressure.

Once triggered, power from the device's battery is directed to electrodes that rapidly heat, causing the polymer layer to expand to about seven times its original size within 10-15 seconds. This crushes the vital components inside the device, destroying any stored information.

One engineer believes the phone will see adoption in the intelligence and financial communities first, though it can also be retrofitted to existing phones for about $15.

Phone Battery Grabbers - The component that uses the most energy on your smartphone is the screen. The more you use it, the faster your battery drains. Using the auto dimming feature helps use less battery. You can also shorten the delay time to turn screen off when you are finished using it.

Watching a streaming video movie requires your phone's screen to be on continuously, to maintain an active Internet connection, and the phone's processor and graphics processor also use juice to decode the video and audio.

Streaming music also uses more battery than music stored on the phone, due to network activity of streaming.

Using maps for long trips and your phone's screen is on, and the app forces the phone's GPS circuitry to refresh at a more frequent rate than in normal usage. It is also making heavier use of cellular and Wi-Fi connections in order to aid in pinpointing your location.

Pop up ads use much processor and waste battery use as much as twice as what it would if you used an ad blocker.

Push messages also use up the battery faster. Why not set the email to only check once every thirty minutes, or each hour, or never, and check mail when you want to, not when someone decides to interrupt you. Same with contacts updates and calendar changes. You can always switch back if you do not notice a noticeable increase in battery life.

Keep your phone relatively warm. Cold weather (below about 60F) is a major battery drainer for any battery, not just phone batteries.

If you do not need it, turn GPS and WiFi off until you need them. The constant pinging wastes a battery charge. If you are in a store or another place you do not wish to be disturbed, skip the vibrate mode and just turn on Airplane Mode. All your messages, mail, etc., will arrive when you turn Airplane Mode off.

If you have a battery saving mode on your phone, use it. You will not lose features, it will just keep the automatic pinging and background apps to a minimum.

You can check your settings to see which apps are gobbling most of your resources and turn them off or delete them if you do not need them. You can also turn off GPS or WiFi access for those apps that really do not need these features.

Last, if you are in an area of bad reception, your phone works overtime to find a signal. Use Airplane Mode until you move closer to populated areas. *Incidentally, if you notice your battery draining faster than normal and your usage or apps have not changed, might be time to buy a new battery.*

Robo Call Blockers - I hate robo calls. A very annoying thing about my phone is that when I block a robo caller, it still lets the caller go to voice mail. So I went looking for a solution. Two apps might help. Truecaller for iPhone and Android, and Nomorobo for VOIP home phones.

Nomoromo blocks known robo and spam callers and you can add your own numbers to block. Truecaller allows saved contacts and blocks spam callers and telemarketers. It also searches for any name or number not in your contacts, so you do not incorrectly block numbers from a school or doctor's office. Bottom line, seems a bit intrusive with checking your contact list, but blocks robos and spammers.

Block My Name - If you do not want someone to know you are calling them. Just type *67 or #31# before the ten-digit mobile number of the person you are calling. Some providers will provide a confirmation beep or tone after you dial *67, so wait for the regular dial tone to return before dialing the 10-digit number you wish to call. Some countries have different codes, such as 141 in the United Kingdom or 1831 in Australia.

Landline Call Blocking - AT&T, Verizon, and others have a feature for home landline phones that blocks 'Anonymous' and 'Private' callers. It will not block 'Unknown' or 'Out-of-Area' callers, so aunt Bertha's call will get through.

Pick up your phone and dial *77. This will activate the Anonymous Call Rejection feature on your landline. Anonymous and private numbers will not cause your phone to ring. When Anonymous Call Rejection is turned on, private callers will hear an automated message. The automated message will prompt them to hang up, unblock or "un-private" their number, and call again. If the caller makes their number visible and calls again, your phone will ring. If they remain private, your phone will never ring.

To turn off this feature, pick up your phone and dial *87.

There are also other options, such as dialing *60 for AT&T landline phones to block 10 local numbers, but the company charges a monthly fee for the privilege.

Wordology

WORDOLOGY

Adage, Axiom, Epigram, and Idiom - An *adage* is a traditional saying or proverb that states a piece of wisdom or a general truth. An adage is usually something that has been repeated for so long that it is a cliché, such as 'less is more'.

An *axiom* is a statement or principle that is accepted as being true, self-evidently true, or proven true by virtue of experience. An axiom can be the foundation for further study or knowledge. Axiom and adage are interchangeable and are usually sayings that have been repeated, often over many generations. Mathematicians make heavy use of axioms and maxims. An Aphorism can be a short Axiom.

An *epigram* is a short, witty, saying or remark expressed with brevity and sometimes paradoxically. An epigram is usually an original saying or remark, such as 'I can resist everything but temptation'. Many famous quotes are epigrams.

An *idiom* is a word or phrase whose meaning cannot be understood outside its cultural context. These expressions are usually figurative, such as 'cut to the chase', 'rule of thumb', etc. Idioms generally convey a casual tone and are known culturally, so other cultures may not understand the phrase or meaning. Many adages, axioms, and epigrams can also be considered idioms if not universally known.

Pronunciation Poem - The following is the beginning of a poem "The Chaos" The only way it makes sense is if you know how to correctly pronounce the words. If you can pronounce correctly every word in this poem, you will be speaking English better than 90% of the native English speakers in the world.

The poem was written during 1922 by Gerard Nolst Trenité.

Dearest creature in creation
Studying English pronunciation,
  I will teach you in my verse
  Sounds like corpse, corps, horse and worse.

I will keep you, Susy, busy,
Make your head with heat grow dizzy;
  Tear in eye, your dress you'll tear;
  Queer, fair seer, hear my prayer.

Pray, console your loving poet,
Make my coat look new, dear, sew it!
   Just compare heart, hear and heard,
   Dies and diet, lord and word.

Sword and sward, retain and Britain
(Mind the latter how it's written).
   Made has not the sound of bade,
   Say-said, pay-paid, laid but plaid.

Now I surely will not plague you
With such words as vague and ague,
   But be careful how you speak,
   Say: gush, bush, steak, streak, break, bleak,

Previous, precious, fuchsia, via
Recipe, pipe, studding-sail, choir;
   Woven, oven, how and low,
   Script, receipt, shoe, poem, toe.

> There are more libraries in Britain's prisons than there are in its schools.

Egg Someone On - This is one of those idioms where you think the etymology would be obvious, but this phrase has nothing to do with eggs.

The egg in this expression is a verb meaning "to goad" or "to incite" which is derived from the Old Germanic dialect word, eggia. The word is related to the Old English word, ecg, meaning "an edge." It is also related to the Middle Low German eggen, meaning "to harrow." Therefore, this may suggest that someone is "egged" on in fear of being prodded with something sharp, but this is only a vaguely implied connection.

The word came into English around the year 1200, originally in the sense of provoking or tempting a person. Today, the phrase means to encourage someone to do something, usually of a risky, foolish, or dangerous nature. In other words, people egg one another on to get a reaction.

Difference Between French Bread and Italian Bread - Both Italy and France are countries that specialize in bread making. Bread is essential to almost every meal in Italy and France. However, the two countries approach bread-making quite differently from one another.

When we think of French bread, the "the French stick" usually comes to mind. It is a long, thin crusty loaf that is typically referred to as a "baguette," which directly translates into "a stick." The Baguette may be the most popular type of bread in France. It is eaten throughout almost every province in the country. Other types of ordinary French white bread include the couronne, which is bread in the shape of a ring, or "country bread" (pain de campagne) that often incorporates whole wheat or rye flour in its ingredients.

In terms of Italian bread making, they allow the yeast to fully rise over the course of a few hours, resulting in a very thin-crusted loaf. The interior of Italian bread is typically extremely moist and absorbent to better to soak up olive oil and tomatoes. Types of Italian bread include ciabatta, made of wheat flour and yeast, piadina, made of flour, lard and slat, and panettone, a bread that is native to Milan.

Both countries make delicious loaves, but the similarities between Italian and French bread end the moment you compare the two side by side. The first way to distinguish Italian from French bread is to simply eyeball the two. To broadly generalize, while French bread is long with rounded edges, Italian bread comes in a more overall circular shape.

French bread is typically baked in a long, thin shape and has become the major food symbol of the country. The baguette can be baked as long as 30 inches and is a staple in almost every region.

Italian bread is known to be baked in more a flat and round shape. Italian loaves are also shorter and typically thicker than their French counterparts. Although it is possible to get baguette-type looking bread in an Italian bakery, on average, most Italian bread is shaped into larger rounds.

There are endless variations in size and shape for bread in each country, but there are indicators that will distinguish the two. In France, breads are usually given as a starter. French brioche, a sweet bread, is sometimes eaten in the morning with breakfast meals. The French also employ the baguette as a multipurpose bread, used for sandwiches and as the base for canapés. Italian breads are usually served as a supplement to pasta or other main courses. Italians eat bread to absorb the flavors of olive oils or thick sauces in a rich meal.

Both are made with the same ingredients in a similar fashion. However, one major difference in ingredients is that bread making in France is more tightly controlled than in Italy. By law in France, bread cannot have added oil or fat. French baguettes, for instance, must be made from water, flour, yeast, and salt. Italian bread often contains a little bit more milk, olive oil, and sometimes sugar in its contents.

Accumagate - When an individual, while under the influence of alcohol, stumbles over his or her words and accidentally invents a new one, he or she has accumagated, such as while trying to say 'communicate' you accidentally say 'accumagate'. *It goes with the next morning feeling crapulous.*

Bollard - A bollard was originally a wooden or metal post that was used to moor a ship. In the 20th century, a bollard became a post meant to obstruct cars and other traffic or to separate cars from people, cars from buildings, etc. Many places decorate them to give visual appeal.

In New York, bollards are most often found by fire hydrants. Wellington, New Zealand, has bollards with their tops curled into the spiral shape of plants. For decades, Amsterdam used bollards to distinguish people spaces from car spaces on streets without elevated sidewalks. In Mexico City some bollards are shaped like little pyramids.

Food Marketing Expense - Seventy percent of food manufacturers' marketing budgets goes to trade promotion fees, which is money paid to supermarkets to obtain better product placement and promotion. The other thirty percent is for advertising and product packaging.

Brand awareness only goes so far and packaging, a fine art, is used to entice us to buy, but ultimately we are swayed by what is in front of us.

Beauty really is in the eye of the beholder and we buy what we see first in the store.

Perfume, Cologne, Toilette, and Other Fragrances - Fragrances are complex mixtures of what people in the industry refer to as raw materials. These raw materials can be extracts from natural sources or synthetic raw materials.

Oils are dissolved in a solvent (usually alcohol), to preserve pleasant scents. The higher the concentration of oils, the greater the strength of the fragrance. The strength determines how long an application lasts on your skin.

All fragrances are largely the same, but they are given a name based on the concentration of oil in alcohol and water, such as:

> The shelf life of an average bottle of perfume is 3-5 years from the date of manufacture.

Eau Fraiche – The most diluted version of fragrance, usually with 1% – 3% perfume oil in alcohol and water. Usually lasts for less than an hour.

Cologne (Eau de Cologne) – Oldest term for perfume, used in North America for masculine scents. Light, fresh and fruity, typically composed of 2% – 4% perfume oils in alcohol and water. Usually lasts for about 2 hours.

Toilette (Eau de Toilette) – A light spray composition with 5% – 15% pure perfume essence dissolved in alcohol. Usually lasts for about 3 hours.

Perfume (Eau de Parfum) – Historically genderless, used to describe both men's and women's fragrances. The best term used to describe a fragrance. Contains 15% – 20% pure perfume essence and lasts for about 5 to 8 hours.

Perfume (Parfum)– A corruption of the Latin phrase per fumum (through smoke). The most concentrated and expensive of all fragrance options. Slightly oilier, perfume is composed of 20% – 30% pure perfume essence. A single application of perfume can last up to 24 hours.

Usually, the amount of concentrate a fragrance contains will affect its price.

Major brands create perfumes that are part science and part marketing. They have a familiar feel to all their perfumes. Ralph

Lauren perfumes are made to have a family of familiar scents, such as the newest Polo perfume should smell comfortable, even though it is not the same original scent.

More money does not necessarily mean better colognes or perfumes. Some of the most popular fragrances are relatively cheap. It is possible to mix expensive raw materials and create bad fragrances. Most often price is determined by the marketing cost and the image associated with a brand, but not necessarily the cost of raw materials comprising the scent. *Buy the scent, not the name.*

Pareidolia - Pronounced par-i-DOH-lee-a. This is a psychological phenomenon involving a stimulus (an image or a sound) wherein the mind perceives a familiar pattern of something where none actually exists. Things leap to mind, like the man in the moon, Jesus Chicken, and Michael Jackson in a pan.

Cannabis vs. Hemp vs. Marijuana - The two subspecies of cannabis are known as Cannabis indica (hemp) and Cannabis sativa (hemp and marijuana). A third type found mainly in Russia, Cannabis ruderalis has a lower THC content than either C. sativa or C. indica, so it is rarely grown for recreational use and the shorter stature of C. ruderalis limits its application for hemp production. Cannabis ruderalis strains are high in the cannabinoid cannabidiol, so they are grown by some medical marijuana users. (The term, marijuana originally spelled as "marihuana", "mariguana", etc., originated in Mexican Spanish.) Marijuana is now mostly an American term.

Tall, sturdy cannabis plants were grown by early civilizations to make a variety of foods, oils, and textiles. These plants were bred with other plants with the same characteristics, leading to the type of cannabis known as hemp. It is virtually impossible to get high on hemp, although it does have some medicinal benefits.

Other plants were recognized for being psychoactive and were bred selectively for medical and religious purposes. This led to unique varieties of cannabis.

The core agricultural differences between medical cannabis and hemp are largely in their genetic parentage and cultivation environment. Marijuana growers usually try to maintain stable light, temperature, humidity, CO_2, and oxygen levels, among other things. Hemp is usually grown outdoors to maximize its size and yield, and less attention is paid to individual plants.

Cannabis plants contain unique compounds called cannabinoids. Current research has revealed over 60 different cannabinoids so far, but THC is the most well known. THC is credited with causing the marijuana high. While marijuana plants contain high levels of THC, hemp contains very little.

Countries like Canada have set the maximum THC content of hemp at 0.3%. Any cannabis with higher THC levels is considered marijuana. Medical marijuana produces anywhere between 5-20% THC on average, with some strains up to 25-30% THC.

Before 1910 Bristol-Meyer's Squib and Eli Lilly included cannabis and cannabis extracts in their medicines to cure common household ailments. The US Bureau of Narcotics, during the 1930s, used the name "marijuana" when campaigning against the plant, and showing its new "foreign" identity. The Marihuana (sic) Tax Act of 1937 federally criminalized the cannabis plant in every US state.

All cannabis is federally illegal to produce in the United States. Both hemp and marijuana are classified as Schedule I drugs under the Controlled Substances Act (non-psychoactive hemp is not included in Schedule I). It is legal to import hemp products into the United States. The US Drug Enforcement Administration is considering whether cannabis should be reclassified under federal law.

In the US, 29 states allow people with certain medical conditions to use marijuana. Seventeen states have passed laws opening the door to marijuana use as long as the drug is extremely low in THC, the intoxicating ingredient. Five states have removed the potential for jail time for those caught with small amounts of the drug. Some states both have approved marijuana use by sick people and removed jail sentences for recreational users, including California, Connecticut, Delaware, Maine, Maryland, Massachusetts, Minnesota, Nevada and Rhode Island. Eight states and Washington, D.C., allow marijuana possession in small amounts by adults over 21 for any reason, including Alaska, Colorado, Oregon, Washington.

> Thomas Jefferson drafted both the Declaration of Independence and the U.S. Constitution on hemp paper.

Outside the US, hemp is grown in more than 30 countries. In 2011, the top hemp-producing country was China, followed by Chile and the European Union. Hemp production is also expanding in Canada.

Marijuana remains illegal in most countries, but a few, such as Israel and Canada, have recently started to regulate marijuana as a medicine. Legalization supporters consider possession either legal or tolerated in Argentina, Bangladesh, Cambodia, Canada, Chile, Colombia, the Czech Republic, India, Jamaica, Jordan, Mexico, Portugal, Spain, Uruguay, Germany, and the Netherlands.

Hemp can be made into wax, plastic, resin, rope, cloth paper, fuel, detergent, paint, snacks, flour, beer, insulation, carpeting, paneling, auto parts, and an estimated 25,000 products.

Salubrious - Some words just roll off the tongue and you can almost taste them. This word means promoting health.

My sincerest wishes for a salubriously beneficial and gratifyingly pleasurable period between dawn and sunset. *In other words, have a happy day.*

Twelve Words Turning 40 - Words that are forty years old during 2016 include:

BEER GUT
While beer belly had been around since 1942, beer gut arrived in 1976.

> Your lips do not touch when you say 'touch', but they do touch when you say 'apart'.

BOLLYWOOD
This blend of Bombay and Hollywood, used to refer to the Indian film industry, was first used in a 1976 Inspector Ghote mystery novel by H.R.F. Keating.

BOOMER
While we already had baby boom to describe the increase in births after World War II, and were already referring to the members of this generation as baby boomers by 1970, during 1976 the generational label was shortened to just boomers.

TREKKIE
The first citation we have for Trekkie, (an admirer of the U.S. science fiction television program Star Trek) comes from a 1976 New Yorker caption reading, "Of course, I didn't know George was a Trekkie when I married him."

CHICKEN NUGGET
The earliest citation for chicken nugget is from a 1976 ad in a Jackson, Missouri phone book for Troy's Fish House. "Catfish 'All You Can Eat.' Shrimp—Oysters—Steak. Chicken Nuggets—Burgers." It wasn't until the early '80s that the McDonald's Chicken McNugget was introduced.

HACKER
Hackers were calling themselves hackers before 1976, but the first print citation of hacker showed up that year and was defined by various publications around that period as a "compulsive programmer," a "home-computer nut," or "someone who spends much of his time writing computer programs."

EBOLA
The first Ebola outbreak occurred in a village near the Ebola River in the Democratic Republic of Congo in 1976, and the virus was identified and named after the river.

PMS
PMS was first used as an abbreviation for "the premenstrual syndrome," in a 1976 Lancet (medical journal) article

EXIT POLL

It was during the 1976 presidential election race between Jimmy Carter and Gerald Ford that the term 'exit poll' was used to describe a poll asking how individuals leaving a polling station had voted. It is used to predict the result of an election.

SUPER TUESDAY

The phrase Super Tuesday was first used to refer to the general election, but during the 1976 presidential race it was in reference to the primaries. From a New York Times article about how "New York would open up a string of victories on super-Tuesday, June 8, in California, Ohio and New Jersey."

MEME (pronounced meem)

Richard Dawkins introduced the word meme in his 1976 book The Selfish Gene: "We need a name for the new replicator, a noun which conveys the idea of a unit of cultural transmission, or a unit of imitation. Mimeme comes from a suitable Greek root, but I want a monosyllable that sounds a bit like gene. I hope my classicist friends will forgive me if I abbreviate mimeme to meme. Examples of memes are tunes, ideas, catch-phrases, clothes fashions, ways of making pots or of building arches."

ICONIC

Iconic is an old word for "pertaining to an icon or image," but it was 40 years ago that it first came to be used as a way to refer to a person or thing regarded as representative of a culture or movement; important or influential in a particular cultural context.

Turning a Blind Eye - Turning a blind eye is an idiom describing the ignoring of undesirable information.

The phrase to turn a blind eye is attributed to an incident in the life of Admiral Horatio Nelson. Nelson was blinded in one eye early in his Royal Navy career. During the Battle of Copenhagen in 1801 the cautious Admiral Sir Hyde Parker, in overall command of the British forces, sent a signal to Nelson's forces ordering them to discontinue the action.

Knots and Bends
A 'knot' is something tied in a single piece of rope or line.
Something that joins two ropes together is a 'bend'.

At the time, naval orders were transmitted via a system of signal flags at that time. When this order was given to the more aggressive

Nelson's attention, he lifted his telescope up to his blind eye, said, "I really do not see the signal," and most of his forces continued to press home the attack. The frigates supporting the line-of-battle ships did break off, in one case suffering severe losses in the retreat.

There is a misconception that the order was to be obeyed at Nelson's discretion, but this is contradicted by the fact that it was a general order to all the attacking ships, and later that day Nelson openly stated that he had 'fought contrary to orders'. Sir Hyde Parker was recalled in disgrace and Nelson appointed Commander-in-Chief of the fleet following the battle.

Winning Hands Down - In horse racing, a jockey who is winning by a wide margin does not need to whip his horse to go faster, and can win with his hands down. The phrase soon caught on outside the sporting world.

Words That are Their Own Opposite - English is so much fun. Here are some words that are difficult to define without context.
Apology: A statement of contrition for an action, or a defense of one.
Bill: A payment, or an invoice for payment.
Bolt: To secure, or to flee.
Bound: Heading to a destination, or restrained from movement.
Buckle: To connect, or to break or collapse.
Cleave: To adhere, or to separate.
Clip: To fasten, or detach.
Consult: To offer advice, or to obtain it.
Continue: To keep doing an action, or to suspend an action.
Custom: A common practice, or a special treatment.
Dike: A wall to prevent flooding, or a ditch.
Discursive: Moving in an orderly fashion among topics, or proceeding aimlessly in a discussion.
Dollop: A large amount (British English), or a small amount.
Dust: To add fine particles, or to remove them.
First degree: Most severe in the case of a murder charge, or least severe in reference to a burn.

Barding vs. Cauling - *Barding* is the wrapping of fat, such as bacon around meat to cover the meat in a layer of taste and texture.

Cauling is the act of wrapping caul around meat and is similar to barding.

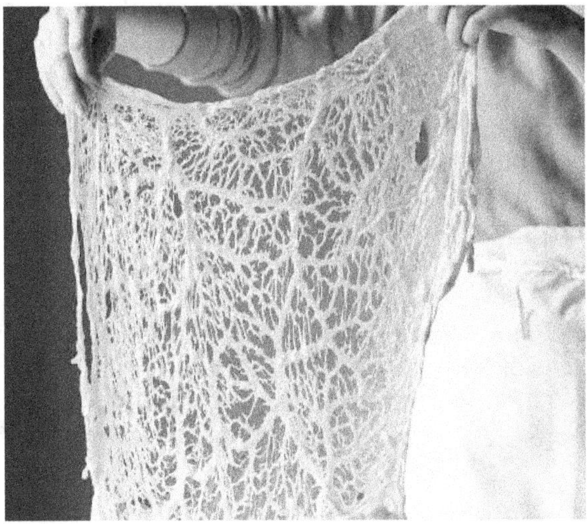

Picture of caul

Since caul is thin, as opposed to the thicker layer of fat used in barding, a cauled dish has a delicately rendered layer of fat that can accent a dish without overtaking it, as bacon might. It can be kept frozen for a long time and should be brought back to room temperature before it is used.

Tantalize - The word "tantalize" comes from the plight of the mythological Tantalus, son of Zeus who so offended the gods by stealing ambrosia that he was condemned in the afterlife to an eternity of hunger and thirst. He was made to stand in a pool in Tartarus, the Underworld zone of punishment. Each time he reached down for the water that beckoned to his parched lips, it drained away. Overhanging the pool were boughs laden with luscious fruit, but each time Tantalus stretched to pluck a juicy fruit, the boughs receded from his grasp.

Its meaning is to cause someone to feel interest or excitement about something that is very attractive, appealing, etc. It also means to tease or torment by presenting something desirable to the view, but continually keeping it out of reach.

Deja Vu, Jamais Vu, and Presque Vu - *Deja vu,* literally 'already seen' is having the strong sensation that an event or experience currently being experienced has already been experienced in the past.

Jamais vu, literally 'never seen' is experiencing a situation that one recognizes, but seems very unfamiliar, such as not remembering something you always see. It is most commonly experienced when a person momentarily does not recognize a word or, less commonly, a person or place, that he or she knows.

Presque vu, literally 'almost seen' is a failure to remember something, with the sense that recall is imminent. In English it is equivalent to 'tip of the tongue', failing to retrieve a word from memory, combined with partial recall and the feeling that retrieval is imminent.

Hazard and Risk - *Hazard* refers to potential for harm and *risk* refers to chances of being harmed under real-world conditions. Sharks are a hazard. They are fierce predators with sharp teeth, and have attacked humans in the past, but for most people, sharks are not a risk.

If you are swimming in a tank full of sharks, your risk is high. If you are mowing your lawn, your risk is low. The hazard does not change.

Whet One's Appetite - This means to arouse interest in something, usually food. The whet in 'whet one's appetite' refers to a sharpening, as in sharpening one's interest in something. Someone may whet your appetite by providing a small taste, an example or enticing description that makes you want more of the item in question or to know more about a subject. Whet one's appetite dates back to the early 1600s to describe stimulating an appetite for food. Whet is a verb, to sharpen, as on a whetstone, or to make more aware.

Bisect vs. Dissect - *Bisect* means to divide into two equal parts, to cut in two. Bisect comes from the prefix bi- which means two, and the Latin word sect, derived from the word secare which means to cut.

Dissect means to cut apart methodically in order to learn about the internal workings of something, especially a dead animal or plant. Dissect is also used figuratively to mean to analyze something piece by piece. Dissect comes from the prefix dis- which means apart and the Latin word sect, derived from the word secare which means to cut.

Screw This - Since at least 1725 screw has meant to copulate. Not having your head screwed on right has been an expression since at least 1821. The screwball as a pitch dates back to 1866. Since 1900 it has meant to cheat or defraud. Screw-up as a person began during 1933. "To screw up" dates from 1942. Finally the screwdriver cocktail traces its roots to 1956.

The six great simple machines are the screw, the inclined plane, the lever, the pulley, the wedge, and the wheel and axle.

Red Tape - The practice of referring to "excessive bureaucratic rigmarole" as red tape dates back more than 400 years to the court of the Holy Roman Emperor and King of Spain, Charles V, 1500-1558, heir to three of Europe's most powerful dynasties (Habsburg, Valois-Burgundy, and Trastámara).

At the time, administrative documents were bound in some fashion, either with rope, string, ribbon, or cloth. During the early 16th century, in order to distinguish the most important documents that required immediate discussion at the highest levels of government from those of less significance, Charles' ministers began tying important papers together with red string or red ribbon.

Seeing the efficacy of such a system, the method was soon adopted across Europe, and England's Henry VIII used red string, ribbon, or cloth to secure the petitions he sent to Pope Clement VII requesting annulment of his marriage to Catherine of Aragon in 1527.

The term 'red tape', in reference to this string for important papers dates back to the late 17th century where it was written in Maryland Laws: "The Map . . . upon the Backside thereof sealed with his Excellency's Seal at Arms on a Red Cross with Red Tape."

The Oxford English Dictionary dates its current meaning to 1736 and John Hervey's Poetical Epistle to the Queen: "Let Wilmington, with grave, contracted brow, Red tape and wisdom at the Council show."

Lock, Stock, and Barrel - This means everything, the whole thing. The term lock, stock, and barrel refers to the parts of a gun. There are three major parts of a gun, the lock or firing mechanism, the stock or wood handle, and the barrel which the bullet travels through. If one has a lock, stock, and barrel, then one has everything that makes up a gun. In time, the phrase came to be used figuratively to mean the whole thing.

Luthier - A luthier (loo ti ur) is someone who builds or repairs string instruments generally consisting of a neck and a sound box. The word "luthier" comes from the French word luth, which means lute. The term originally referred to makers of lutes and is now used interchangeably with any term that refers to makers of a specific, or specialty, type of stringed instrument, such as violin maker, guitar maker, or lute maker.

Antonio Stradivari was an Italian luthier who lived between 1644 and 1737. Throughout his life he made around 1,100 instruments, 650 of which are still around today. Out of these, about 500 are violins. Five out of 12 of the most expensive violins in the world today were made by him, and the most expensive one, called "The Messiah Stradivarius" is worth $20 million. How he was able to craft them so perfectly still baffles luthiers today.

Carousel vs. Merry-go-round - They are the same. In England and much of Europe, these rides usually go clockwise. In the US they move counterclockwise. To some Americans, a merry-go-round is a simple spinning playground fixture for children and a carousel is a more elaborate ride, with music, fancy horses, and other creatures.

They both can be a revolving circular platform fitted with seats, often in the form of animals, ridden for amusement, or a piece of playground equipment consisting of a small circular platform that revolves when pushed or pedaled.

Another definition of carousel is a tournament in which groups of knights took part in chariot races and other demonstrations of equestrian skills. Still one more is a continuously revolving belt, track or other device on which items are placed for later retrieval, such as a food or luggage carousel.

On Accident, By Accident - A survey by Indiana State University indicates that people born after 1990 almost always say 'on accident', and are not aware that 'by accident' is proper usage. Those born before 1970 almost always say 'by accident'.

Chorale, Choral, and Corral - A *chorale* is a slow, dignified hymn that employs harmony. In the United States, a chorale is also a choir or chorus of people. Chorale comes from the German word Choral which means metrical hymn in Reformed church.

Choral is the adjective form of chorale, meaning written for or sung by a chorale or group of singers.

A *corral* is a fenced enclosure used to hold livestock, especially horses or cattle. Corral is also used as a transitive verb, which is a verb that takes an object, to mean 'to contain livestock in a fenced enclosure or to round up'. Corral is an American word, based on the Spanish word corro which means ring.

Clementines, Mandarins, Tangerines, and Oranges - A *Mandarin* is a small, loose-skinned, orange-yellow to deep orange-red citrus fruit. While many refer to mandarins as oranges, they are technically tangerines.

A *Clementine* is a deep red-orange, often seedless mandarin orange.

A *Tangerine* is a widely cultivated variety of mandarin orange having deep red-orange fruit with easily separated segments. Tangerines have seeds. A tangerine is smaller, less round, sweeter, and contains less acid than an orange. They have virtually the same nutritional values. Tangerines are smaller than oranges and the peel comes off easily.

> All Clementines and Tangerines are Mandarins, but not all Mandarins are Clementines or Tangerines.

Oranges are larger, as well as more tart and sweet than tangerines. Orange zest is the orange layer on the outside and the rind is the white underneath.

A *Satsuma* is a seedless tangerine native to Japan and the hardiest commercial citrus fruit.

Clementines look like small oranges: they are actually a cross between navel oranges and mandarin oranges. They are a great source of vitamin C and provide a natural sweet, honey-like flavor. They have shiny tight skins and make a great display as a centerpiece. Clementines are often confused with Satsumas, which have a looser skin.

Navel oranges are the most common type of oranges for eating. These sweet oranges are baseball sized, seedless, and sweet. The thick skins make these oranges easy to peel.

Blood oranges have a deep red color of the flesh that distinguishes them. They are smaller than navel oranges and are very sweet.

Valencia oranges are the classic orange for juicing. They have a thin skin and seeds. Valencia oranges are delicious to eat as a fruit, but more difficult to peel than navel oranges.

Seville and other sour oranges make great marmalade. They can be used to add acid when cooking, for cocktails, and in salad dressing. You can replace lemon or lime juice in recipes with the juice of a Seville or sour orange.

Whale, Wail, and Wale - A *whale* is a large marine mammal, one of the larger cetacean mammals that has flippers, a streamlined body, and a blowhole. The word whale may also be used as an adjective to signify something outstanding or impressive, and used as a verb to mean to thrash soundly, to beat upon, or to go fishing for whales. The word whale is derived from the Old English word hwæl.

A *wail* is a high-pitched cry of grief, anger, or pain. Wail may be used as a noun or a verb. Wail is also used by American jazz musicians to mean 'play well', as in, he can sure wail on that sax. Wail comes from the Old Norse word væla, which means to lament.

A *wale* is the welt that raises up on the skin after a whipping. Wale may also be used to refer to a ridge of corduroy fabric or the weave of a fabric in general. Wale also refers to the horizontal band on a basket. Wale is derived from the Old English word walu, which means ridge of earth or stone, as well as stripe or weal.

Denote and Connote - The difference between denotation and connotation is easy to confuse, because they describe related concepts. Both denotation and connotation stem from the Latin word notāre, meaning 'to note'.

The *denotation* of a word or phrase is its explicit, direct meaning.

The *connotation* of a word or phrase is an associated, secondary meaning. It can be something suggested or implied by a word or thing, rather than being explicitly named or described.

For example, the words home and house have similar denotations or primary meanings: a home is "a shelter that is the usual residence of a person, family, or household," and a house is "a building in which people live." However, both of these words carry different secondary meanings, or connotations. A home connotes a sense of belonging and comfort and house conveys little more than a structure.

One way to remember the difference between the terms is to take a hint from the prefix: 'con' comes from Latin and means 'together; with'. The connotation of a word works together with its denotation or explicit meaning.

Picosecond - Computers are becoming faster than ever and scientists are working on devices that are a thousand times faster than current technology. A picosecond, one trillionth of a second, is about the time it would take for a beam of light, traveling at 186,000 miles per second, to pass through two pieces of paper.

Part and Parcel - Although not used in everyday discussions as it was in the past, this idiom is still used in the legal system. In this reduplicative phrase, common since the 14th century, the nouns 'part' and 'parcel' are synonyms. It comes from the ancient legal practice of including words of closely similar meaning to make sure that the sense covers all eventualities. The expression part and parcel was originally used in a sense that was frequently preceded by every, to mean all parts of something, even the smallest.

A parcel is part of a larger whole, such as parcel of land, parcel of weather, parcel of equipment, etc. Part is a division or portion of something and has the same meaning.

Recently it has come to imply the sense of something being a necessary part of some larger containing thing and the implication that this particular part may not be desirable, but cannot be avoided if you want the thing it is part of. For instance, we understand that some inconveniences are still part and parcel of modern travel. Other similar words include: nooks and crannies, aid and abet, etc.

Incidentally, the Southern US variation, passel comes from the old pronunciation of parcel and is often preceded by whole, suggesting a large group of people or things, such as a passel of problems, or passel of experts.

SMAC - This new acronym (initialism) comes from the technology industry and we will be hearing it more often. The future is all about SMAC: social, mobile, analytics, and cloud.

Recto and Obverse - The front side of a page in a book is the recto page and the front side of a coin is the obverse.

The back side of a page in a book is the verso page and the back side of a coin is the reverse.

Dictionary Update - The venerable Oxford English Dictionary has added some new words for us to remember. The dictionary is updated every three months, and a recent update marks the centenary of the birth of children's book author Roald Dahl. It has added vocabulary described by another newly added word, 'Dahlesque'.

'*Splendiferous*', as we have read in Roald Dahl children's books means full of or abounding in splendor.

'*Yogalates*', a fitness routine combining yoga techniques with pilates exercises.

'*Moobs*', the scourge of older men, is finally defined as unusually prominent breasts on a man, or a contraction of man boobs.

'*Gender-fluid*' may sound like leaking, due to too much drinking, however, it really means a person with a fluid or unfixed gender mental identity, which can change from day to day.

'*YOLO*' is an acronym for You Only Live Once. *Sorry, Shirley MacLaine.*

Broker vs. Realtor vs. Real Estate Agent - A *real estate agent* is a real estate professional who has taken and passed all required real estate classes and passed the real estate licensing exam in the state in which he or she intends to work. It is the most encompassing of the titles, since it is the starting point for most real estate professionals. Agents are also referred to as real estate associates.

A *realtor* is a real estate agent who is a member of the National Association of Realtors. To become a member, a real estate agent has to agree to abide by the association's standards and uphold the code of ethics.

A *real estate broker* has continued his or her education past the real estate agent level and passed the real estate broker license. Real estate brokers can work as independent real estate agents or have other agents working for them.

The biggest distinction between the three is that a broker can work on his or her own, while an agent or associate has to work under a licensed broker. A hybrid position, referred to as a real estate associate broker, is an agent who is working toward achieving a broker's license. Associate brokers have to work under a licensed broker, but may share in the brokerage profits above and beyond the usual agent commission.

ASMR - This is becoming an advertisers dream way to soft sell. YouTube is littered with hundreds of thousands of ASMR videos. Bob Ross, the late painter is, to some, the epitome of ASMR as his soft spoken, almost whispering way of describing brush strokes and the feeling evoked by his art. It is both auditory and visually stimulating in an almost sensuous manner.

Autonomous Sensory Meridian Response is described as a "euphoric experience characterized by a static-like or tingling sensation on the skin that typically begins on the scalp and moves down the back of the neck and upper spine, precipitating relaxation." It comes from hearing soft voices and sensual sounds, such as tapping objects with fingernails. Think of it as the opposite of scratching nails on a chalkboard.

Too much ASMR can have the opposite effect for me, but a bit is a welcome change from the in-your-face 'buy me in the next ten minutes or else'.

I do not usually like ads, but here is one with George Hamilton doing a soft spoken, almost whisper as Colonel Sanders for KFC. The ad is pure ASMR and uses pocket squares as the tag, with him eating chicken tossed in between. You might also like to see the queen of ASMR and her GentleWhispering channel. Search YouTube for ASMR.

Androids, Robots, and Cyborgs - These words are often used interchangeably, but actually, there are differences. One common assumption is that a robot can, but does not necessarily need to be in the form of a human, but an android always has the form of a human. Neither are required to have, although more recently many do have artificial intelligence built in.

Androids and robots are both electromechanical devices and can be controlled by remote control or internal software. Physical characteristics are not part of the robot definition.

Authors have used the term android in more diverse ways than robot or cyborg. In some fictional works, the difference between a robot and

A fembot is a humanoid robot that is gendered feminine. It is also known as a gynoid.

android is only its appearance, with androids being made to look like humans on the outside, but with robot internal mechanics. Wikipedia says, an android is a robot or synthetic organism designed to look and act like a human. The term 'android' appears in US patents as early as 1863 in reference to miniature human-like toy automatons.

A *cyborg* is a human, animal, etc., with one or more electronic parts, such as artificial hands, eyes, or other parts, usually to extend or enhance its capabilities. It may also referred to as bionic, a portmanteau from biology and electronics. In its strictest definition, a person with a pacemaker can be termed to be a cyborg.

Origin of Android, Cyborg, and Robot - The word robot was coined by artist Josef Čapek. His brother introduced the word in a play called R.U.R. The full title translating into English as Rossum's Universal Robots, debuted in January of 1921. Josef suggested 'roboti', which gave rise to the English 'robot'. 'Roboti' derives from the Old Church Slavanic 'rabota', meaning 'servitude', which in turn comes from 'rabu', meaning 'slave'.

The first documented mention of the word 'android' is in the 18th century Ephraim Chambers' Cyclopaedia. Android derives from the Greek (andro-), meaning 'man', and the suffix (-eides), meaning "form, likeness, appearance, or resemblance". The definition of android being "automaton resembling a human being.

During 1960, Manfred Clynes coined the word "cyborg" to describe an emerging hybrid of man's machines and man himself. The word itself combined cybernetics, the then-emerging discipline of feedback, control, and organism.

Strand - The name of the famous street near the River Thames in London comes from the German word 'Strand', which means beach in modern German, but also once referred to river banks.

That is also why, if you are left on a desert island beach helpless and alone, you would be described as 'stranded'.

Common Pronunciations - Here is a quick list to help you correctly pronounce common words that are not obvious from the spelling.

FOODS
açaí: ah-sigh-EE
bánh mì: bahn MEE
bouillon: BOOL-yen or BOOL-yon (with a very light l sound)
bruschetta: broo-SKEH-tah
endive: EN-dive or AHN-deev
gyro: YEE-roh
kefir: kuh-FEER
phở: fuh
quinoa: KEEN-wah

FOOD BRANDS
Fage: FAH-yay
Hoegaarden: HOO-gar-duhn
Laphroaig: la-FROYG
Moët & Chandon: Mwett eh SHA(n)-doh
Stolichnaya: stoh-LEECH-nye-a

FASHION DESIGNERS
Bulgari: BUHL-guh-ree
Givenchy: zhee-VON-she
Hermès: AIR-mehz
Ralph Lauren: LOR-uhn [not lor-EN]
Louboutin: loo-boo-TAH(n), with a soft n
Yves Saint Laurent: eev sahn LOR-uhn
Louis Vuitton: LOO-ee VWEE-tah(n), with a soft n

LOCATIONS
Budapest: boo-da-PESHT
Colombia: co-LOHM-bee-ya
Qatar: kuh-tahr
Uranus: YOOR-uh-nuss (updated pronunciation)

Honing vs. Sharpening - When most people at home use a honing steel or butcher's steel, or that long metal rod that comes in the center of a knife block, to sharpen their knives, what they are really doing is honing them.

The difference is that a honing steel straightens out the blade of a knife, making the edge straight, free of burrs, and ready to use. As you use a knife, the tip of the blade will eventually bend and curl so you do not get a real blade-on cut at the very tip. The best you can really do at home is to hone your knives regularly to keep the cutting edge straight. For most at-home cooks, this makes the knives feel sharper. To sharpen a blade, you need a knife sharpener, or stone.

Exercise vs. Exorcise - Sometimes it is difficult to distinguish between the pronunciation of these two words and content of the rest of a sentence is key to understanding. We exercise to stay fit, but we also exercise to get rid of fat and we exercise to develop skills. We exorcise demons to get rid of them.

Many people have a fear of public speaking, but we can both exercise (develop skills), and exorcise, to get rid of public speaking demons.

GMT and UTC - Greenwich Mean Time (GMT) is often confused with Coordinated Universal Time (UTC). GMT and UTC share the same current time in practice, but there is a basic difference between the two.

> GMT is a
> time zone
> and
> UTC is a
> time standard.

GMT is a time zone officially used in some European, African, and other countries. The time can be displayed using both the 24-hour format (0 - 24) or the 12-hour format (1 - 12 am/pm).

UTC is not a time zone, but a time standard that is the basis for civil time and time zones worldwide. This means that no country or territory officially uses UTC as a local time.

Neither UTC nor GMT ever change for Daylight Saving Time. However, some of the countries that use GMT switch to different time zones during their Daylight Saving Time periods. For example, the United Kingdom is not on GMT all year, it uses British Summer Time (BST), which is one hour ahead of GMT, during the summer months. *Seems to me all Daylight Saving Time should adopt the British acronym and call it for what it is - BST, for Bull S... Time.*

Delicatessen - Most of us are familiar with the word Deli, which conjures up sliced sausage and cheese piled high on rolls and ordered at the counter. The term also brings to mind baguettes and camembert, or olives and prosciutto. The term deli comes from delicatessen shops, which came from the German 'Delikatesse'.

The shops called delicatessens were first opened in New York and London by German proprietors, such as Lingner's Delicatessen on London's Old Compton Road in Soho, recorded in 1877.

The German word has its roots in Latin "delicatus" and the French word "délicatesse". The French term for a fine foods shop is "une épicerie fine".

Nickel - The name for this metal began during 18th century by Swedish mineralogist Axel von Cronstedt from the Swedish 'kopparnickel', which was taken from the German 'Kupfernickel'.

Copper miners named this different metal ore Kupfernickel, which literally translates as copper-devil. The German word Nickel, related to the name Nicholas, an antiquated term for a mythological spirit that haunts houses, caves, and mines. They used this term because they were often fooled into thinking that nickel ore was copper.

During the second half of the 19th century, people began to refer to small coins as nickels, because they were made of nickel rather than copper. Today a US nickel is 75% copper and 25% nickel.

Dietitian vs. Nutritionist - Now that the holidays are over and you made your New Year resolution to drop some post-holiday weight, think about this. A *dietitian* is an expert in prescribing therapeutic nutrition. A dietitian is accredited by the Academy of Nutrition and Dietetics (formerly the American Dietetic Association). A Registered Dietitian Nutritionist has completed an undergraduate program in nutrition and also a one year clinical internship program. Registered Dietitian Nutritionists must pass a national exam administered by the Academy of Nutrition and Dietetics and maintain their registered status through continuing education.

A *nutritionist* is a non-accredited title that may apply to somebody who has done a short course in nutrition or who has given themselves this title. The term nutritionist is not protected by law in almost all countries so people with different levels of knowledge can call themselves a nutritionist. A nutritionist can also be someone who completes an undergraduate or graduate degree in nutrition. Some individuals market themselves as nutritionists with little or no training in nutrition. Before you take nutrition advice, be sure to check out the professional background and training of the individual giving it.

Incidentally, 'Dietitian' spelling is preferred over 'Dietician' in the dietetics world, and the term Registered Dietitian has been updated to Registered Dietitian Nutritionist, further confusing the distinction.

Things and Stuff - George Carlin had a great bit about Stuff. He talked about his stuff, your stuff, and everybody's stuff. He talked about stuff, but he neglected to mention things.

We distinguish between these two classes of existence. We can count things, but stuff forms a sort of cumulative mass. Things are made of stuff (cars are made of steel), but stuff is made of things (gold is made of molecules).

Chairs, dogs, balloons, and flowers are things. If I have one dog and add another, I have two dogs. My chair did not exist until it was assembled into that form. If a balloon pops, it is no longer a balloon.

Helium, gravy, wood, and music are stuff. If some helium escapes my balloon, it seems wrong to say that I lost a thing. If I divide my gravy into two portions, it is still gravy. If I chop my cabin into firewood, the amount of wood in the world has not changed.

Linguistically, we distinguish between thing terms and stuff terms, where a thing is a count noun, and stuff is a mass noun. Syntactically, thing functions as a term that refers to a single "entity" and hence takes "a" and "every" and is subject to pluralization, while stuff functions refers to a plurality of "entities" and hence takes some and is not subject to pluralization. *Bottom line, we have some things and some stuff.*

Vicious Circle - Election campaigns have sometimes been referred to as a vicious circle. The term vicious circle or vicious cycle refers to a complex chain of events which reinforce themselves through a feedback loop. A chain of events in which the response to one difficulty creates a new problem that aggravates the original difficulty.

During the feedback loop each iteration of the cycle reinforces the previous one. These cycles will continue in the direction of their momentum until an external factor intervenes and breaks the cycle.

Incidentally, A <u>virtuous</u> circle has favorable results, while a <u>vicious</u> circle has detrimental results.

Nasothek - A collection of noses is a Nasothek.

Classical statues tend to lose their noses, and during the 19th century museums would commonly replace them with "restoration" noses, to preserve the appearance of the original sculpture.

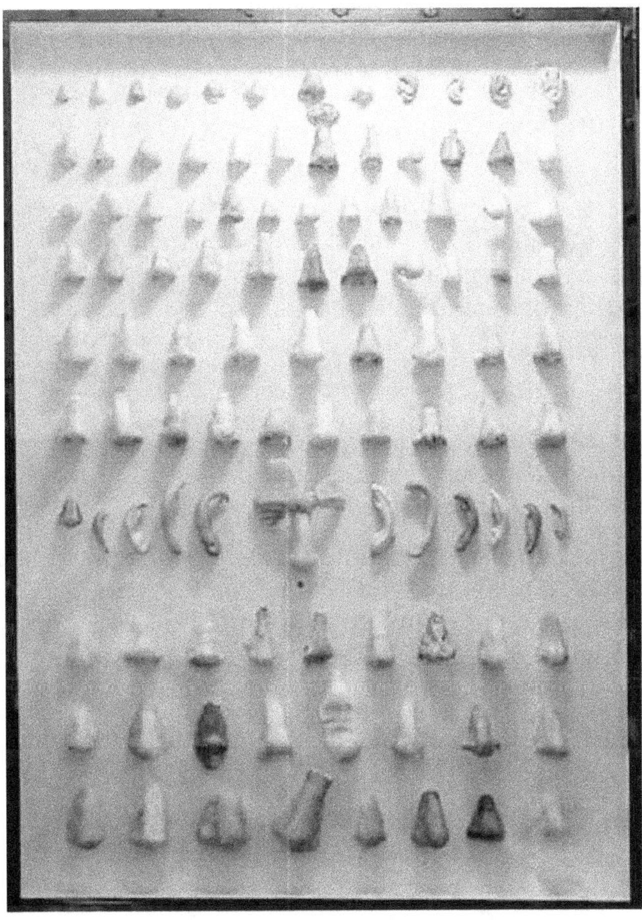

During the 20th century some museums changed philosophies and "de-restored" their collections, thinking it better to present each piece in its authentic state. This created a excess of noses, and some museums collect these into displays of their own. *I make no claims about which one might resemble mine.*

Incidentally, Gutzon Borglum, who also sculpted Mount Rushmore, sculpted the Capitol bust of Abraham Lincoln - with just one ear. He believed that the dualities of Lincoln's personality (hard as rock, soft as velvet) were reflected in the opposite sides of his face, with the right strong and masculine, the left soft and feminine. Borglum said of Lincoln's face, "You see half-smile, half-sadness; half anger, half-

forgiveness; half-determination, half-pause; a mixture of expression that drew accurately the middle course he would follow." If you look at the left side, you do not see an ear. Borglum explained that he purposely omitted the ear because he wished attention to be drawn to the stronger right side of the face.

Roughshod - We see this word in the expression "to run/ride roughshod" over somebody or something, meaning to tyrannize or treat harshly.

It came about as a way to describe the 17th century version of snow tires. A "rough-shod" horse had its shoes attached with protruding nail heads in order to get a better grip on slippery roads. It was great for keeping the horse on its feet, but not so great for anyone the horse might step on.

Artisanal, Bespoke, and Handcrafted - These words have increasing play on social media and are often used interchangeably, but there are subtle differences.

Artisanal is an adjective, pertaining to a person skilled in an applied art. Men were taught artisanal skills such as clothes-making and carpentry, etc. Also, pertaining to a high-quality or distinctive product made in small quantities, usually by hand or using traditional methods.

Bespoke is another adjective relating to goods, especially clothing made to order, such as a bespoke suit.

Handcrafted is a past participle verb meaning to make skillfully by hand, such as a handcrafted rocking chair.

Newts and Salamanders - Newt and salamander are often used interchangeably, but there are subtle distinctions between the two. Newts are a type of salamander, belonging to a subfamily called Pleurodelinae of the family Salamandridae. Both are able to regenerate nearly all parts of the body, such as limbs, tail, eyes, intestines, heart, and spinal cord.

Newts have three metamorphoses throughout their life, an aquatic larva, a terrestrial juvenile stage called an eft, and an adult stage. As adults, newts live a semi-aquatic to aquatic life. Most newts have webbed feet and a paddle-like tail, which make it easier to live in the water. Newts usually have rougher skin than salamanders. During the breeding season, they develop a flat tail.

Adult *salamanders* live a mostly terrestrial life except when breeding and laying eggs. A salamander is pregnant for only a few days. Salamanders typically have longer and more rounded tails with well-developed toes for digging in soil. Salamanders have smooth, wet skin like a frog. There are over 600 different species of salamanders.

> All newts are salamanders, but not all salamanders are newts, just like a toad is a frog, but all frogs are not toads.

Resilience - A new non-dictionary political term for Climate Change. To be resilient now means to encompass all previous climate change strategies: to resist, to mitigate, and to adapt. Its use in climate research and US academic papers has multiplied over time.

The 2015 US PREPARE Act, a bill to help the federal government recover from extreme weather events, does not mention climate change or global warming, but it uses the term 'resilience' 40 times. The word has also begun to show up in individual state plans to 'mitigate flooding' rather than to 'deal with sea level rise affects of climate change'. - *A rose by any other name. . .*

Noisome - (noy some) It comes from Middle English noysome, from noy- shortened annoyance, alteration of anoi, from Anglo-French anui, from anuier to harass, annoy. Noisome sounds like it might be a synonym of noisy, but it is not. Something noisome is disgusting, offensive, or harmful, often in its smell. Also highly obnoxious or objectionable as noisome habits. English words annoy and annoyance are also related to noisome.

Portmanteau - [pawrt-man-toh] It would be a terrible shame if portmanteau were not itself a portmanteau. The word originally referred to a large traveling case made of stiff leather, derived from a combination of the French porter, meaning "to carry," and manteau, meaning "mantle" or "cloak." From Lewis Carroll in 'Through the Looking-Glass', Humpty Dumpty explains to Alice that the strange compound words she hears in Wonderland are "like a portmanteau-- there are two meanings packed up into one word."

MacGuffin - A MacGuffin is an object, event, or person that the characters in a story value greatly. Almost the whole plot revolves around it, even though the thing itself isn't actually important to the unfolding story. The most common type of MacGuffin is a person, place, or thing, such as money or an object of value.

Think of the falcon in the Maltese Falcon movie. The black falcon statuette, called the "Maltese Falcon" is the MacGuffin in the movie and the plot revolves around ownership and finding it. The Rabbit's Foot in Mission: Impossible III is a modern MacGuffin.

Scenario editor Angus MacPhail established the term MacGuffin for the unknown plot objective which you did not need to choose until the story planning was complete. Some say it comes from the word guff, which is defined as meaning nonsense and MacPhail added Mac from his name to the front of it. Alfred Hitchcock adopted and used the word to the end of his career.

Graffiti - Both "graffiti" and its occasional singular form "graffito" are from the Italian word graffiato 'scratched'. The term graffiti originally referred to the inscriptions, figure drawings, etc., found on the walls of ancient sepulchers or ruins, such as the Catacombs of Rome. Use of the word has evolved to include any graphics applied to surfaces in a manner that usually constitutes vandalism.

Graffiti are writing or drawings that have been scribbled, scratched, or painted, mostly illicitly on a wall or other surface, often within public view. Graffiti range from simple written words to elaborate wall paintings, and have existed since ancient times, with examples dating back to Ancient Egypt, Ancient Greece, and the Roman Empire.

> Both "graffiti" and its occasional singular form "graffito" are from the Italian word graffiato ("scratched").

Cornicione - The outer edge of pizza is called the cornicione, pronounced - "cor-nee-cho-nay," which means cornice or molding. The crust is the name for the base that the toppings are added to.

Donnybrook - A donnybrook is a free-for-all or brawl and is usually a public quarrel or dispute. Usage of the word stems from history of a place in Ireland. The word donnybrook comes from Domhnach Broc, meaning 'The Church of Saint Broc'. A donnybrook is larger than a fight, but smaller than a brouhaha or hubbub.

The Donnybrook Fair was an annual eight to fourteen day event held in Donnybrook, Ireland from the 1200s to the mid 1800s. The fair was legendary for the vast quantities of liquor consumed, the number of hasty marriages performed during the week following it, and for the frequent brawls that erupted throughout it. From the 1790s on there were campaigns against the drunken brawl the fair had become. The event was abolished in 1855, but not before its name had become a generic term for a free-for-all.

Incidentally, there is an annual Donnybrook Fair held in Walsh, Ontario, Canada named after the Dublin fair.

Origin of Golf Terms - The website ScottishGolfHistory.org cites a golf glossary published in 1857 that included the word fore. Historians at the British Golf Museum have surmised that the term 'fore', as a warning in golf, evolved from forecaddie. A forecaddie is a person who accompanies a grouping of golfers around the golf course, going forward on each hole to be in a position to pinpoint the locations of the group members' shots.

Mary Queen of Scots was likely the first woman to play golf. It was during her reign that the famous golf course at St. Andrews was built, in 1552. Mary coined the term caddie by calling her assistants cadets. Of course, le cadet is French for youngster of the family. Some argue French military 'cadets' carried clubs for golfing royalty and this practice came to Scotland when Queen Mary Stuart returned in 1561.

One of the most common misconceptions is that the word GOLF is an acronym for Gentlemen Only Ladies Forbidden. The first documented mention of the word 'golf' is in Edinburgh on 6th March 1457, when King James II banned 'ye golf', in an attempt to encourage archery practice, which was being neglected. During 1460, Sir Gilbert Hay translated an old French poem into the Scottish language. It uses the word 'golf' twice. "Therefore I am sending you a ball to play with and a 'golf staff' to hit it with, as children do round the streets."

Incidentally, according to Grammarist the most correct spelling is caddie (an attendant who carries the golf clubs for a player), not caddy (a can for storing tea). Although the word caddy is currently loosely accepted for caddie.

Pounds and Ounces - These words must seem weird to those who follow the metric system, so a bit of history might help explain. The Latin word Libra is abbreviated to 'lb'. Libra is widely known as the astrological sign for balance, but it was also part of the Roman unit of weight, libra pond, which translates to "pound weight." Britain derived pound from that expression as its unit of measurement and also as a term for its currency, because centuries ago a pound in money was considered equal to the value of a pound of silver.

Ounces - The Spanish ounce (Onza) was 1/16 of a pound. It is a unit of mass used in most British systems of measurement. It is most pervasive in the retail sale of groceries in the United States, but is also used in many other matters of domestic and international trade between imperial or customary measurement driven countries.

Muselet - It comes from the French: myz.le. It derives its name from the French museler, to muzzle and is a wire cage that fits over the cork of a bottle just below the annulus, of champagne, sparkling wine, or beer to prevent the cork from emerging under the pressure of the carbonated contents. The muselet often has a metal cap (plaque) incorporated in the design which may show the drink maker's emblem.

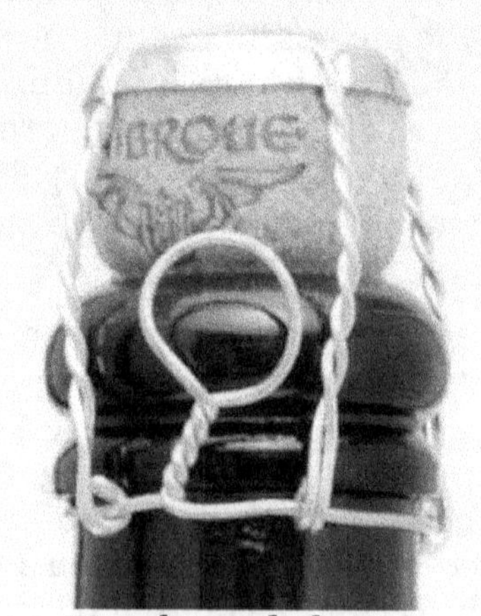

Muselet and plaque

Muselets are also known as wirehoods or Champagne wires. Another term sometimes used is agrafe. In Champagne, this was a large metal clip used to secure the cork before capsules were invented, typically during the second fermentation and aging in bottle. A bottle secured with this clip is said to be agrafé. Some French refer to muselet as an agrafe (French for staple), a cork, and a disk. Corks have been used as stoppers since about 1718.

Agrafe

When opening a bottle of champagne you need to remove the muselet that sits on top of the cork. It is loosened by removing the foil and turning the wire counter-clockwise. It takes exactly six turns, or three 360 degree turns to remove the muselet.

It is unclear on who invented the muselet, but is clear that Dom Perignon and Adolphe Jacqueson made important contributions. Dom Perignon is believed to have made important improvements to the production process of champagne. Including a wire caging on the cork. At that time many bottles were lost during production because the cork or the bottle was unable to withstand the pressure of the Champagne. Dom Perignon's invention made it better. During 1844 Adolphe Jacqueson made the muselet in the shape and form we know today.

Collecting the caps of Champagne and other sparkling wine is called Placomusophilia. The small, dome-shaped, often colorfully decorated metal cap that protects the outer end of the cork are called 'plaque' or 'plaque de muselet'.

Achaplinarse - This is a Chilean word meaning to run about in the style of Charlie Chaplin. In Spanish it means to hesitate, turn back, or change direction in a chaplinesque manner.

Incidentally, In 1915, Charlie Chaplin entered a Charlie Chaplin lookalike contest in San Francisco. He did not win and he failed to make the finals.

Pizza Peel - You may think it is odd to peel a pizza, but that is not what this is.

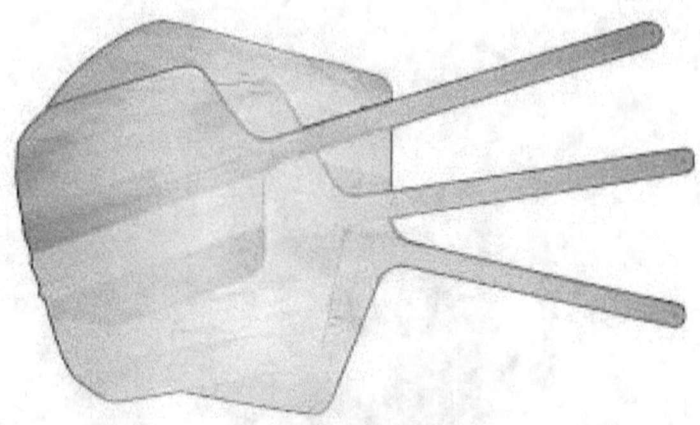

It is the instrument that pizzerias and cooks around the world use to shove a pizza into the oven and to remove it from the oven. Kind of like peeling off the oven floor.

Empty Calories - Many people associate alcohol calories with empty calories. They think empty calories are less fattening than regular calories. Empty calories are empty because they have no vitamins, minerals, or nutrients associated with them.

Alcohol calories are treated differently in the body than food calories. Alcohol calories get used for energy like any other calorie. However, alcohol is treated as a toxin by the body, and is given first priority for metabolism, so food calories must wait to be burned until after the liver deals with the alcohol calories. Food calories are stored as fat until used after the alcohol calories are used and that (simplified) is why alcoholics suffer from liver cirrhosis, or fatty liver, which is deadly.

Calorie Defined - The official definition of calorie is: A measurement of energy, the amount of energy needed to raise 1 gram of water 1 degree Celsius at standard atmospheric pressure. Calories in food are actually measured in kilocalories, so 1,000 actual calories for every 1 Calorie listed on food packages. Europe uses the actual kilocalories or kilojoules.

During the 1880s, Wilbur O. Atwater decided to determine how much energy different types of foods contained. He decided to treat different foods just like coal and burn them to ash in a furnace and measure how much heat (or calories) each one produced. He gave a numerical value to the calories produced by each food. He measured nine calories per gram from high-fat foods, and about four calories per gram from carbohydrates and proteins. We still use this system, to an extent.

During 2003, a US university team of nutritionists tested two slimming diets with the same number of calories on a group of overweight women. One diet was very low-fat and relatively high in carbohydrate. The other was high in fat, but low in carbohydrate. The low-fat dieters lost 3.9kg (almost 9lb), but the high-fat dieters lost more than twice as much weight at 8.5kg (almost 19lb).

The calories are the same, but the body reacts differently when it uses them. Maybe it is time to rethink how we count calories.

Calories listed on food labels are only an approximation. The US FDA allows food manufacturers to look at their ingredients and determine how many grams of fat, carbohydrates, and protein they contain, and then assume that each gram of protein and carbohydrates gives 4 kilocalories, each gram of fat gives 9, etc. Then they subtract 4 kilocalories for every gram of fiber, and that is the official, government sanctioned calorie measurement.

In addition to the above, different bodies deal with Calories differently. Genetic conditions, illnesses, and other factors can cause foods to be metabolized differently by some people vs. others. A 100 Calorie snack for you, might only be an 80 Calorie snack for someone else.

Bottom line, since Calories are an approximation, ingesting a few hundred more or less on any given day is not going to make much difference on your weight.

Dox - Here is an interesting word that has been floating around the web for the past bunch of years. Doxing or doxxing, from abbreviating the word documents, is an Internet-based practice of researching and broadcasting private or personal identifiable information about an individual or organization. It is usually done to humiliate or expose someone.

Doxing is the act of finding one's personal information through research and discovery, with little to no information to start with. You may have seen doxing in the news, for instance when not so long ago, hacker team Anonymous doxed and reported thousands of twitter accounts related to ISIS.

Doxxing is easy to accomplish using common internet sites. Social media, phone number databases, housing information, etc., are all readily and freely available. Linkedin, Twitter, Facebook, and Google+, etc. are treasure troves of personal information, such as relatives, friends, coworkers, pictures, nicknames, employer name, job title, school information, addresses, and much more.

Hackers, police officers, and amateur detectives can harvest the information from the internet about individuals. There is no particular structure in place for doxing, meaning a hacker may seek out any kind of information related to the target.

Anime vs. Manga - Anime (pronounced ann e mae) is animation of a cartoon show. The word is the abbreviated pronunciation of "animation" in Japanese, where this term references all animation. Anime is usually, but not always, the animated version of popular manga.

Manga is book of pictures or comics. Manga are comics created in Japan or by creators in the Japanese language, conforming to a style developed in Japan in the late 19th century. They have a long and complex pre-history in earlier Japanese art.

Lidar - The word is an acronym for Light Detection and Ranging. The US military and NASA invented the Lidar technology during the early 1960s for measuring distance in space. Its first commercial usage did not occur until 1995.

It uses ultraviolet, visible, or near infrared light from lasers. Radar (Radio Detection and Ranging) uses radio or electromagnetic waves.

Lidar used in cars is low powered and classed as 'eye-safe' allowing it to be used with few safety precautions.

Some refer to Lidar as laser radar, however it is not. It is more precise than radar, because the speed of light is a constant, so a laser can make extremely precise measurements of distance by computing the time between when the device emits a laser pulse and when it detects the reflection. Sound travels about 1,000 feet (300 meters) per second and light travels about 984,000,000 feet per second (300,000,000 meters). Also, radar wavelengths suffer from atmospheric conditions, such as humidity, fog, rain, snow, and temperature, but do perform better in smokey or dusty conditions.

A laser unit fires a short pulse of light. The pulse rebounds off a point, such as the rear of the car in front and is detected by a sensor in the laser unit. A computer connected to the unit measures the time between the initial pulse and the light return and, using the speed of light, calculates the distance the light has traveled. It creates a high-resolution 3D map of the surrounding environment. The best sensors can see details of a few centimeters at distances of more than 330 feet or 100 meters.

Currently most autonomous cars use some combination of Lidar, Radar, and camera. Lidar is precise, Radar is good at motion, and cameras are good for depiction. Each technology has strengths and weaknesses, so automakers and others are trying to find the best combination of strengths at the lowest cost.

Knickerbockers - Knickers is actually a standard word for underwear, mainly in Britain. Knickers derives from knickerbockers, or "loose-fitting short pants gathered at the knee." Because the city's early Dutch settlers wore those pants, "New Yorkers" became known as "Knickerbockers." The Knickerbockers, now more commonly "The Knicks" is the name of New York's NBA team. It does not have a picture of knickerbockers in its logo.

Psychopath vs. Sociopath - The terms "psychopath" and "sociopath" often get used interchangeably, but they are not exactly the same. It is not completely nature or nurture, but a complex combination of genetics, neurology, and environment. They are both classified as Antisocial Personality Disorders. They both show a disregard for laws and social mores, a disregard for the rights of others, a failure to feel remorse or guilt, and a tendency to display violent behavior.

> Psychopathy is the largely the result of genetics, while sociopathy is more likely the result of the environment.

Psychopathy is related to a physiological defect that results in the underdevelopment of the part of the brain responsible for impulse control and emotions. Psychopaths are unable to form emotional attachments or feel real empathy with others. Traits include a total freedom from fear, anxiety, or guilt. They can be charming, outgoing, and charismatic. They thrive on power and control and are self centered and impulsive.

Sociopathy is likely the product of childhood trauma and physical/emotional abuse. Sociopathy can also be acquired, such as by dementia or a head injury. Sociopaths have a less severe form of lack of empathy and lack of guilt. Sociopaths may be able to form some deep bonds while a psychopath cannot. A sociopath would feel no guilt about hurting a stranger, but may feel guilt and remorse over hurting someone with which they share a bond. A sociopath is less organized in demeanor and might be nervous, easily agitated, and quick to display anger. Sociopaths are often crusaders or martyrs for a perceived cause and may see their wild acts as necessary.

Psychopaths are confident, social, and dominant, but sociopaths are reserved and inhibited, sometimes loners.

Psychopaths are exempt from negative emotion, but sociopaths do experience anxiety and rejection.

Psychopaths have no morals, but sociopaths have a sense of morality and a conscience however, it is skewed.

Bottom line, all psychopaths are sociopaths, but not all sociopaths are psychopaths.

Terrific - John Milton, author of Paradise Lost came up with many new words. One of them is the word terrific, but it had a different meaning for Milton. He used the word terrific to mean something that was terrifying, as in terrif fic.

Wamblecropt - It sounds just like it means. It means overcome with indigestion. You might have observed your stomach was wambling a bit. If the wambles (indigestion) got so bad you could not move, you were wamblecropt. Sad that such a descriptive word has gone out of favor.

Riot, Rout, and Unlawful Assembly - Riot, rout, and unlawful assembly are related offenses, but are separate and distinct. A *rout* differs from a riot in that the persons involved do not actually execute their purpose, but merely move toward it. The degree of execution that converts a rout into a riot is often difficult to determine.

A *riot* is a form of civil disorder commonly characterized by a group lashing out in a violent public disturbance against authority, property, or people. To be considered a riot in England and Wales it must legally involve a minimum of twelve people. Under US federal law it is only three people, in New York, US ten people, Lynchburg, VA, US, three people, and in Nevada, US only two people can constitute a riot.

An *unlawful assembly* transpires when persons convene for a purpose, if executed would make them rioters, but who separate without performing any act in furtherance of their purpose.

Peruse - Peruse has a controversial double meaning due to common misuse. Even dictionaries do not all agree on the meaning of the word.

The primary meaning for the word peruse is to read or look at carefully or thoroughly. Its original meaning is synonymous with words like examine or inspect. The new definition addressing the misuse cropped up rather recently, sometime late in the last century.

The new meaning for the word is to skim, to look through in a casual or selective manner. These definitions have one suggesting a thorough examination and the other a few simple glances.

A word with two potential, opposite meanings is called a contronym, an autoantonym, or a Janus word. Others include: "To bolt" can mean "to run away," but it can also mean "to hold in place." "Sanction" can mean "to approve" or "to boycott."

I understand that all of you peruse my Friday Thoughts, some reading and digesting every word, while others do a quick skim looking for a little tidbit to impress others at the office.

Fulsome - By far, its most common use is in the expression "fulsome praise," which would seem like a good thing. The word sounds positive, drawing mental associations to "full" and "wholesome." At one point, this was exactly what the word meant.

Then Samuel Johnson, considered the father of the English dictionary came along. He and Noah Webster thought that the word "fulsome," which mostly held a positive connotation for hundreds of years (meaning "copious" or "abundant"), drew its roots from the word "foul" and "fulsome" gained its negative connotation. Many have fought and continue to fight for its original use, even as far back as 1868.

The word simultaneously retains both definitions, and even former president Barack Obama used the word in its much older, positive sense. He came under some scrutiny for that and for the fact that he misused "enormity". It is another word that may create an entirely new definition, because people incorrectly associate it with size.

"Fulsome praise" usually means "disgustingly over-the-top and insincere praise, but some have assumed its meaning to be more positive.

Hispanic vs. Latino - Many people use the terms "Hispanic" and "Latino" interchangeably, they actually have different meanings. There is significant overlap between the terms, but their differences may make only one term correct in certain circumstances.

Hispanic and Latino are often mistakenly used to refer to race or color. Instead, these terms actually describe ethnicity.

Hispanic is a term that focuses on language and describes the culture and people of areas formerly ruled by the Spanish Empire. The common thread among Hispanics is the shared common language of Spanish. This would include areas such as Mexico, Central America, and most of South America.

Latino (or Latina for females), on the other hand, focuses on geography and describes people of Latin American descent. This would include countries in South America, Central America, the Caribbean, and North America whose people speak Romance languages, such as Spanish, French, Italian, and Portuguese.

Based upon those definitions, it is easy to see how much overlap there is between the terms Hispanic and Latino. To see where the two terms differ, consider the people of Brazilian descent. Since the people of Brazil speak Portuguese rather than Spanish, they would be considered Latino, but not Hispanic.

So, the terms have much overlap, but they are not completely interchangeable. Hispanics and Latinos generally choose not to use either term. Instead, most prefer to be referred to simply as Americans or by their family's national origin, such as Mexican-American, Cuban-American, etc.

Today, there are more than 56 million Hispanic and Latino people in the United States, over 17% of the US population.

> "Hispanic" comes from the Latin word for "Spain,"
> Latino comes from the Spanish word for "Latin."

Corpsing - On stage 'dead' actors involuntarily laughing is such a big problem, that in British theater it is known as 'corpsing'. This has become generalized to any situation where an actor laughs inappropriately; any time you see a reference to an actor "corpsing", it means they ruined the shot by laughing.

Rasceta - The creases on the inside of wrist. (ras setta)

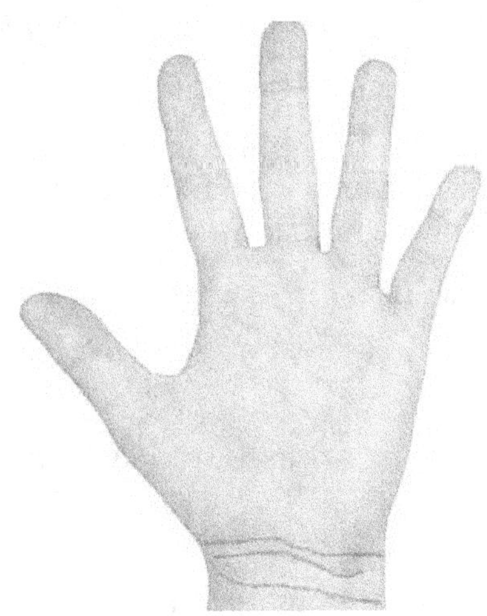

Terminal Velocity - You close your eyes and jump. You feel yourself in free fall, hurtling toward Earth, open your eyes and see the ground slowly getting closer. You seem to be picking up speed as you fall and soon you hit terminal velocity. It is the velocity at which you stop accelerating. It describes a physical reality based upon Newton's First Law of Motion.

When an object falls freely through a medium, such as water or air, the force of gravity pulls it toward Earth. As the object falls, its velocity increases as it accelerates toward Earth.

Gravity is not the only force working on the object. Air molecules collide with the falling object, pushing it upward against gravity. Scientists call this force air resistance. As the velocity of the falling object increases, so does air resistance.

Eventually, air resistance will equal the weight of the object in free fall. When this occurs, the object reaches terminal velocity. This means the falling object has reached its maximum velocity. The object will continue to fall at the same speed (terminal velocity) for the remainder of its free fall, until it hits Earth or a parachute opens.

Terminal velocity can be affected by a few different factors. For example, a heavier object will generally have a higher terminal velocity and a smaller surface area will have a higher terminal velocity than a larger surface area.

Most skydivers reach a terminal velocity of about 125 miles per hour. Experienced skydivers who streamline their bodies during free fall have reached speeds of over 200 miles per hour.

During October, 2012, Austrian skydiver Felix Baumgartner jumped from a helium balloon in the stratosphere, twenty four miles above Earth. Because the atmosphere at that height is so thin, there is next to no air resistance at the beginning of the free fall. This allows the skydiver to reach a much higher terminal velocity before encountering Earth's normal atmosphere far below.

On Baumgartner's skydive, he reached an estimated top speed of approximately 843.6 miles per hour.

Laughing Hyena - This is used to describe someone cackling: "laughing like a hyena."

Scientists who have studied hyenas will tell you the unique sounds they make are not actually laughing. Hyenas do indeed make loud barking noises that sound like cackling laughter, but it is not because they are amused by anything.

Instead, a hyena's sound is actually a form of communication used to convey frustration, excitement, warning, or fear. Most often, you hear this unique vocalization during a hunt or when the animals are feeding on prey as a group.

What sounds like maniacal giggling to humans lets other hyenas know that one of the other members of their pack has either made a kill or been attacked. When sharing a fresh kill, the sound might also indicate frustration on the part of a younger animal that did not get its fair share yet. Likewise, the animal in possession of the meat might also 'laugh' as a warning to others that it is not ready to share yet.

There are several species of hyenas, and they all have a variety of unique vocalizations. Only one of these species, the spotted hyena makes the laughing sound that has become synonymous with hyenas, in general.

Researchers have also learned that the pitch of a hyena's sound usually varies dependent upon its social status. Hyena packs are matrilineal, which means that females are dominant and lead the pack. There is intense competition for food within a pack, and the subordinate animals, often male tend to make the sound more frequently with a higher pitch.

Manicule - A manicule is a unique symbol. Literally it takes the form of a hand with an outstretched index figure, gesturing towards a particularly pertinent piece of text or a direction.

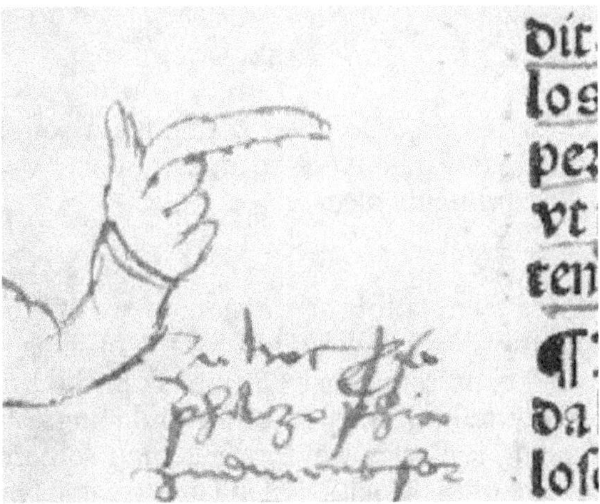

Although manicules are still visible today in old signage and retro décor, their heyday was in medieval and Renaissance Europe.

Despite its centuries-long popularity, the first-ever use of a manicule is surprisingly difficult to find. They were reportedly used in the Domesday Book of 1066, a record of land ownership in England and Wales. Widespread use began around the 12th century. The name comes from the Latin word manicula, meaning little hand, but the punctuation mark has had other synonyms, including bishop's fist, pointing hand, digit, and fist.

As far as punctuation marks go, the manicule's function was fairly self-explanatory. Usually drawn in the margin of a page (and sometimes between columns of text or sentences), it was a way for the reader to note a particularly significant paragraph of text. They were essentially the medieval version of a highlighter.

The use and dynamic of manicules changed once books began to be printed. This new technology allowed writers and publishers to highlight what they believed to be significant. The little hands with outstretched finger make it easy to find the key points without re-reading the whole text.

Ultracrepidarian - One who gives opinions on something beyond his or her knowledge. Someone who does not know what they are talking about. *No comments please.*

O'clock - The long form of this expression is 'two of the clock' or 'two on the clock' and the apostrophe stands for the missing letters. Two of the clock is an old expression that dates back to the time of sundials and other means of telling time. In order to distinguish the fact that one was referencing a clock's time, rather than something else, one would say, "It is two of the clock," which later became two o'clock.

WHAT'S IN A NAME

Chuck Berry - I usually do not do news items, but this interested me. St. Louis rock 'n' roll pioneer Chuck Berry celebrated his 90th birthday. He was soon to release his first new studio album in almost 40 years. The album, titled 'Chuck' was announced to be available during 2017 through Dualtone Records. It consists mostly of originals written and arranged by him. On it, he is backed up by 'The Blueberry Hill Band'.

The songwriter and guitar player was in the first class of Rock and Roll Hall of Fame inductees in 1986. He passed away March, 2017.

Duct Tape - It was invented by Johnson & Johnson during World War II. Their original creation for the United States military was a green waterproof tape that could be used for sealing ammunition cases to keep water out.

Soldiers soon learned the tape was good at fixing any type of rip or tear they might encounter for tents, vehicle seats, and even uniforms. After the war, returning soldiers introduced it to friends and neighbors back home.

One of the first uses for the tape was to repair or seal the ductwork in home heating and cooling systems. To match the color of ductwork, the company changed the color of the tape to silver and began to call it duct tape.

Many people believe that the tape was called duck tape, because its ability to repel water reminded of the similar property of duck feathers. There is a brand of tape named Duck tape that is sometimes confused with the original.

Duct tape comes in many different colors, although the most popular are silver and black. It is so strong, because it is made of three different layers. The bottom layer is a strong rubber-based adhesive. The middle layer is a web of cloth fabric that adds durability. The top layer is soft, waterproof plastic.

Lake Baikal - If the rest of the planet's fresh water disappeared, there would be enough left in Lake Baikal, Russia to supply humanity for 50 years. It is world's oldest (25 million years old) and deepest (over a mile deep) freshwater lake and contains about 23% of the world's fresh surface water. In Mongolian it means "the Nature Lake." *Appears the screams about running out of fresh water are a bit premature.*

Alcatraz Facts - Its name came from Spanish explorer Juan Manuel de Ayala in 1775: La Isla de los Alcatraces or "Island of the Pelicans."

In 1850, US President Fillmore converted the island to military use. A fortress was built, cannons were installed, and the West Coast's first operational lighthouse was constructed.

The US Army also began to use Alcatraz to house military prisoners. It was the perfect spot for a prison, because it was isolated and everyone assumed no prisoner could successfully escape by swimming across the frigid waters of San Francisco Bay.

During the early 1900s, military prisoners helped to build a new, 600-cell jail, as well as a hospital, cafeteria, and other prison buildings. Over time Alcatraz was transferred to the US Justice Department for use as a federal prison for prisoners too dangerous to be kept at other penitentiaries. Alcatraz usually held between 260-275 prisoners. Each prisoner had his own cell, and there was one guard for about every three prisoners.

There were 14 known escape attempts involving 36 prisoners. Of those attempting to escape, 23 were captured, six were shot and killed during their attempt, two drowned, and five went missing and were officially presumed dead.

Alcatraz was shut down during 1963, because it was too expensive to keep operating. Now it is thriving again as a tourist attraction.

Dos Equis - Now that the most interesting man in the world (Jonathon Goldsmith) is going to Mars and not coming back, thought it is time to look into him and the brand. Two interesting abilities he has, among many others, are parallel-parking a train, and slamming a revolving door. "His only regret is not knowing what regret feels like."

Dos Equis (XX) Mexican beer was first brewed in 1900 and was originally named "Siglo XX" (twentieth Century) to signify the new millennium. It is brewed in the Cuauhtémoc Moctezuma Brewery. Now it is simply called Dos Equis XX. Dos equis translates to two X's.

Frisbie - William Russell Frisbie bought a bakery in Connecticut in the late 19th century, which he called the Frisbie Pie Company. After Frisbie's death, his company continued to flourish and it 1956 reached a peak production of 80,000 pies per day. Pies and cookies made by the company came with plate-shaped tin bearing the name 'Frisbee Pies'.

Yale students discovered a second use for the tins, and began to hurl them around the university campus. As the flying disk approached its target, the thrower would shout "Frisbie" as a warning. *The slightly different spelling "frisbee" is now used for the toy.*

The Real Popeye - Frank "Rocky" Fiegel (January 27, 1868 - March 24, 1947) was a real-life person from Chester, Illinois who inspired the Thimble Theatre character, Popeye.

Rocky was a well-known Chester individual and something of a local legend. He supposedly had an inordinate strength and often participated in fights. Like Popeye, he smoked a pipe and was toothless. He is said to have been kind to children as well. *Incidentally, Wimpy and Olive Oyl were also based on real people.*

Wikipedia - Wikipedia is based on two words, the Hawaiian word Wiki, meaning quick and encyclopedia, with pedia being the Greek term for knowledge: "quick knowledge."

Jimmy Carter Peanut Statue - The Jimmy Carter Peanut stands 4 meters (13 ft) tall with a wide, toothy smile and no eyes. The peanut can be found on the side of the road in Plains, Georgia (Jimmy's hometown). The structure started out being constructed in Indiana in 1976 to honor Jimmy Carter's visit to the state during his presidential campaign tour.

Before he was president, Carter was a peanut farmer. The statue has the same grin that was known so fondly as one of Carter's traits during his years in office. It is the most photographed thing in Plains.

Subway Origins - Subway opened in 1965, when 17-year-old Fred DeLuca received a $1,000 investment from a friend of his family, Dr. Peter Buck. Buck suggested using the money to open up a sub shop, because it would be a good way for DeLuca to pay for college and medical school.

On August 28, 1965 DeLuca opened Pete's Super Submarines in Bridgeport, Connecticut. However, on the radio ads, it sounded like "Pizza Marine," so they changed the name to Pete's Subway and later to Subway.

In 1974, DeLuca started franchising and he went through a bit of a learning curve, but he was soon able to jump from 16 stores to 200. Since 1987, 1,000 Subways open every year. For a while, as of mid-

2015, Subway was the biggest restaurant chain, with the most franchises in the world.

Emergency Goaltender - All NHL teams must have an emergency goaltender on call, in the event that one of the two goalies on the roster can't play.

The league keeps a list of willing and able goalies in each city. When Anders Lindback was injured before the Arizona Coyotes played Montreal, the team called up Nathan Schoenfeld, a local bank manager. Schoenfeld rode the bench all night and got the best seat in the house for Coyotes' 6-2 win. He also received $500 and a jersey.

Interesting Food Names - Menus need to convey the right kind of information about a dish as concisely as possible. Short descriptions are used as advertising elements to entice customers. Sautéed shrimp in garlic butter is a good basic description, while zesty garlic butter might make a dish seem even more delicious. Adjectives such as 'tasty', 'fresh', or 'hot' go a long way in persuading a customer to try something. Words that actually refer to taste, such as 'bitter', 'salty', or 'sour' are rarely used. Fanciful participles such as 'married', 'kissed', 'accented', and 'hand-crafted' suggest high quality cooking or ingredients without really saying anything substantive about the dish. Below are a few regional food descriptions.

Toad in the hole (sausages baked in a batter),
Ants on a log (raisins on peanut butter on a celery stick),
Devil/Angel on horseback (dates or oysters wrapped in bacon),
Bubble and Squeak (fried potato and cabbage),
Pigs in a blanket (a sausage wrapped in dough or bacon)
Spotted Dick (a pudding with raisins and custard),
Hush puppies (deep fried cornbread balls),
Love in disguise (a Welsh dish of stuffed and boiled heart).

Incidentally, during 1972-73 the American Food for Peace Program sent tons of yellow corn from the United States to Botswana for distribution in schools as drought relief. The shamed and humiliated secondary school students in Serowe rioted, burned the headmaster's car, and destroyed stockpiles of the corn. Seems only white maize is fit for human consumption there. Yellow is fed to animals.

Sikhs - Many people in the US confuse Sikhs and Muslims. However, 99 percent of people wearing turbans in the US are Sikhs from India. There are about 700,000 Sikhs in the US today.

Sikhism is an Indian religion and the world's fifth largest religion with 25.8 million adherents worldwide. Sikhs believe in one God, equality, freedom of religion, and community service.

The word Sikh (pronounced 'seekh') means 'student', 'disciple', or 'learner.' The Sikh religion was founded in Northern India in 1469 by Guru Nanak Dev Ji. Sikhism is monotheistic and stresses the equality of all men and women. Sikhs believe in three basic principles; meditating on the name of God (praying), earning a living by honest means as well as sharing the fruits of one's labor with others. Sikhism rejects all distinctions based on caste, creed, gender, color, race, or national origin and emphasizes service to humanity.

Sikhs have no food taboos except those that stem from one simple injunction – a life of moderation in which they shun all that harms the body or the mind. This also means all intoxicants, tobacco, alcohol, or any mind altering drugs are forbidden.

Additional facts:

Sikhism is a distinct religion, separate from Hinduism and Islam.
In Sikhism, the influences of ego, anger, greed, attachment, and lust, known as the Five Thieves, are believed to be particularly distracting and hurtful.
Sikhs have a baptism ceremony.
Sikhism does not have priests. Liturgical service employs people for a salary to sing hymns, officiate marriage, and perform services.
Sikhs cover their uncut hair with a turban. The Sikh turban represents a commitment to equality and justice.
Women are not required to wear compulsory veil.
Religious ceremonies, or idol worship are of little use and Sikhs are discouraged from fasting or going on pilgrimages.
Sikhs do not believe in converting people, but converts to Sikhism by choice are welcomed.
The morning and evening prayers take about two hours a day, starting in the early morning hours.

Facts about Aldi - It was founded by brothers Karl and Theo Albrecht in 1946 when they took over their mother's store in Essen, Germany which had been in operation since 1913. It is one of the world's largest privately owned companies. The name is a syllabic abbreviation for Albrecht Diskont.

The German discount supermarket chain is the ninth largest retailer in the world, following Walmart, Tesco, Costco, Carrefour, Kroger, Lidl, Metro AG, and Home Depot. Target is number ten. Five of the top ten are American and three of the top ten are German owned.

Nine of ten items Aldi sells are store brands.

You must bring your own bags.

You must pay 25 cent deposit for cart (you get it back when returned).

Aldi accepts no coupons.

Items at Aldi are, on average, 53% cheaper than at Walmart.

Aldi owns Trader Joe's.

J.R. Simplot - J.R. Simplot was a high school dropout who developed the first freeze-dried potatoes and vegetables for the US Army, during WWII in Europe. The longer shelf-life and easy reconstitution of Simplot's frozen vegetables helped ensure troops overseas could be kept stocked with food needed during the war.

At the end of the war Simplot signed a contract with Ray Kroc at Mc Donald's to provide frozen French fries. It provides McDonald's with more than 50% of its French fries worldwide.

Stetson - John Batterson Stetson came from a long line of hatters, and when he was diagnosed with tuberculosis, he headed west during the 1860s. After setting up shop in Missouri, Stetson created the original cowboy hat - the Boss of the Plains hat.

It looks little like what we might imagine for the typical cowboy hat, with a round brim and uncreased crown. Originally made from beaver fur and designed to be lightweight and waterproof, it was not until the Boss of the Plains hat was already popular that it began to morph into something closer to the cowboy hats we think of today.

Wearers in different areas started customizing their hats, and the creases and folds of the hats developed into their own type of language. They defined status, occupation, and where a person was from, until Stetson adopted the five most popular creases into his official line.

Notable people who wore Stetson hats included Colonel William F. "Buffalo Bill" Cody, Calamity Jane, Will Rogers, and Annie Oakley.

Emma Morano - Emma Morano died 15 April 2017 at 117 years old. The Italian Supercentenarian was the last person alive to have been born in the 19th century. She was born in northern Italy on November 29, 1899 when Queen Victoria and Oscar Wilde were still alive. A world that had never known global war, and where the automobile was still a fancy toy for rich folk. No human had ever successfully flown a plane. At that moment, Emma was closer in time to the Battle of Waterloo than she was to her twilight years in 2017.

Ten Things You Never Knew the Name of -
Barm: the foam on a beer.
Columella nasi: the space between your nostrils.
Griffonage: unreadable handwriting.
Ideolocator: a "you are here" sign.
Keeper: the loop on a belt that keeps the end in place after it has passed through the buckle.
Obelus: the division sign ($\div$).
Phloem bundles: those long stringy things you see when peeling a banana.
Punt: the bottom of a wine bottle.

Irene Triplett - When the US Civil War ended in 1865, the US government promised a monthly stipend to the wives and children of Yankee soldiers. 152 years later Irene Triplett was still receiving her Civil War pension.

During the 1920s, Mose Triplett – a Confederate soldier who had defected to the Union in 1862, married Irene's mother, Elida. Irene was born to Mose Triplett and his second wife, Elida, in 1930. Mose, whose first wife Mary died in the 1920s, fathered five children with Elida, who was 50 years younger than he was. Mose died in 1938.

During 2013, after breaking her hip, Irene, the last child moved into a Wilkesboro skilled-nursing facility. She collected $73.13 each month from her father's military pension until her passing July 4, 2017 at the age of 90 in Spencer, Iowa.

Incidentally, about 15 children of veterans from the Spanish-American War of 1898 still receive benefits.

Frank Hayes - Frank Hayes was a horse trainer and jockey during the early 1900s. During 1923, at the age of 35, Hayes had an opportunity to compete in a steeplechase in Belmont Park, New York. He had never won a race before that. The horse that he was going to race was named Sweet Kiss, a 20-1 underdog.

In spite of the long odds of winning, and despite the fact that Hayes had little experience as a jockey since he was a horse trainer by profession, Hayes and Sweet Kiss ended up victorious.

The owner of the horse, elated with the win, approached Hayes afterward only to find out that Hayes was dead. It appeared at some point during the middle of the race, Hayes suffered a heart attack and died. Sweet Kiss somehow managed to hop the final fence and cross the finish line ahead of everyone while carrying literal dead weight.

The track physician speculated that his death may have been caused by a pre-existing heart disease. Hayes is in the Guinness Book of Records as the first, and so far the only, deceased jockey to win a race.

Diesel - Diesel is used in about 50 percent of cars in Europe, but only in about three percent of the market in the US. The German word Diesel was named after the German inventor and mechanical engineer Rudolf Diesel, who patented the idea for his new engine in 1895 that used diesel fuel rather than gas (petrol).

The engine works by compressing only the air and therefore does not use a spark plug to ignite the air-fuel mixture. Although the diesel engine and German car industry has taken a serious hit recently with Volkswagen's diesel emissions scandal, diesel engines are still very common across Europe.

Email - Here is a tip to track marketing of your email. When you sign up to a new web site for any reason, use the website name as part of

your real name. When you begin getting more junk mail (as you will)
at least you will know which site sold your email address.

Newfoundland and Labrador - Newfoundland and Labrador is
the name of a Canadian Province on the East Coast of Canada.
Labrador is the Northern portion and Newfoundland Island is
Southeast. They are also the names of two different breeds of related
dogs. Newfoundlands were originally bred and used as a working dog
for fishermen in Newfoundland, Canada. They are famously known for
their giant size, tremendous strength, sweet dispositions, and loyalty.

Labrador Retrievers were originally black and initially bred for
retrieving small downed waterfowl. They are also adept at a number of
other jobs including leading the blind, acting as hearing dogs, and
used for police and military work. The name "Labrador" was given to
this dog by British breeders in order to differentiate between the two
types. The retriever was originally called the 'lesser Newfoundland' or
'St. John's Dog'.

*Incidentally, St. John's is a city on the Island and is the capital of
Newfoundland and Labrador.*

Lucille - In the winter of 1949, BB King played at a dance hall in Twist, Arkansas. The hall was heated by a barrel half-filled with burning kerosene, a fairly common practice at the time. During a performance, two men began to fight, knocking over the barrel and sending burning fuel across the floor. The hall burst into flames, and the building was evacuated.

Once outside, King realized that he had left his guitar inside so he went back into the burning building to retrieve his beloved $30 Gibson guitar. King learned the next day that the two men that started the fire had been fighting over a woman who worked at the hall named Lucille. King named that guitar, and every guitar he subsequently owned, Lucille, as a reminder never again to do something as stupid as run into a burning building or fight over a woman.

Amethyst - It is a semiprecious stone and is the traditional birthstone for February.

1250-1300; Latin amethystus, Greek améthystos not intoxicating, not intoxicated (so called from a belief that it prevented drunkenness).

The ancient Greeks wore amethyst and made drinking vessels decorated with it in the belief that it would prevent intoxication. It is one of several forms of quartz.

Father and Son - John Scott Harrison was a member of the United States House of Representatives from Ohio and the only person to be both the child and the parent of US Presidents. He was also the grandson of Declaration of Independence signer, Benjamin Harrison V. He was the father of thirteen children.

His father, William Henry Harrison was the ninth President in 1841 and his son, Benjamin Harrison, was the 23rd President from 1889 to 1893. Harrison did not live to see his son become President.

Snow White - One of the most famous fables, variations of Snow White appear in more than 400 versions of fairy tales around the world. The most well-known version is actually called " Snowdrop" and comes from Grimms' Children's and Household Tales . It was later tweaked into a more familiar format by the folklorist Andrew Lang and eventually adapted by Walt Disney.

In this version, the queen wished for a child and a baby girl was born; her hair was as dark as ebony and her skin was so fair and pure that her mother named her Snow White. After the queen died, her father married a woman who was vain and wicked, who would stand in front of a magic mirror asking who was the fairest woman in the land. The mirror always replied "My Queen, you are the fairest one of all", until one day an answer came that threw her into a rage – Snow White was now the fairest woman in all the land.

Snow White's step-mother, furious at what the mirror had told her, ordered a huntsman to take Snow White into the forest and kill her, taking the girl's heart as a proof. The huntsman felt sympathy for Snow White and let her free, bringing the Evil Queen a deer's heart instead. Snow White came upon a small cottage and, exhausted, collapsed into one of the beds and fell into a deep sleep. When she awoke, seven dwarfs were looking down upon her. They told Snow White she could stay with them as long as she cleaned and cooked.

Snow White and the dwarfs lived in contentment, until one day when the magic mirror told the Queen that Snow White was alive and was still the fairest of them all. The Queen disguised herself as an old woman and presented Snow White with a poisoned apple. After taking a bite of the apple, Snow White fell unconscious. The dwarfs, assuming she was dead, built a glass coffin and placed her inside.

In the animated movie, the prince convinced the dwarfs to let him give her one last kiss - that became the most popular version. She awakened and the prince declared his love for her. They were married, and as all fairy tales go, they lived happily ever after.

Other versions include, "Gold-Tree and Silver-Tree" - "Maria, the Wicked Stepmother, and the Seven Robbers" - "Snow-White and Rose-Red" and "The Young Slave."

Incidentally, Disney announced a live-action feature retelling Snow White's tale from her sister's perspective, Rose Red.

Name Changes - When the Anglo-Saxons conquered Britain in the 5th Century, they transformed not only its society, but its language, which we now know as Old English. Remnants of their rule remain inscribed in maps of not only London, but Britain; the Anglo-Saxon suffix '-ham' (as in Birmingham) meant homestead, for example, while '-ton' (like Brighton) referred to a farm. The ending '-ing', meant belonging to or associated with someone, or their followers. So Paddington was the farmstead belonging to Padda or his clan, Kennington was that of Cēna's people.

> **Elsie the Cow**
> Elsie is the name of the cow used as the symbol on Elmer's products. She is the spouse of Elmer, the bull, after whom the company is named.

When the Normans invaded in 1066, though, they seized Saxon properties to hand out among their loyalists... and tacked on new names accordingly. One winner in the land-grab was the abbey of Bec-Hellouin, in Normandy, which was granted the land that once belonged to a Saxon chief named Tota. All of which turned into the name today, Tooting.

Around 190, London was Londinium.

Forth Bridge - During March 1890, the Forth railway bridge, connecting Edinburgh to Fife over the Firth of Forth, opened, becoming an internationally recognized Scottish landmark. *So, the tongue twisting Forth bridge over the Firth of Forth connects to Fife.*

Piccadilly Circus - The London landmark gets its name from the alternate meaning of 'circus' referring to a round junction where several streets meet.

(This also explains Oxford Circus, the Tube station just a half mile northwest). The other half of its name, meanwhile, is a centuries-old bit of snark.

A 'piccadill' is a large, ruffled collar that was the height of fashion in the late 16th and early 17th Centuries – think portraits of Queen Elizabeth I. Creating piccadills was how one London tailor, Robert Baker, made his fortune... and funded the construction of his grand house here in 1611. Apparently it was seen as a little too grand for a 'lowly' tailor, since it came to be known as Pickadilly Hall. The witty put-down stuck: when the junction was built there in 1819, it was called Piccadilly Circus. So, of course, was the Underground station when it opened in 1906.

Java Jacket - Your fancy coffee cup holder was originally named Java Jacket, and now it has been morphed into the modern-day names as a coffee sleeve, coffee cozy, or coffee clutch.

They are also called paper zarfs. A zarf was originally a metal chalice keep your hot coffee from burning your fingers. The fancy cup holder has morphed into the modern-day cardboard sleeve that comes wrapped around your hot coffee cup. Next time you are in Starbucks, ask them if the zarf is free. It might be fun to watch the reaction from your barrister.

Al Capone - A famous crime boss during prohibition in the US was jailed for income tax evasion. He was released from Alcatraz prison on November 16, 1939 and died January 25, 1947 with few of his friends attending his modest funeral.

He died penniless after once earning $40 million a year. He struggled to support his family on an income of $600 a week, which was provided by former associates of the Chicago Outfit. After his death, his wife, Mae, whom he married in 1918, was forced to sell their home due to financial constraints. She died during 1986.

Wyatt Earp and John Wayne - Wyatt Earp was not satisfied sticking to one job for too long. During his life he was a lawman, buffalo hunter, brothel keeper, miner, and boxing referee among others. But he was best known for being an infinitely tough cowboy.

Earp took part in the most famous shootout in the history of the American Wild West, the Gunfight at the O.K. Corral, a 30-second gun battle that has inspired dozens of feature-length films. What you might not realize is that, unlike most people involved in that event, Earp lived long enough to see the earliest movies inspired by his exploits.

Toward the end of his life, Earp settled in California and tried to break into Hollywood. Perhaps noticing an alarming lack of westerns where his character was always surrounded by naked ladies, Earp decided he wanted to tell his story from his own perspective. Unfortunately, the closest he got was reportedly a background part in a single scene of an obscure 1915 film. However, Earp did get to befriend some Hollywood actors, including a 17-year-old nobody called Marion Morrison, whose stage name was John Wayne.

> **Mickey**
> In the film industry, a 'mickey' is a gentle forward camera move. It is named for Mickey Rooney (a 'little creep').

While hanging out on movie sets, casually choreographing historical gunfights for directors like John Ford, Earp would share stories from the Wild West with the actors. The future Wayne, then an extra and prop man, soaked them up. He also paid close attention to the way Earp talked and carried himself.

Freddie Mercury - The late Farrokh Bulsara (Freddie Mercury) was proud of his Zoroastrian heritage. "I'll always walk around like a Persian popinjay and no one's gonna stop me, honey," he once said. His sister Karishma Cooke also talked about the role of Zoroastrianism in the family. "We as a family were very proud of being Zoroastrian. I think what [Freddie's] Zoroastrian faith gave him was to work hard, to persevere, and to follow your dreams."

First Martini - Like many drink recipes, Martini origins are fuzzy. The precise origins of the martini remain obscure, with a number of people and locations vying for the honor of being home to the cocktail. The town of Martinez, California put up a plaque to proclaim itself the birthplace of the Martini. According to the plaque, situated at 911 Alhambra Avenue, the very first Martini was mixed on that spot.

The plaque records the story: "On this site in 1874, Julio Richelieu, bartender, served up the first Martini when a miner came into his saloon with a fistful of nuggets and asked for something special. He was served a 'Martinez Special'. After three or four drinks, however, the 'Z' would get in the way. The drink consisted of 2/3 gin, 1/3 vermouth, a dash of orange bitters, poured over crushed ice and served with an olive."

> *Lawrence Tureaud is the full name of Mr. T.*

Another theory suggests it evolved from a cocktail called the Martinez served sometime in the early 1860s at the Occidental Hotel in San Francisco, which people frequented before taking an evening ferry to the nearby town of Martinez.

Others assert that the drink was named after "Martini & Rossi" vermouth, which was first created during the mid-1800s. Apparently in the interest of brevity, the drink became known as the 'Martini'.

Simpson's Names - Many of the characters on the Simpsons show were named by Matt Groening and are named after people in his family. He did refuse to name the grandfather after his own grandfather, Abraham, and asked the writers to choose a name. The writers, who had no knowledge of his grandfather's name, chose Abraham. The full name is Abraham Jedediah "Abe" Simpson II, but he is commonly called grampa. His parents were Orville J. Simpson and Yuma Hickman.

O. J. Simpson - No relation to the above. His full name is Orenthal James Simpson. His nickname from football days is The Juice. He had a parole hearing July 20, 2017 in Nevada, and was released during October, 2017.

Groundhog - The groundhog (Marmota monax), also known as a woodchuck, or whistlepig, is a rodent of the family Sciuridae, belonging to the group of large ground squirrels known as marmots. It was first scientifically described by Carl Linnaeus in 1758. The groundhog is also referred to as a chuck, wood-shock, groundpig, whistler, thickwood badger, Canada marmot, monax, moonack, weenusk, and red monk. The name "thickwood badger" was given in the Northwest to distinguish the animal from the prairie badger.

Monax was a Native American name of the woodchuck, which meant "the digger".

Whisky - Whisky is a spirit distilled from malted grain, barley, or rye. The word whisky is originated from the Old English word usquebae. The word is derived from the words uisce, which means water, and bethu, which translates to life. Summing it up, the word whisky basically means 'water of life'.

Genghis Khan - That was his title, his name was Temüjin, which means "of iron" or "blacksmith." He was the Great Khan and founder of the Mongol Empire, which became the largest contiguous empire in history after his death. First Khagan (Great Kahn) of the Mongol Empire and Supreme Khan of the Mongols, the King of Kings.

Between 1206 and his death in 1227, the Mongol leader Genghis Khan conquered nearly 12 million square miles of territory, more than any individual in history. He was responsible for the deaths of as many as 40 million people.

He came to power by uniting many of the nomadic tribes of Northeast Asia. After founding the Empire and being proclaimed "Genghis Khan," he launched the Mongol invasions that conquered most of Eurasia.

The Mongol Empire ended up ruling, or at least briefly conquering, large parts of modern day China, Mongolia, Russia, Azerbaijan, Armenia, Georgia, Iraq, Iran, Turkey, Kazakhstan, Kyrgyzstan, Uzbekistan, Pakistan, Tajikistan, Afghanistan, Kuwait, Turkmenistan, and Moldova. Many of these invasions repeated the earlier large-scale slaughters of local populations.

Gas is Not a Gas - Soon after oil was found in Pennsylvania during 1859, John Cassell, publisher and coffee merchant, began importing it to London. Cassell came up with a name for the substance, inspired by his own name, Cazeline. On 27 November 1862 he placed an advertisement in The Times that stated, "The Patent Cazeline Oil, safe, economical, and brilliant ... possesses all the requisites which have so long been desired as a means of powerful artificial light.

The first use of gasoline to be found in America is in an 1864 Act of Congress which declared a tax on the oil.

Cassell discovered a shopkeeper in Dublin, Samuel Boyd selling counterfeit cazeline and wrote to him to ask him to stop. Boyd did not reply, but instead went through his stock, changing with a single dash of his pen, every 'C' into a 'G' and gazeline was born.

7Up - 7Up is a brand of lemon-lime flavored, non-caffeinated soft drink. The rights to the brand are held by Dr Pepper Snapple Group in the United States, and PepsiCo in the rest of the world. Creative marketing during prohibition moved the product to underground speakeasies. Like other products such as ginger ale and tonic, 7UP quickly became a popular mixer for alcoholic drinks. After prohibition was repealed, it was still marketed as a mixer. By the late 1940s, 7UP had become the third best-selling soft drink in the world.

Westinghouse bought 7Up in 1969 and sold it in 1978 to Philip Morris, which then during 1986 sold it to a group led by Hicks & Haas. 7Up merged with Dr Pepper in 1988. Cadbury Schweppes bought the combined company in 1995. The Dr Pepper Snapple Group was spun off from Cadbury Schweppes in 2008.

7Up was created by Charles Grigg, who came up with the formula for a lemon-lime soft drink in 1929. The product, originally named "Bib-Label Lithiated Lemon-Lime Soda" contained lithium citrate, a mood-stabilizing drug. "Bib-label" referred to the use of paper labels that were placed on the plain bottles.

The US Food and Drug Administration banned the use of lithium in beer and soft drinks in 1948, and 7Up was reformulated two years later. Its name was later shortened to "7Up Lithiated Lemon Soda" before being further shortened to just "7Up" during 1936.

The actual origin of the 7Up name is unclear, as is the origin or meaning of the red dot. It contains no sugar, preservatives, caffeine or coloring.

Medical and Healthcare

HEALTH INFORMATION

Third Leading Cause of Death in US - Research estimates up to 440,000 Americans die annually from preventable hospital errors. This puts medical errors as the third leading cause of death in the United States.

Leapfrog, an independent, national nonprofit organization that administers the Score, is an advocate for patient safety nationwide. "We are burying a population the size of Miami every year from medical errors that can be prevented. A number of hospitals have improved by one or even two grades, indicating hospitals are taking steps toward safer practices, but these efforts aren't enough," says Leah Binder, president and CEO of Leapfrog.

Key Findings:
On average, there was no improvement in hospitals' reported performance on the measures included in the score. Of the 2,539 general hospitals issued a Hospital Safety Score, 813 earned an "A," 661 earned a "B," 893 earned a "C," 150 earned a "D" and 22 earned an "F."

The states with the smallest percentage of "A" hospitals include New Hampshire, Arkansas, and Nebraska. No hospitals in New Mexico or the District of Columbia received an "A" grade.

Maine claimed the number-one spot for the state with the highest percentage of "A" hospitals.

Kaiser and Sentara were among the hospital systems where 100 percent of their hospitals received an "A."

2013 (latest causes of death available) -
Heart disease: 611,105
Cancer (all types): 584,881
Hospital preventable error deaths: 440,000
Chronic lower respiratory diseases: 149,205
Accidents (unintentional injuries): 130,557
Stroke (brain diseases): 128,978
Alzheimer's disease: 84,767
Diabetes: 75,578
Influenza and Pneumonia: 56,979
Nephritis, nephrotic syndrome, and nephrosis (kidney related): 47,112
Intentional self-harm (suicide): 41,149.

Leading Causes of Death 1900 and 2014 - For all of the advances in modern medicine, it seems like many things remain the same. Politics, headlines, and funding appear to have as much influence as medicine and science for finding cures. Case in point, HIV/AIDS threatened to wipe out millions, yet it is not shown in either list. It became a cause *célèbre*, was well funded, and today is a mere blip in the grand scheme of leading causes of death.

During 1900, leading causes of death were: Pneumonia or influenza, Tuberculosis, Gastrointestinal infections, Heart disease, Cerebrovascular disease (stroke), Nephropathies (causes are Diabetes, Alcohol abuse, Vitamin deficiencies, Infections, and Autoimmune disease), Accidents, and Cancer.

During 1940, leading causes of death were: Diseases of the heart, Cancer and other malignant tumors, Intracranial lesions of vascular origin, Nephritis (all forms), Pneumonia and influenza, Accidents excluding motor-vehicle, Tuberculosis, Diabetes mellitus.

During 2014, leading causes of death among Americans under age 80 were: Heart disease, cancer, stroke, chronic lower respiratory diseases, such as asthma, bronchitis and emphysema; and accidents. Nearly two-thirds of deaths in the United States were caused by these five diseases or conditions.

Thirty percent of heart disease deaths, 15 percent of cancer deaths, 28 percent of stroke deaths, 36 percent of chronic lower respiratory disease deaths, and 43 percent of accident deaths were preventable, according to the CDC.

It appears we have become much better at defining causes, but not developing cures. To a politician, the problem is the healthcare system, but to a patient, the problem is the disease. To a politician, the symptom is the size of the wallet, but to a patient, the symptom is the size of the tumor.

Medical Robots - The first robot-assisted surgery was performed during 1983. There were 1,000 robot-assisted surgeries performed in 2000 and by 2014, there were 570,000 robot-assisted surgeries. The list of robot types and surgeries performed are too numerous to list here. *Incidentally, all robot systems are projected to triple during the next five years.*

Dutch Doors - There is a Dutch senior facility that attached life size pictures of previous home front doors to the resident's room doors. It helps patients with dementia have a familiar look and assist them to find their room.

That is a truly caring facility.

Zika Virus Facts - Much fear-mongering has recently been spread about the Zika virus, but here are a few facts to keep things in perspective. It is not all that bad, certainly is not life threatening, and most people will not even know if they get it.

Zika virus was first discovered in 1947 and is named after the Zika forest in Uganda. In 1952, the first human cases of Zika were detected. Since then, outbreaks of Zika have been reported in tropical Africa, Southeast Asia, the Pacific Islands, and Brazil.

Eighty percent of Zika cases will not be diagnosed. Most people infected with Zika virus will not even know they have the disease, because they will not have symptoms. The most common symptoms of Zika are fever, rash, joint pain, or conjunctivitis (red eyes). Other common symptoms include muscle pain and headache. The incubation period, from exposure to symptoms for Zika virus disease is not known, but is likely to be a few days to a week.

There is no vaccine to treat or prevent Zika virus.

Zika in the U.S. as of March 23, 2016:
Locally acquired vector-borne cases reported: 0
Travel-associated Zika virus disease cases reported: 273 (of the 273

travel-associated infections, 19 were in pregnant women and 6 were sexually transmitted.)

It may be "on occasion" spread through sexual contact or blood transfusions. The CDC has received 15 reports of possible spread of Zika through sex, meaning a person traveled to an area where Zika has broken out, acquired the virus, and gave the virus to a sexual partner who did not travel. Brazilian scientists have found the virus in saliva and urine of infected people.

The illness is usually mild with symptoms lasting for several days to a week after being bitten by an infected mosquito. Zika virus usually remains in the blood of an infected person for about a week, but it can be found longer in some people.

Once a person has been infected, he or she is likely to be protected from future infections.

There have been reports of congenital microcephaly in babies of mothers who were infected with Zika virus while pregnant. Zika virus infections have been confirmed in several infants with microcephaly. It is not known how many of the microcephaly cases are associated with Zika virus infection. A pregnant woman can pass Zika virus to her fetus during pregnancy. There is no evidence that prior Zika virus infection poses a risk of birth defects in future pregnancies.

Zika Virus Update - There are 346 cases of Zika confirmed in the continental United States, all in people who had recently traveled to Zika-prone countries, according to the most recent CDC report.

A Brazilian study recently released also links Zika to a second autoimmune disorder that resembles multiple sclerosis and involves a swelling of the brain and spinal cord. "Though our study is small, it may provide evidence that in this case, the virus has different effects on the brain than those identified in current studies," said Dr. Maria Lucia Brito, a neurologist at Restoration Hospital in Recife, Brazil. Six of 151 patients tested positive for Zika.

Scientists reported in the April edition of the New England Journal of Medicine that while evidence gathered does not provide conclusive proof that Zika causes microcephaly and other birth defects, an increasing amount of scientific research suggests that is the case. *Still no need for panic.*

Addyi two Years Later - So, my friend Jeff Flanagan asked another puzzler this week, "What happened to Addyi?" Addyi is the brand name for a little pink pill called flibanserin and known as the 'female Viagra'. It received approval from the FDA, in August, 2015. It is a non-hormonal serotonin to treat a little or no sexual desire disorder in pre-menopausal women. The manufacturer states that flibanserin corrects an imbalance of dopamine and norepinephrine, both responsible for sexual excitement, while decreasing levels of serotonin, responsible for sexual inhibition.

The difference between Addyi and Viagra type drugs is that the men's medications are physiological. Addyi targets lack of libido and affects the balance of certain chemicals in the brain. It also requires a daily (taken at bedtime) dose. JAMA reported a benefit for flibanserin over a placebo.

One study showed marginal results for women, compared to Viagra's immediate physical results for men. Severe adverse reactions have been observed, including dizziness, low blood pressure, and passing out after taking the drug along with much alcohol. High cost also contributes to lack of widespread use.

Incidentally, in English the meaning of the name Addy is ardent (characterized by intense emotion).

More Sun, Longer Life - Research from 2016 finds that women who sunbathe are likely to live longer than those who avoid the sun, even though sunbathers are at an increased risk of developing skin cancer.

An analysis of information on 29,518 Swedish women who were followed for 20 years revealed that "Longer life expectancy among women with active sun exposure habits was related to a decrease in heart disease and non-cancer non–heart disease deaths, causing the relative contribution of death due to cancer to increase." Whether the positive effect of sun exposure demonstrated in this observational study is mediated by vitamin D, another mechanism related to UV radiation, or by unmeasured bias could not be determined.

"We found smokers in the highest sun exposure group were at a similar risk as non-smokers avoiding sun exposure, indicating avoidance of sun exposure to be a risk factor of the same magnitude as smoking," said Dr. Pelle Lindqvist, lead author of the Journal of Internal Medicine study. "Guidelines being too restrictive regarding sun exposure may do more harm than good for health." *In other words, get out and enjoy some sunshine, just do not overdo it.*

Aspirin and Heart Attack - Your chest feels heavy, as if you are in a vise and the pain is spreading to your jaw and shoulder. What to do, call 911, then chew a single uncoated full-size 325-mg aspirin.

The reason you need aspirin is the same reason you should call 911. A heart attack is a dynamic event, and early intervention can limit damage. Paramedics can give you oxygen and medication, and they will monitor your blood pressure and heart rhythm to forestall complications. In the hospital, doctors take EKGs and blood tests to see if you are having a heart attack; if so, they will usually try to open the blocked artery with an angioplasty and stent or a clot-busting drug.

Most heart attacks develop when a cholesterol-laden plaque in a coronary artery ruptures. Relatively small plaques, which produce partial blockages, are the ones most likely to rupture. When they do, they attract platelets to their surface. Platelets are the tiny blood cells that trigger blood clotting. A clot builds up on the ruptured plaque. As the clot grows, it blocks the artery. If the blockage is complete, it deprives a portion of the heart muscle of oxygen. As a result, muscle cells die, a heart attack.

Aspirin helps by inhibiting platelets and just a tiny amount is needed to inhibit all the platelets in the bloodstream. Since the clot grows minute by minute, time is of the essence.

Studies show that a chewed aspirin needs only five minutes to reduce TxB2 concentrations by 50% and 14 minutes for the chewed tablet to produce maximal platelet inhibition, versus 26 minutes for an unchewed aspirin swallowed with water.

Aspirin can also help prevent heart attacks in patients with coronary artery disease and in healthy men over 50 years of age. Low doses, between 81 and 325 mg a day, are needed.

Sunscreen Facts - Summer means it is time to slather on some sunscreen - do it early and do it often. The US FDA, which regulates sunscreen, among other stuff too numerous to mention says, any sunscreen that is (Sun Protection Factor) SPF15 or above, and carries the label "broad spectrum," must provide protection from both UV-A and UV-B light. Any sunscreen SPF14 or below, or that is not labeled "broad spectrum," is primarily only useful for protection from UV-B light and against sunburn only. Other countries have started providing measurements for UV-A protection on their products, but not the US, yet.

Broad spectrum protection blocks both UV-B and UV-A light, which means you reduce your risk of sunburn as well as skin cancer. UV-A light, which has a much longer wavelength and penetrates deeper into the skin can also cause skin cancer.

SPF numbers are a simple metric, if you could stay in the sun for 10 minutes without getting a sunburn, SPF15 sunscreen would increases the length of time you can stay out in the sun by 15, so you should be able to stay in the sun for 150 minutes without getting burned. In addition, a higher SPF should prevent more UV light from affecting your skin.

SPF15 absorbs 93.3 percent of UVB rays, SPF30 absorbs 96.7 percent, and SPF50 absorbs 98%. Anything above SPF30 is probably not necessary and 50 or more is essentially a waste of money with little additional protection.

There are two basic kinds of sunscreens: physical blockers and chemical blockers. *Physical blockers* use minerals to deflect the UV rays away from the skin. *Chemical blockers* absorb and filter the light to prevent its damaging effects.

Sunscreen manufacturers are no longer allowed to claim their products are "waterproof," because none are. They can claim that their sunscreens are water resistant for instance 40 minutes, after which it should be reapplied.

Interesting to note that Australia is the skin cancer capital of the world with two in three getting skin cancer before age 70.

Bottom line, Consumer Reports found 74 percent of the physical blockers they tested failed to match their labeled SPF. For best results, go for broad spectrum SPF 30 to 50. *Unlike politicians, sunscreen is better when you lay it on thick - and often.*

DEET Facts - Experts are now saying that it is okay for all pregnant women to use insect repellents that contain DEET.

DEET is the most tested insect repellent available on the market. Concerns over the safety of DEET first emerged during the 1980s after reports of encephalopathy following DEET exposure, particularly in children. However, the role of DEET in either the illness or deaths was and remains purely speculative, says a recent meta-study about the safety of DEET.

A 2015 paper on insect repellent said, "During the 1980s and 1990s there were several reports of encephalopathy following DEET exposure in children. However, risk assessments by both the US Environmental Protection Agency and independent publications, as well as a clinical trial, found no association between encephalopathy and DEET use, and no toxological risk or severe effects except after inappropriate use (ingestion, direct inhalation, or eye exposure)."

The Division of Toxicology and Human Health Sciences looked into the health effects of DEET, as well, and found that over 40 years of use, from 1961 to 2002, eight DEET-related deaths occurred. Three were of people intentionally drinking it, two were of adults wearing it, and three were of girls under 6 who underwent "heavy" use.

DEET is the safest bug repellent, according to both the CDC and the EPA. It is also one of the few OK for use on babies as young as two months, and on pregnant women in their second and third trimesters.

Because people are worried about this type of thing, most bottles of DEET tell you to wash it off after use. This step is to minimize excess exposure.

Picaridin has not been safety-tested nearly as much as DEET, though it may be just as effective. Oil of lemon eucalyptus is most often a synthesized, lab-made compound also known as PMD. According to the CDC, neither type is suitable for use on children younger than 3, because they are severe eye irritants and children that young tend to rub their eyes a lot. PMD is not the same as the "pure" oil of lemon eucalyptus, which is not recommended for use as a repellent as it has not been tested for efficacy.

Phone and Medical Info - There is an app that is pre-loaded on iPhone and available for Android that could save your life or the life of someone you love.

It is the Health app, which includes Medical ID. You can use Medical ID to list the names of your emergency contacts, their phone numbers, special instructions, your health ailments, and any medications you are taking or allergic to, that emergency personnel should know about.

Paramedics may not have time to access this information on your phone in an emergency, so it is not meant to replace a medical ID bracelet. However, if time is available, emergency personnel usually know they can swipe for this information.

For iPhones, Tap on Medical ID > Edit. Then turn on Show When Locked. This ensures that first responders can see your medical information even when your iPhone screen is locked. To make an emergency call or to see your Medical ID, wake up your phone by swiping left to right > tap Emergency > make emergency call or tap Medical ID to see the stored medical information.

For Android users solutions vary by manufacturer. Under Settings, look for an Emergency Contact-type feature. It may be under My Information. If so, fill in your medical information and emergency contact numbers.

To add an Emergency Contact to your phone lock screen, tap Settings > Lock Screen > check mark Owner Info > Tap the small icon to the right of Owner Info > type in your emergency contact name and phone number after owner name. This information will scroll across your lock screen even when it is locked.

Energy Drink Ingredients - Here are some of the most common energy drink ingredients, and where they rate on usefulness and safety. I covered energy drinks before, but this offers more detail.

Ginseng is used most commonly in Chinese medicine. Ginseng is an herb that has been used traditionally to treat numerous ailments. It is generally thought to boost immunity and improve overall health. Research doesn't conclusively back up these claims, but short-term use is thought to be safe.

Taurine is an amino acid found in protein, meat, fish, and breast milk. It helps us maintain neurological function and regulate fluid levels. There are some claims that taking a taurine supplement can improve athletic performance, but not much data exists on its efficacy or its safety as either a supplement or energy drink ingredient.

Guarana is an herb that is often used as a stimulant in teas, either added or naturally occurring. Its major component is caffeine. It has been associated with increased energy and enhancement of physical performance.

Ginko biloba is another herb, added to supposedly increase alertness. It has been used medicinally for thousands of years, according to the Mayo Clinic, and research supports its use for some medical conditions including dementia, anxiety, and schizophrenia. For other uses, evidence is lacking or mixed.

Carnitine is naturally produced by our bodies and is a substance that is used to turn fat into energy. You can also buy it as a supplement, and it claims to boost exercise performance. Some studies suggest carnitine may be promising in treating various health problems, like certain heart conditions, kidney disease, and hyperthyroidism, but in all cases, more research needs to be done.

Medical July Effect - This documented phenomenon is known as the July Effect: when all the almost-docs get to swap their med school scrubs for white coats and stethoscopes, hospitals are temporarily at higher risk of the sort of silly slip-ups and errors, as well as making hospitals the third leading killer of Americans each year.

The coincidence of med school graduations in the month has been directly linked to a ten percent spike in hospital errors, involving everything from mixing up medications to not knowing how to work a defibrillator. Experts agree that, if at all possible, it is best to avoid hospitals throughout the summer.

Researchers from the University of California at San Diego investigated more than 62 million US death certificates between 1979 and 2006. Of those, 244,388 deaths were caused by medication errors in hospitals.

Month to month, the statistics showed a relatively equal chance for a fatal medication error, except at teaching hospitals in the month of July. The study found that fatal medication errors spiked by ten percent in July in counties with a high number of teaching hospitals, but stayed the same in areas without teaching hospitals. The findings appear in a recent issue of the Journal of General Internal Medicine. *Hospital errors are the third leading cause of death in US.*

Sweet Urine - In 1647, English physician Dr. Thomas Willis was the first in modern medical literature to discover that urine from those who had diabetes tasted sweet, comparing the flavor to that of honey.

Willis described the flavor as, "wonderfully sweet as if it were imbued with honey or sugar." Although such a discovery is off-putting and disgusting to most, it broke down barriers to the understanding of diabetes. Ultimately, it led to the term "mellitus" as in "diabetes mellitus," a Latin word for "honey" which Willis coined.

LEDs Making us Fat? - Am thinking they are trying way too hard to get headlines. According to the American Medical Association, which represents about 15% of physicians, "Recent large surveys found that brighter residential nighttime lighting is associated with reduced sleep times, dissatisfaction with sleep quality, excessive sleepiness, impaired daytime functioning, and obesity." It says, "the effect of streetlight LEDs on drivers and passengers lingers even after we have locked our cars and headed indoors, especially if we have LEDs in our houses."

Incidentally, Doximity, a social network for doctors founded in 2011 now has more members than the AMA.

Blood Pressure History - In 1628, Dr. Harvey published Exercitatio Anatomica de Motu Cordis et Sanguinis in Animalibus ("On the Movement of the Heart and Blood in Animals"), which was the foundation for work on the circulatory system.

Over 100 years later in 1733, Reverend Stephen Hales recorded the first blood pressure measurement after developing a further understanding of the correlation between the heart and pulse and how it applies to blood pressure and volume.

This new knowledge allowed for the invention of the first sphygmomanometer (blood pressure monitor) in 1881 by Samuel Siegfried Karl Ritter von Basch.

However, it was not until 1905 that Dr. Nikolai Korotkoff discovered the difference between systolic and diastolic blood pressures, further improving the sphygmomanometer by using a cuff that could be placed around the arm to provide equal pressure. Korotkoff discovered the varying sounds within the arteries as pressure was applied and released, and this remains the standard of blood pressure measurement to this day.

Here is what the US National Institution of Health says, Blood pressure can identify potential heart disease, stroke, eye problems, or chronic kidney disease. All adults should have their blood pressure checked:

- Every 2 years if your blood pressure was less than 120/80 mm Hg at the most recent reading.
- Yearly if your last reading was 120 to 139/80 to 89 mm Hg or if you have high blood pressure, diabetes, heart disease, kidney problems.

Wow, modern medical technology with a silly name and over a hundred years old.

Chemotherapy Origin - During the early 1900s, German chemist Paul Ehrlich focused his attention on immunology as well as combating infectious diseases through the use of drugs. Ehrlich coined the term 'chemotherapy', which he described as a process of treating diseases with chemicals.

He tested his chemicals on animal models and was the first person to show the potential effect that drugs could have. In 1908, Ehrlich used arsenicals to treat syphilis in a live rabbit, which he cured before penicillin was created in 1929.

In time, he turned his interest to the cure of cancer, ultimately using the first alkylating agents and aniline dyes that proved to be effective. His pioneering research and the therapies that he discovered, such as using chemicals that combated not only diseases, but tumors as well led to groundbreaking contributions that gave birth to modern chemotherapy.

Free Gym Membership - Before you sign up or renew your health club/gym membership, check your health insurance policy. Many reimburse for health club membership fees.

Alkaline Water - This type of water is supposedly an extra-healthy type of water to drink, with claims that it slows the aging process, increases energy, helps cure fertility issues, regulates the body's pH level, has antioxidant features, cleanses organs, and prevents chronic diseases like cancer.

Proponents of alkaline water believe it works by making our bodies less acidic. Many people believe that the American diet contributes to chronic low-grade acidosis, associated with health issues including hormonal problems, loss of bone, and metabolic problems.

In your stomach, where the stomach acids digest your food, the pH is 1.5 to 3.5 (acidic). Antacids, like Tums contain alkaline ions that can cancel out acidity and neutralize stomach gastric acid. Under normal circumstances, stomach acid is essential for food digestion.

There are two types of alkaline water: artificial alkaline water, which is generally tap water run through an electrical ionizer to make the pH more alkaline and bottled spring or mineral water. Natural spring water passes through rocks and soil and picks up various minerals, which affect its pH. Naturally-occurring mineral water contains alkalizing compounds, such as calcium, silica, potassium, magnesium, and bicarbonate.

For people who have a kidney condition or people who are taking medication that alters kidney functions, the minerals in alkaline water could start to accumulate in their bodies. Drinking too much alkaline water, or drinking water with a high pH, may disrupt the body's normal pH. This can lead to a condition called metabolic alkalosis, which may cause confusion, nausea, vomiting, hand tremors, muscle twitching, and tingling in the face, hands or feet.

You can purchase water ionizing machines, which use titanium or platinum to make water alkaline, and they do not introduce natural minerals.

There are no peer-reviewed studies demonstrating that consuming alkaline water can reduce a person's cancer risk or help them to better fight cancer and the American Cancer Society does not make a recommendation for consumption of alkaline water.

It is possible that alkaline water may provide some health benefits, to some people, in some circumstances, such as with acid reflux disease.

No studies, to date have proven there is any benefit to health by drinking alkaline water. According to Mayo Clinic, regular water is best and there is no scientific evidence that verifies the claims made by alkaline water proponents. *Caveat Emptor!*

Ultrasound vs. Sonogram - A sonogram is the image generated during ultrasonography, which is a diagnostic imaging technique that uses ultrasound to visualize anything inside the body.

Ultrasound is sound with a frequency above the range audible to humans, about 20 kHz. Both words are used to refer to the ultrasonography procedure.

When ultrasound waves are sent into the human body some of them bounce back when they hit tissues of differing density. The time it takes the reflected ultrasound waves to return to the machine is translated into an image of the internal organ, or of a fetus. This image is called a sonogram.

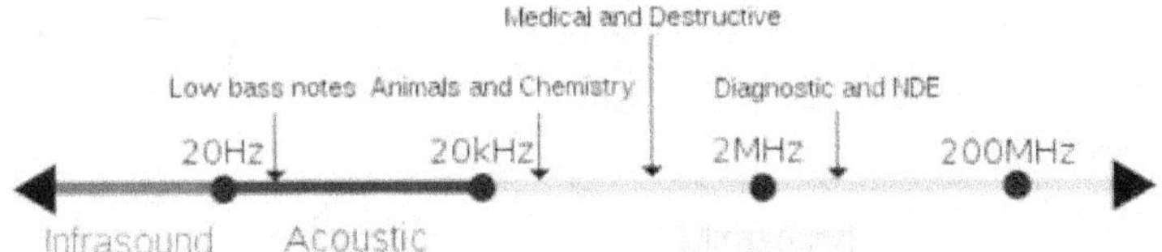

Ultrasound is used in industry to measure the purity or uniformity of liquid, to measure the depth of water, and to search for underwater objects such as submarines. Whales and dolphins use ultrasound to communicate.

Preauricular sinus - I have a Preauricular sinus and never knew it. These are common congenital malformations first described by Heusinger in 1864. Both sexes can have one. In females, it is commonly found outside the right ear.

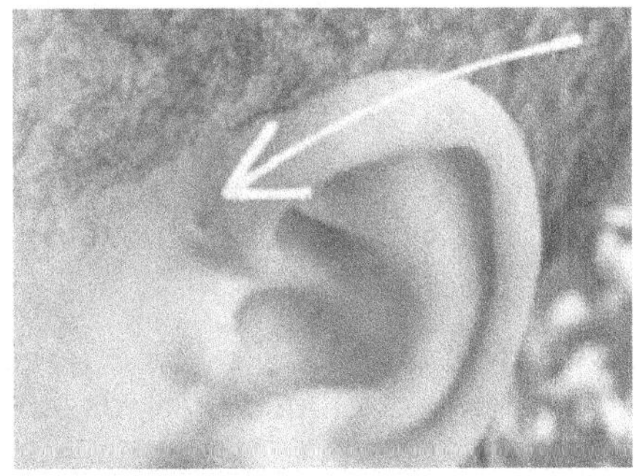

Theories of origin of preauricular sinus (also known as a congenital auricular fistula) includes: defective or incomplete fusion of the beginnings of the external ears at the embryonic stage. Just one third of folks even know they have one.

The sinus may be bilateral (both ears) in 25-50% of cases, and bilateral sinuses are more likely to be hereditary. In unilateral cases, the left side is more commonly affected. They are usually benign and do not change through life.

On Facebook, people with a preauricular sinus believe they are special. Neil Shubin, an evolutionary biologist, has a highly speculative theory that the holes could be an "evolutionary remnant of fish gills."

In Taiwan, the incidence of preauricular sinuses is estimated to be 1.6-2.5%; in Scotland, 0.06%; and in Hungary, 0.47%. In some parts of Asia and Africa, the incidence is estimated to be 4-10%. Just 0.1

percent of the population have it in the US, and 0.9 percent in the UK. *Bottom line, I always knew I was special, now I can prove it. Ha*

FODMAP - Have been seeing ads lately for something called FODMAP. I never heard the term before, so thought I would do some research. It is an acronym for **F**ermentable **O**ligosaccharides (eg. Fructans and Galacto-oligosaccharides (GOS) **D**isaccharides (eg. Lactose) **M**onosaccharides (eg. excess Fructose) and **P**olyols (eg. Sorbitol, Mannitol, Maltitol, Xylitol and Isomalt). The name alone raised my latest-fad-diet-of-the-week antenna.

A FODMAP is one of a group of compounds thought to contribute to the symptoms of irritable bowel syndrome and similar gastrointestinal disorders. The term is used mainly with reference to a diet that is low in these compounds.

Foods high in FODMAPs include barley, yogurt, many fruits, honey, almost all beans, garlic, onions, foods that contain wheat, beer, coconut milk, rum, soy milk, tea, cheese, milk, ice cream, and cauliflower.

Blackberries bad, blueberries good. Celery less than 5cm of stalk good, Celery more than 5cm of stalk bad.

It is a relatively new concept and was first published in 2005. The low FODMAP diet was originally developed by a research team at Monash University in Melbourne, Australia. When looking for some proof, only found a few published papers and each contained the same author Susan J Shepherd, an Advanced Accredited Practicing Dietitian and Accredited Nutritionist who is director of a private practice Shepherd Works. She also has a line of low FODMAP products.

The foods to avoid is too long to include here. *For me, the name alone gives me IBS.*

Finger Fact - The ratio between the lengths of one's index and ring fingers is usually quite different in men and women. Men tend to have shorter index fingers than ring fingers; women tend to have their index fingers either the same length or longer than their ring fingers. *I saw you checking.*

Cold or Flu - This is the time of year there are many bugs going around to make us miserable. Worse yet, some come back during the same season. In general, flu symptoms tend to be more severe than cold symptoms, but do not last as long. Here are a few ways to tell whether you have a cold or the flu.

Symptoms of a cold usually come on gradually, but symptoms of the flu can appear suddenly.

Symptoms such as sneezing, stuffy nose, and sore throat are more common with colds than with the flu.

People with the flu usually develop a fever, but people with colds rarely do.

The flu often causes body aches and headaches, which can be severe. If you have a cold, aches are usually mild.

The flu can cause serious complications, such as pneumonia or bacterial infections, but such compilations are rare with colds.

You can get a seasonal flu vaccine to reduce the severity of flu each year, but there is no vaccine to protect from the common cold.

Washing your hands frequently can help prevent either cold or flu.

There is no cure for the common cold, but relief includes: stay hydrated, get rest, soothe a sore throat, combat stuffiness, relieve pain. etc. All are common sense, and should help you feel better for the week or two it takes to shake that nasty cold. Antibiotics attack bacteria, but they are no help against cold viruses.

Antiviral medications do not cure, but can help alleviate some of flu symptoms, and many of the remedies for cold apply to the flu as well, including taking medicine for headaches. Flu symptoms usually are gone in a short time and do not linger as a cold does.

Regardless of whether you have a cold or the flu, the illness will usually go away on its own, but you should visit your doctor if your symptoms change or get worse. *If you get either a cold or flu, please stay home and do not share.*

Zinc and Colds - It is one of the few ingredients linked to shortening a cold. Unlike Vitamin C, which studies have found likely does nothing to prevent or treat the common cold, zinc may actually be worth it. The mineral seems to interfere with the replication of rhinoviruses, the bugs that cause the common cold.

In a 2011 review of studies of people who recently became ill, researchers looked at those who started taking zinc and compared them with those who just took a placebo. The ones on the zinc had shorter colds and less severe symptoms.

Uninsured vs. Insured - Did a comparison on the number of US uninsured vs. insured between 2007 (before the Patient Protection and Affordable Care Act) and 2016. Medicare and Medicaid added 18.7 million more people than the uninsured reduction.

In addition, this does not count the number of insured, whose premiums are being subsidized by the Affordable Care Act.

	Millions		
	2007	2016	diff
Uninsured	45.7	27.3	-18.4
Medicaid	46.4	70.5	24.1
Medicare	44	57	13

As the chart shows, Uninsured dropped by 18.4 million people. However, the number of people covered by Medicaid and Medicare increased by 37.1 million during the same period. Medicaid, alone added 5.7 million more people than were dropped from the uninsured rolls. At the same time, Medicare added an additional 13 million people.

Bottom line, the pea shuffle of uninsured numbers looks like all is well, except the rest of us are paying more for Medicaid, more for Medicare, more for subsidies to cover insurance for the poor - and more for increases in the cost of our own health insurance.

Talking Bandages - Bandages now can detect how a wound is healing and send messages back to a doctor. 3-D printing is used to manufacture the dressings. Nano-sensors within the bandages report to doctors about events such as detected infections and blood clotting.

The work on smart bandages is at Swansea University, and could be set for trials within the next twelve months. The smart bandage effort is part of a 5G test hub for digital innovation. Professor Marc Clement said experts at the Welsh Wound Innovation Centre are also involved in the project.

Care by the Numbers - Medicaid and Medicare are similar programs that are publicly run. They cover 70 million and 57 million Americans, respectively. They each use their large membership to negotiate lower prices with hospitals and doctors. Medicaid tends to have the lowest payment rates. On average, Medicaid pays 66 percent of what Medicare pays doctors.

Medical Paperwork - A PricewaterhouseCoopers study for the American Hospital Association chronicled more than 40 layers of paperwork associated with caring for a typical Medicare patient who arrives at an emergency room with a broken hip and receives treatment until recuperation. Some of the findings:

> The US Census Bureau as of 2016 shows population of about 323 million Americans.

Roughly 60 minutes of paperwork were performed for every hour of emergency department care, 36 minutes of paperwork for every hour of surgery and acute inpatient care, 30 minutes of paperwork for every hour of skilled nursing care, and 48 minutes of paperwork for every hour of home healthcare.

"Each time a physician orders a test or a procedure, the physician documents the order in the patient's record, and the government requires additional documentation to prove the necessity for the test or procedure." "Many forms ... must be completed daily by clinical staff to submit to the government to justify the care provided to skilled nursing facility patients."

Medicare and Medicaid "rules and instructions" are more than 130,000 pages and "medical records must be reviewed by at least four people to ensure compliance" with Medicare program requirements.

"A Medicare patient arriving at the emergency department is required to review and sign eight different forms, just for Medicare."

"Each time a patient is discharged, even if only from the acute unit of the hospital to an on-site skilled nursing unit, multiple care providers must write a discharge plan for the patient. This documentation, as long as 30 pages, applies to all patients, regardless of the complexity of care received within the hospital or required post-hospital setting."

In addition to regulation by state agencies, local agencies, private accrediting organizations, and insurers, hospitals are regulated by more 30 federal agencies.

Three Strange Job Illnesses - *Chimney sweep's cancer,* also called soot wart, and chimney sweep's scrotum is a squamous cell carcinoma of the skin of the scrotum. Warts caused by the irritation from soot particles, if not excised, developed into a scrotal cancer, then enlarged the testicle and proceeded up the spermatic cord into the abdomen where it proved fatal. It is the first reported form of occupational cancer, and was first identified during 1775. It was initially noticed as being prevalent among chimney sweeps.

Bagpiper's Fungus - Bagpipes are made of sheepskin traditionally coated in treacle or honey on the lining to keep it airtight. The inside is sticky, dark and damp, making it a breeding ground for spores and fungus. Pipers breath in those bacteria and develop pneumonia, respiratory infections, and more.

Wool Sorter's Disease - This condition usually afflicts those working with wool, like sheep shearers. What the name does not suggest is just how bad this disease actually is. The more common name is anthrax. A person can contract meningitis, high fever, and severe abdominal pain, before finally suffering a fatal respiratory collapse - all from breathing in the bacteria hidden in sheep's wool.

Medicare Birthday - On July 30, 1965, at a public ceremony in Independence, MO., President Lyndon Baines Johnson signed Medicare into law. Moments later, the 36th president of the United States presented America's 33rd president, Harry S. Truman, then 81 years old — the nation's first Medicare card.

Medicare provides health insurance to Americans age 65 and older and to younger people with certain disabilities or health conditions. At its creation, Medicare consisted of two parts: Medicare Part A hospital insurance coverage and Medicare Part B, an optional medical insurance program.

Medicare's first beneficiaries paid a $40 annual deductible for Part A. The monthly premium for Part B was $3.

CT, MRI, PET, and SPECT Scans - Had a chance to sample some of this technology recently and realized many folks are not aware of what the terms actually mean. Each requires a distinct type of radiology equipment used to perform mostly medical procedures. Each piece of equipment costs millions of dollars and data shows that more machines cause more tests to be performed. Various pieces of equipment may look different, due to company design and age of the equipment.

A CT (computed axial tomography) scan uses X-rays, an MRI (Magnetic resonance imaging) scan uses magnetic and radio waves, a PET (Positron emission tomography) scan uses a radioactive substance injected in the body and gamma rays, and SPECT (Single photon emission computed tomography) scan uses a radioactive substance injected into the body and a gamma camera. Tomography is a technique for displaying a representation of a cross section through a human body or other solid object using a penetrating wave.

A CT scan is better suited to cancer, pneumonia, abnormal chest x-rays, and bleeding in the brain, especially after an injury. A CT scan shows organ tear and organ injury more quickly, so is more suitable for trauma cases. Broken bones and vertebrae are more clearly visible on a CT scan. CT scans provide a better image of the lungs and organs in the chest cavity between the lungs.

An MRI is better for examining the spinal cord. An MRI shows a more visible brain tumor.

A CT scan does not show tendons and ligaments, but an MRI does.

A CT or MRI scan can assess the size and shape of body organs and tissue, but they cannot assess how these work.

The PET system detects pairs of gamma rays emitted indirectly by a positron-emitting radionuclide (tracer), which is introduced into the body. Three-dimensional images of tracer concentration within the body are then constructed by computer analysis.

A PET scan can show how an organ works, and is often used with a CT or MRI scan. PET scans are used to diagnose a condition or to track how it is developing. PET scans are used to investigate epilepsy, Alzheimer's disease, cancer, and heart disease.

The SPECT system works like a PET, but uses gamma rays to show a tracer dose of radioactive material injected into the body. The material moves to areas of bone and elsewhere highlighting healing or cancer progression as it is usually lit up on SPECT scans.

Cancer Stages and Grades - Cancer is the name given to a collection of related diseases. In all types of cancer, some of the body's cells begin to divide without stopping and spread into surrounding tissues.

Too many of us are aware of the prevalence of cancer in our society. Two words often come up, but are not universally understood. Staging is for the cancer itself and grade references the actual tumor. Beyond that, things get confusing, because there are different grading systems for different types of cancer. For instance, there is Gleason for prostate cancer, Bloom-Richardson for breast cancer, Fuhrman for kidney cancer, etc.

Cancer stage refers to the size and/or reach of the original (primary) tumor and whether or not cancer cells have spread (metastasized) elsewhere in the body. Stages do not change from initial diagnosis, even if the cancer becomes more aggressive. This is important for consistent statistical analysis.

Stage 0 (zero) Abnormal cells are present, but have not spread to nearby tissue. Stages I, II, and III Cancer is present. The higher the number, the larger the cancer tumor and the more it has spread into nearby tissues.

Stage IV The cancer has spread to distant parts of the body.

Staging is usually based on the TNM system of classifying cancer. In the TNM system, each cancer is assigned a letter or number to describe the **t**umor, **n**ode, and **m**etastases. T stands for the original (primary) tumor. N stands for nodes and tells whether the cancer has spread to the nearby lymph nodes. M stands for metastasis.

Tumor grade is the description of a tumor based on how abnormal the tumor cells and tumor tissue look under a microscope. There are four grades G1 Well differentiated (low grade), G2 Moderately differentiated (intermediate grade), G3 Poorly differentiated (high grade), and G4 Undifferentiated (high grade). Grade 3 and 4 tumors tend to grow rapidly and spread faster than tumors with a lower grade.

Low-grade cancer cells look more like normal cells and tend to grow and spread more slowly than high-grade cancer cells. Cancer grade may be used to help plan treatment and determine prognosis.

In addition, there are two tumor types, *benign,* such as moles and warts and *malignant,* where the cells invade the surrounding tissue and organs.

Generally, there are five cancer stages, four tumor grades, and two tumor types, benign and malignant. *Unlike school, a high stage or grade is not good.*

HEALTH AND HAPPINESS

Happiness Study - For the study, published in Social Psychology and Personality Science, researchers Aaron Weidman and Elizabeth Dunn from the University of British Columbia gave 67 participants $20 to spend on either an experiential or material purchase of their choice, and then to report one experiential or material gift they had recently received. Then they quizzed them about their happiness levels through text messages and questionnaires.

They found that the study subjects derived more frequent momentary happiness from material goods, but more intense momentary happiness from the experiences. In other words, they enjoyed their material goods on a greater number of occasions than they did their experiences, even though the happiness felt from the experiences was slightly more intense.

People who want the most happiness for their buck should buy experiences, not things. The idea is that the joy of an experience begins before it even starts, and continues when you look back on the fancy dinner or vacation fondly. Experiences provide both more anticipatory happiness and afterglow happiness.

Another Happiness Study - In countries worldwide, happiness for most is success in doing the things of everyday life. That might be making a living, raising a family, maintaining good health, and working in an interesting and secure job. These are the things that dominate daily lives everywhere; the things that people care about and which they think they have some ability to control.

> "Laugh a lot, and when you are older, all your wrinkles will be in the right places."

Psychologists have investigated the reliability and validity of the measures and economists have studied the nature and robustness of the results. Support comes from the fact that many countries now officially collect happiness data. The same relationships are found between happiness and a variety of life circumstances in country after country. Those who are significantly less happy are typically the unemployed, those not living with a partner, people in poor health, members of a minority, and the less-educated.

Respondents to surveys clearly recognize the difference between happiness as an emotion and happiness in the sense of life satisfaction.

Happiness Followup - My friend, Deacon Bob passed along this addition to last week's Thoughts. A strong correlation exists between religiosity and personal happiness, according to a new study by the Austin Institute for the Study of Family and Culture.

The study found that people who attend religious services on a weekly basis are nearly twice as likely to describe themselves as "very happy" (45%) than people who never attend (28%). Conversely, those who never worship are twice as likely to say they are "very unhappy" (4%) as those who attend services weekly (2%).

Laughing - Did you know that laughing stimulates neurotransmitters in the brain that improve learning and increase attention span.

Medicine and Humor - The International Journal of Psychiatry in Medicine says, "A highly significant increase in survival was due to the psychological variables of block three [quality of life and sense of humor] essentially accounted for by sense of humor. Those who scored above the median in sense of humor increased their odds for survival by on average 31%. Conclusions: Sense of humor appeared to mediate better coping and therefore, protected against detrimental effects of disease-related stressors upon survival."

This finding is in line with the notions that stress weakens the immune system and humor can reduce stress.

Researchers are using the idea that stress reduces blood flow and laughter increases blood flow. A preliminary study by Michael Miller, M.D., and others (all from the University of Maryland School of Medicine, Baltimore, US) used violent and comedic movie scenes with twenty patients. In 2005 Miller reported that "average blood flow increased twenty two percent during laughter, and decreased 35 percent during mental stress." Miller said we still need to exercise regularly, but 15 minutes of laughter on a daily basis is probably good for the vascular system.

> Laughing for fifteen minutes has the same benefit as getting two extra hours of sleep.

Bottom line, laughter can improve your health.

Laughter and Exercise - According to researchers at Georgia State University, forced laughter incorporated into an exercise program increases the health benefits and makes older adults more likely to exercise more. Simulated laughter techniques added to a strength, balance, and flexibility workout improved older adults' performance in an exercise program and significantly improved their enjoyment.

> A hearty belly laugh leads to a natural boost in blood pressure and heart rate, which can overpower the midday fatigue.
> ~ Dr. Robert Provine

Laughter has physical benefits, and in many cases has an effect on the muscles used during exercise programs. Forced laughter, or choosing to laugh, rather than as a response to something funny gave way to actual laughter and enjoyment for most participants in classes with laughing incorporated into physical exercises.

Laughter is an enjoyable activity and has many health benefits. In a recent study, participants experienced improvement in mental health, aerobic endurance, and outcome expectation for exercise, with 96.2 percent of participants saying laughter made exercise more enjoyable, 88.9 percent saying it made exercise more accessible and 89.9 percent saying it would motivate them to participate in more exercise classes or activities. *We all need a good laugh for better health and to clear out the cobwebs of our mind.*

Benefits of Laughter - Laughter reduces the level of stress hormones like cortisol, adrenaline, dopamine, and growth hormone. It also increases the level of health-enhancing hormones like endorphins. Laughter increases the number of antibody-producing cells and enhances the effectiveness of T cells. All this means a stronger immune system, as well as fewer physical effects of stress.

A good belly laugh exercises the diaphragm, contracts the abs and even works out the shoulders, leaving muscles more relaxed afterward. It even provides a good workout for the heart.

Laughter provides distraction and brings focus away from anger, guilt, stress, and negative emotions in a more beneficial way than other distractions.

Studies show that our response to stressful events can be altered by whether we view something as a 'threat' or a 'challenge'. Humor can give us a more lighthearted perspective and help us view events as 'challenges', thereby making them less threatening and more positive.

Laughter connects us with others. Just as with smiling and kindness, most people find that laughter is contagious, so if you bring more laughter into your life, you can most likely help others around you to laugh more, and realize these benefits as well. By elevating the mood of those around you, you can reduce their stress levels, and perhaps improve the quality of social interaction you experience with them.

Quote - "Like a welcome summer rain, humor may suddenly cleanse and cool the earth, the air and you." ~ Langston Hughes

----

Quick Clean Humor - I told my girlfriend she drew her eyebrows too high.
She seemed surprised.

What's the difference between in-laws and outlaws?
Outlaws are wanted.

And God said to John, come forth and you shall be granted eternal life.

John came fifth and won a toaster.

I bought some shoes from a drug dealer. I don't know what he laced them with, but I have been tripping all day.

I bought the world's worst thesaurus yesterday.
Not only is it terrible, it is terrible.

> I believe that laughing is the best calorie burner.
> I believe that happy girls are the prettiest girls.
> ~Audrey Hepburn

Older is Better - Research has shown getting older could also mean getting happier. During 2016, research from the UK Office for National Statistics concluded the most joyful age bracket was 65-79.

The survey looked at more than 300,000 adults across the UK and found life satisfaction peaked at that age before declining over 80. However, those in their 40s were shown to be less happy and with the highest levels of anxiety.

In a blog post on Psychology Today, Dr. Romeo Vitelli says that happiness can be a tricky thing to define. It can mean the kind of joy that only occurs at key moments in our lives, or it can simply be the amount of positive emotion we happen to feel at any given time. There appears to be an upswing as we get older.

A United States research project found happiness was relatively stable for people in their mid-20s to late 30s, then it declined during the 40s and slowly rose to a peak from 60 to 69 years old.

It is all relative, and there is no set rule for how happy anyone will be at certain times in life. *I believe, regardless of age, you can be as happy as you choose to be.*

Quote - "I love people who make me laugh. I honestly think it's the thing I like most, to laugh. It cures a multitude of ills. It's probably the most important thing in a person." ~Audrey Hepburn

One minute of anger weakens the immune system for 4 to 5 hours.

One minute of laughter boosts the immune system for 24 hours.

CANNABIS

Indica vs. Sativa vs. Hybrid - Another sea change is beginning. It stems from a number of states approving legislation for the legalization of marijuana, either for recreational or medical purposes.

It seems odd to me that any substance can be classified as either medical or recreational. I guess that pouring vodka on a wound to cleanse it might be considered medical use and drinking it might be considered recreational. However, marijuana can be ingested the same way for both purposes.

Cannabis classification has been around for a long time. Early taxonomic distinctions between Cannabis indica and Cannabis sativa began in the 18th century when differences between their structure and resin production were first noted. The hybrid category was adopted later on, as growers began mixing genetics from different geographic locations. In addition to the major strains, each can have many minor strains that produce different effects.

Indica strains are known for being physically sedating, perfect for relaxing with a movie or as a nightcap before bed.

Sativas typically provide more invigorating, uplifting cerebral effects that pair well with physical activity, social gatherings, and creative projects.

Hybrids tend to fall somewhere in between the indica-sativa spectrum, depending on the traits they inherit from their parent strains.

Other unique attributes:
Indica and sativa plants have differences in appearance.
Sativa plants have a longer maturation cycle than indica plants.
Indica strains tend to produce heavier yields than sativa strains.
Indica and sativa strains tend to have different flavor profiles.

Because of these differences, medical patients using cannabis to treat their symptoms and conditions may also consider a strain's classification. A patient suffering from fatigue or depression may use a sativa during the day, and another treating pain and insomnia will likely choose an indica strain at nighttime.

Incidentally, most countries use the word cannabis vs. the US use of the word marijuana. Also, the US stock market and valuations for cannabis companies is vigorously growing.

Cannabis Genotype vs. Phenotype - There are there are defining characteristics for every strain, but each plant uniquely expresses genes according to its garden environment. That is why the government is so determined to control the production process, from seed to distribution.

Two things influence the structural formation of any given cannabis plant: genetics and environment. The plant's genetic makeup, also called a genotype, acts as a blueprint for growth: it allows a spectrum of physical possibilities, but it is up to the environment to induce these characteristics.

The physical expression of a genotype is referred to as a phenotype, which is simply defined as the traits that the environment pulls out from the plant's genetic code. Everything from color, shape, smell, and resin production are affected by the environment.

Cannabis breeding took a major turn during the 1970s and 1980s when federal anti-cannabis sentiments peaked, driving cultivation from the great outdoors to inside. Indoor gardens, raised by soil, electric lights, and hydroponic systems, produce a bulk of the cannabis in the market today. The plant's phenotypic expression depends on: nutrients, temperature, the amount and angle of light, soil type, photoperiod length, time of harvest, and the distance between the plant and light source. These and other conditions affect a plant's characteristics.

Narrowing diversity even further, growers during this time were primarily motivated by THC content and selectively chose this characteristic over other important chemical constituents like CBD.

CBD vs. THC - Cannabidiol (CBD) and tetrahydrocannabinol (THC) are the two main ingredients in a cannabis plant. Both CBD and THC belong to a unique class of compounds known as cannabinoids.

While many strains of marijuana are known for having abundant levels of THC, high-CBD strains are less common. THC is probably best known for being the psychoactive ingredient in marijuana. CBD is non-psychoactive. In other words, CBD does not get you high. This unique feature of CBD is what makes it so appealing as a medicine.

THC is known to cause some people to feel anxious or paranoid, but CBD is believed to have the opposite effect. Studies show that CBD works to counteract the anxiety caused by ingesting THC. A number of studies also suggest that CBD can reduce anxiety when administered on its own.

In addition to being non-psychoactive, CBD seems to have antipsychotic properties. Researchers believe that CBD may protect marijuana users from getting too high by reducing the psychosis-like effects of THC. On its own, CBD is being tested as an antipsychotic medicine for people with schizophrenia.

One of the most common uses of cannabis is as a sleep aid. THC is believed to be responsible for most of marijuana's sleep-inducing effects. On the other hand, studies suggest CBD acts to promote wakefulness, making CBD a poor choice as a sleep medicine. The opposite effects of CBD and THC on sleep may explain why some strains of cannabis cause users to feel drowsy while others are known to boost energy.

While most countries have strict laws surrounding cannabis and THC, the legal status of CBD is less clear. In the United States, CBD is technically illegal since it is classified as a Schedule I drug under federal law. A pharmaceutical form of CBD, called Epidiolex, was only recently cleared by the FDA to be tested in children with severe epilepsy.

CBD is also found in hemp, which can be legally imported and sold in the US. Some companies have taken advantage of this loophole by importing high-CBD hemp extracts from other countries where hemp is produced.

Recently, research has shown CBD to have analgesic, anti-inflammatory, and anti-anxiety properties without the psychoactive effects, such as getting high. Its use looks promising to combat Crohn's disease, PTSD, multiple sclerosis, and Dravet's Syndrome.

THC is one of over 480 different compounds present in the cannabis plant. So far about 85 have been identified as cannabinoids The most well known of these compounds is the delta-9-tetrahydrocannabinol or THC.

Bottom line, THC is the stuff in cannabis that makes us high, while CBD is the stuff in cannabis that is used for medicinal purposes and does not make us high. Neither has a lethal dose.

Incidentally, marijuana is the most-consumed illegal drug in Germany, but recently, cannabis has expanded medical and legal allowances. German health insurance providers also now must cover the costs of cannabis treatments.

Phytocannabinoids - Prior to the US Marihuana (sic) Tax Act of 1937, phytocannabinoids found in hemp were prevalent in a vast majority of the food supply. Hemp oils and hemp proteins were used to fortify food formulations and consumed daily worldwide. Hemp was used as feed stock for nearly all animals that were consumed. Farmers would feed hemp to chickens, pigs, and cattle for its high protein and essential amino acids. The animals would then pass along to humans phytocannabinoids through their meat or milk and mothers would pass phytocannabinoids to their babies during breast feeding.

Cannabis Sativa, including hemp, is one of the only medicinal plants on Earth that grows naturally on nearly every continent of the world. The history of cannabis can be traced well beyond the beginnings of civilization. It has been used as both food and medicine since people began walking this planet. Humans and animals have evolved a system of cells that are nourished and replenished by phytocannabinoids.

Cannabinoids are active chemicals in cannabis that cause drug-like effects throughout the body, including the central nervous system and the immune system. They are also known as phytocannabinoids. At least 85 different cannabinoids have been isolated from the Cannabis plant.

Other plants that have cannabinoids include: Coneflower (Echinacea), Electric Daisy (Acmella Oleracea), Helichrysum Umbraculigerum, Liverwort (Radula Marginata), Chocolate (Theobroma Cacao), and Black Pepper (Piper Nigrum).

Cannabis History - US Drug Enforcement Administration Museum in Arlington, Virginia, states that the oldest written references to cannabis date back to 2727 B.C., when the Chinese supposedly discovered the substance and used it medicinally. Ancient Taiwanese were using hemp fibers to decorate pottery about 10,000 years ago, according to "The Archaeology of Ancient China." The plant itself was in use in both Europe and Asia more than 10,000 years ago and grew naturally across both continents.

According to a recent study, the world's first-known pot dealers were the nomads of the Eastern European Steppe. The Yamnaya, traders from what is now Russia and Ukraine, may have traded cannabis throughout Europe and East Asia about 5,000 years ago.

Archaeological records show a spike in cannabis use in East Asia around 5,000 years ago, at the time when the nomadic Yamnaya established a trade route across the steppes. Yamnaya sites show signs of cannabis burning, suggesting they may have brought the habit of smoking marijuana with them as they moved about.

The difference between hemp and pot is a single genetic switch. Researchers from the University of Saskatchewan announced that they discovered the genetic alteration that allows psychoactive cannabis plants (cannabis sativa) to give users a high, compared to industrial hemp plants, which do not.

Industrial hemp plants are the same species as marijuana plants, but they do not produce a substance called tetrahydrocannabinolic acid (THCA). This is the precursor to tetrahydrocannabinol (THC), the psychoactive ingredient in pot. Hemp plants fail to produce this substance because they lack a gene that makes an enzyme to produce THCA. *Hemp is rich in non-psychoactive CBDA, while marijuana produces THC.*

In the US, before the 1906 Pure Food and Drug Act, cannabis was a common ingredient in medicinal tinctures, and sellers were not required to mention it on their labels. During the 1920s and 1930s, Mexican immigration to the United States spiked as a result of the Mexican Revolution. People moving from Mexico brought along the custom of using marijuana for recreation, and the drug became linked with public fears of the newcomers.

It is not possible to overdose on marijuana like you can on heroin or cocaine.

Trivia, Facts, and Myths

Summer Outdoor Lighting Tip - Bugs do not fly toward many LEDs, because bugs are attracted to ultraviolet light and most LEDs do not give off this type of light.

Costco Savings Tips - If there is an asterisk * on a Costco price tag, that means the item will not be restocked and what you see is the last in the store. So if your favorite seasonal product is marked with an asterisk, it is time to buy enough to last you till next year.

A plus sign + on the sign means the item is discontinued.

Costco is a great place to visit for end-of-season sales. At the end of summer, Costco does major markdowns of large seasonal items like patio furniture and pool toys to free up room for the next season's products.

Costco's food court charges $1.50 for a hot dog and drink, and $1.99 for a slice of pizza. Costco's prices are coded. If an item ends with $0.99, it is regularly priced merchandise. Items ending with $0.97 have been marked down (usually also has an asterisk), meaning you are probably getting more for your money. If you see a price tag ending in $0.88 or an even dollar, those are usually local markdowns by a manager trying to get rid of a product. Other cents, such as 59, 69, 79, etc. is a special offer from the manufacturer, it reflects competitive pricing over other discount retailers.

> Costco is actually the 14th-largest pizza chain in the US.

Costco sends out an employee to comparison shop to make sure the warehouse is the lowest price on certain foods and big ticket items. They drive around town for two days filling out a clipboard of hundreds of items for comparison.

Costco locations sell restaurant gift cards, movie tickets, and other deals that allow you to get Costco-style discounts at local retailers. Some national deals: $100 worth of Cold Stone Creamery gift cards for $69.99 and a ten-pack of Regal Entertainment movie tickets for $89.99.

You can shop at Costco without a member card if you use a gift card, so you can ask a friend with a membership to get you a gift card and go shopping.

Costco, like Sams, does not offer bags. If you do not want cardboard box, bring your own bags.

Costco Liquor Facts - Costco is the US largest wine seller.

In many states, like Texas you do not need to have a membership to buy liquor.

It sells more bottles of Dom Perignon champagne than any other store in the country.

Costco brand wine, beer, and liquor is Kirkland.

Costco's Kirkland brand vodka scored higher than Grey Goose in blind tastings and its water comes from the same region in France.

Two Amazing Costco Facts - Costco sells over 100 million hot dogs a year, according to the Daily Meal. That is more than all the major league baseball parks combined sell in an entire season. *I also think they are better dogs than sold in many of the stadiums, and they are cheaper.*

Lyft and Uber Size - There are more than 315,000 Lyft drivers operating in 195 cities around the world, according to UC Berkeley. Uber operates in 360 cities in 68 countries, with hundreds of thousands of drivers signing up globally each month.

Films and Colons - Twenty films Hollywood will release in 2016 contain a colon in their title, such as "Captain America: Civil War." Thirteen are sequels, one is a reboot, one is a spinoff, one is based on a TV series, one is a concert film, one is an original comedy, and two are based on books. The colon proliferation is indicative of the industry's reliance on sequels and reboots that need to slightly distinguish themselves from their predecessors.

Butt Bricks - An engineer at RMIT University in Melbourne, has proposed re-purposing waste into bricks for building. Bricks produced using cigarette waste are cheaper and less energy intensive than traditional bricks. The cigarette butts are mixed into traditional clay bricks, reducing the energy required by 58 percent. The resulting bricks are more insulating, which would cut down the cost of heating or cooling a home, and easier to move due to their lighter weight.

He believes that his techniques could make a huge dent in the problem of global pollution. "Incorporating butts into bricks can effectively solve a global litter problem as recycled cigarette butts can be placed in bricks without any fear of leaching or contamination."

New York has its own solution to butts. Assemblyman Michael G. DenDekker, of Queens New York recently found out that cigarette butts can be turned into all kinds of useful things, so he proposed a bill for a cigarette recycling program for New York City. It would charge a one cent deposit on each cigarette to partially fund the recycling program and get those butts off the street. *I presume the remainder of funding will come from all taxpayers, smokers or not.*

> **Eliminate Nasty Paint Smells**
> Add one tablespoon of imitation vanilla extract per quart of freshly-opened paint and mix thoroughly until well-incorporated.

A clothing maker in Brazil turns cigarette butts into fabric.

The Cigarette Waste Brigade pilot project recently began in Vancouver, Canada. The program's first step was to install 110 recycling receptacles in four downtown areas where discarded butts are commonly found. The collected butts will be recycled into usable building materials such as planks and shipping pallets.

Life Hacks - Use permanent marker to write the day of purchase on anything you have that might expire.

If you find yourself with a paper cut, grab a ChapStick, or another type of lip balm, and rub it on the cut. It will help soothe the pain of the cut and it helps the cut heal faster.

When it's opened, hydrogen peroxide only lasts a few months before it becomes ineffective (aka turns to water). Unopened, it should be tossed after a year. You will know when it is bad when it stops fizzing.

Cheap power strips or ones that have been overworked can be a fire hazard, and use much energy in your house. Even good-quality surge protectors are only designed to last for a certain amount of joules, which is the amount of excess electrical surges they absorb. If they start to discolor or become hot to the touch, get a new one. It is generally a good idea to replace them every three to five years to keep you and your electronics safe.

Fire extinguishers expire from five to fifteen years, depending on the type. This is definitely one thing you want to be sure is OK, when you need it.

Bleach loses some if its potency after three months. This should not be a problem for household laundry, but the disinfectant qualities fall below the EPA standards at this time, which means it is no longer effective for cleaning.

Insect repellent loses effectiveness after about two years from the manufacture date, which should be marked on the bottle.

Flights Perspective - When Orville Wright died, (January 30, 1948 age 76), Neil Armstrong was 17 years old (born August 5, 1930).

The American Wright brothers, inventors, and aviation pioneers are generally credited with inventing, building, and flying the world's first successful airplane. They made the first controlled, sustained flight of a powered, heavier-than-air aircraft on December 17, 1903. Neil was the first man to walk on the moon July 20, 1969, sixty six years later. *The first Mars landing was July 21, 1976, seven years later.*

Easy Life Hacks - Did you make a mistake while leaving voicemail? Hit the # (pound or hashtag) button. It allows you to re-record your message. Works on a majority of operating systems.

Good for insurance claims, if you own some expensive things, they probably have some identification number. If so, write it down and save it in a safe place, preferably outside the house. Another idea is to take pictures or videos of the inside of your house, including TV, furniture, jewelry, etc.

If an anyone calls and asks if you have a security system, the answer is always yes. If they are bad guys, you shut them down and if they are sales people you also shut them down.

Pouring sugar on spilled nail polish helps to make it clump for easier cleanup.

Lightning Strikes - Between 2004 and 2013 an average of 33 Americans died each year as a result of lightning strikes. The numbers have been coming down and during 2015 there were only 27 lightning deaths.

Lightning strike Washington Monument Aug 15, 2010.

Nine occurred during the first six months of 2016. On average, about three times as many men are killed as women. About ten percent of people struck by lightning become a fatality.

Energy Credits and Rebates - My area was recently hit with a major hailstorm and it caused much destruction to cars, homes, and specifically roofs, and skylights. Insurance has been very good to pick up most costs, but not always the total cost.

I went looking for other ways to make up the difference and found many energy companies, local, state, and federal government programs that offer credits and rebates. Energy companies favor credits toward future bills. Too many options to list here, but look for your local utility company specifically and federal, state, city, and local county web sites for more info.

It is also wise to ask your contractor if he or she is aware of credits and rebates. It might help when choosing a roof type, adding insulation, etc. A little research can yield big financial benefits.

Grilling Tip - Toss some potato chips or Doritos on top of coals and light them. They will burn for long enough to start your coals and there is no fuel smell.

Helium - We usually think of helium as that stuff that goes in balloons, but it is much more. It is formed by the slow and steady radioactive decay of terrestrial rock and is the second most abundant element in the Universe, but very rare on Earth. Helium is used for keeping satellite instruments cool and to clean out rocket engines. It was also used to cool the liquid oxygen and hydrogen that powered the Apollo space vehicles.

Helium is used as a cooling medium for the Large Hadron Collider and the superconducting magnets in medical MRI scanners. It is often used to fill party balloons, weather balloons, and airships because of its low density. Helium-neon gas lasers are used to scan barcodes at supermarket checkouts.

A mixture of 80% helium and 20% oxygen is used by deep-sea divers and others working under pressurized conditions.

It also makes for fun differences with our vocal cords. When you inhale helium, you are changing the type of gas molecules in your vocal tract and increasing the speed of the sound of your voice and changing the timbre. Your voice sounds higher pitched. In contrast, heavier gases like xenon and sulfur hexafluoride slow the speed of sound and lower your resonant frequencies.

Heineken Bricks - During 1962, Alfred Heineken created a beer bottle that also could function as a brick to build houses in impoverished countries.

Ten Uses For Nail Polish Remover -
1. Wipe away permanent marker from any smooth surface.

2. Erase scuff marks from laminate, tile, or concrete floors.

3. Remove the sticky residue from jar labels.

4. Clean and sanitize your razor.

5. Remove stains from white china.

6. Remove nail polish from the carpet. (Pour a generous amount over the stain and let it sit for about a minute before using a hard-bristled brush to scrub it out.

7. Take stray paint off glass windows.

8. Wipe off stains on your shoes.

9. Wipe off colored printing from plastic containers.

10. Loosen the superglue cap. Use a few drops of nail polish remover to dissolve the glue that is dried on the cap.

Size Matters - The Statue of Liberty is the tallest statue in the US. France paid $250,000 to build the statue, US paid $275,000 to build the stand. It was originally copper color and gradually took on a patina to the current green.

Olympic Trivia - American John Heaton won the silver medal for the Skeleton (like a head first luge) in the 1928 games. He came back 20 years later for the 1948 games and won another silver medal in the Skeleton. He retains the record for the longest span between winning two Olympic medals for the same event. *Incidentally, he also won the bronze medal in the two-man bobsled at the 1932 Lake Placid Winter Games.*

Figure skating debuted in the 1908 Summer Games in London. The other warm weather events were held in April and the figure skating was held at the end of October, which made the London Games the longest in modern Olympics history.

Figure skating returned, along with ice hockey, in the 1920 Summer Games in Antwerp and both events were held in April along with the warm weather sports. Canada was the winner of the first Olympic ice hockey gold medal.

The Winter Olympic Games debuted in 1924 in Chamonix, France. The Winter Games included skiing, bobsledding, and curling, along with figure skating and ice hockey.

Another Use for Toothpaste - Take a damp, soft cloth and a small blob of toothpaste to easily erase minor scratches and scuff marks on your car. It works best if the scratches and/or scuff marks have not fully penetrated the clear coat of paint. Softly rub the toothpaste onto the scuff mark using small, circular motions to cover the blemished area.

Whitening toothpaste seems to work best as it has more abrasives than other types. Toothpaste works to sand down the uneven surface of the glossy sheen and fill in the gaps. Make sure the surface around the area is clean. If there is foreign paint on the outside, the toothpaste will also act as an abrasive to help remove it. *Incidentally, it also works well to buff your smart phone screen scratches.*

Tumbleweeds - What we think of as tumbleweeds are actually Russian thistle, and they first showed up in the US in a shipment of flax-seed that was sent to South Dakota. A few years later, they were found all over the West, from California and North into Canada.

Single plants can get as large as a small car and bear up to 250,000 seeds at once, making the invasive species a problem that was already getting the attention of the US Department of Agriculture in 1880.

Since tumbleweeds can thrive with little water, they were capable of taking over towns and driving people from their homes as they spread across the wide expanse of the West.

Pony Express Facts - The Pony Express (The Central Overland California and Pikes Peak Express) only lasted for 18 months and ended in October 1861 with the development of the telegraph. Since it was so expensive to send mail, around $5 per ounce, it was generally reserved for businesses and official correspondence rather than personal mail. Riders were responsible for carrying the mail the relatively short distance of about 32 kilometers (20 mi), and most riders were boys.

Charlie Chaplin Music - Have written about his many talents before, but keep finding more interesting info about him. Charlie Chaplin composed the music for almost all of his films. In fact, he was the only person to write, produce, direct, compose, conduct, and act in his movies. Charlie was never classically trained in music, but played a number of instruments. He even sang.

Customarily in scoring silent pictures the Wagnerian Leitmotiv system, a distinctive musical theme associated with a character and idea. He wrote the ninety five musical cues in "City Lights" and the passages where the music follows or mimics the action in what is generally known as "mickey-mousing" from its use in the scoring of animated cartoons.

> **Yoda Toes**
> In different movies Yoda has different numbers of toes. In The Phantom Menace he has 3 toes. In The Empire Strikes Back and Return of the Sith he has 4.

Here are a few of his songs: "Smile", "Eternally", "Terry's Theme", "Limelight", "This is My Song", "Oh that Cello", "There's Always Someone You Can't Forget", "Sing a Song", "With you, Dear, in Bombay", "Falling Star", "A Paris Boulevard", "Tango Bitterness", and "Rumba".

A few of his songs have become classics, top ten hits, and endure long after his death on Christmas Day, 1977 (He was born in 1899).

"Smile" was made famous by Nat King Cole and was also covered by Michael Jackson, Timi Yuro, and Tony Bennett.

"Eternally" was covered by many, including Placido Domingo, Englebert Humperdink, Jerry Vale, Vic Damone, and Sarah Vaughn.

"This is My Song" covered, among others by Petula Clark and Judith Durham.

Caterpillar Club - Membership is involuntary in this club that has been around since 1922. It is so named as parachutes were made of silk at the time. The sole requirement for joining the Caterpillar Club is to make an emergency escape from a failing aircraft, then plummet to earth with the aid of a parachute. If you survive, you automatically become a member.

If you qualify, contact Airborne Systems, which owns the parachute producers Irvin Aerospace, GQ Parachutes, Para-Flite and Aircraft Materials, Ltd. In accordance with the Irvin protocols established in the 1920s, the company still issues gold pins and membership cards to Caterpillar Club members.

Incidentally, Charles Lindbergh was a member of the Caterpillar Club.

Another Obscure Olympic Fact - During the 1900 Paris Olympics, golf first appeared at the Olympic Games, and one of the last for over a century. The sport returned to the Olympics for the 2016 Rio Games.

The first American woman, Margaret Abbott to win an Olympic gold medal was not aware of what she won. Records suggest she went her entire life oblivious to her historic achievement. Her mother, Mary Ives Abbott entered the golf competition as well. It was the first and only time in Olympic history that a mother and daughter competed in the same sport, in the same event, at the same time. Margaret Abbott passed away during 1955 unaware of the milestone she had set.

Airplane Windows Shape - Most people have noticed that airplane windows corners are rounded. They were not always rounded. Airplanes used to have square windows, but many planes crashed because of them.

During the 1950s when planes became faster, some of them began to crash unexpectedly. Investigators found the squared-off corners of windows were susceptible to stress. Circular window corners are able to disperse that pressure more evenly.

Eagle Fact
If a bald eagle loses a feather on one wing, it will shed a corresponding feather on the other to stay balanced.

Airplane windows now have three panes: one bears the burden of pressurization, another inner pane acts as a fail safe in case the outer pane fails, one pane faces the occupant.

ABBA Trivia - During the Nazi occupation of Norway, 1940 - 1945, it was "expressly desirable that the German soldiers conceive as many children as possible with Norwegian women, regardless of whether it is within or outside of the bonds of matrimony."

In Norway, as many as 12,000 children born to these unions. The rest of the population did not look too kindly on these pairings, as women involved with German officers could get their heads shaved or be branded with swastikas.

Anni-Frid Synni Lyngstad was born during November 1945 as a result of a liaison between her mother and a German sergeant. Her mother and grandmother were branded as traitors and ostracized in their village in northern Norway. They were forced to emigrate to Sweden, where Anni-Frid's mother died of kidney failure before her daughter was two. She was raised by her grandmother. Frida is the singer with auburn hair from the singing group ABBA. Incidentally, Frida co-designed many of the ABBA stage costumes.

Origins of Things - The famous Hollywood sign was originally a real estate ad.

Gender color of pink for boys and blue for girls was an early 1900s department store way to advertise clothing colors. Customers did not like the choice, so the store changed to blue for boys and pink for girls.

Sweetest Day tradition was started by a panel of candy company owners in the early 1920s as a way to boost sales of candy.

Deodorants were not used until Edna Murphey came along. She had an antiperspirant/deodorant product that her father had used in surgery, to keep his hands from sweating. She got the help of an ad agency and started a marketing campaign to convince people that being sweaty and smelly was absolutely the height of social embarrassment. It worked.

Lobster was once considered a poor person's food. There was an overabundance of it. Indentured servants complained about getting so much lobster that rules were established limiting it to only three meals per week.

As canneries on the coasts became bigger and figured out how to send lobster throughout the country. They began to market it as an exotic delicacy. Before long, demand skyrocketed and the price did also.

Glass Hack - Use glass paint or nail polish to paint a dot or something of a different color on wine or drink glasses so people at a party can remember which glass is theirs. Make sure what you use is dishwasher safe.

Airline Seats and Windows - Have you ever noticed that most airplane windows do no line up with your seat? The reason for this is that the airline manufacturers place windows as they believe is the optimum seating arrangement. Airlines decide on actual seating arrangements, using the flexible tracks in the plane.

While one airline might coincidentally line up seats with windows, others do not. Plane window placements are standard, seating arrangements are not.

> Before you leave on your next trip, use your phone to take a picture of your luggage to assist recovery efforts for lost luggage and reduce possible disputes.
> I always place my business card inside each checked and carry-on bag.

Lost Cat Tip - Was not sure I believed this, but verified it with a few cat sites and it appears to be true. Here are things you can do to assist in having your cat return home. Put the litter box or scoop of used litter outside along with any of the following: articles of your own worn clothing, a slept on pillowcase, a used bath mat or towel, a vacuum bag or canister and kitty's favorite bed or blanket. These will be familiar scents that will appeal to kitty. It is said they can smell from long distances. Putting out cat food does not work.

Incidentally, statistics show many cats return from 8pm to 2am and from 4am to 7am.

Ms. Pearl the Squirrel - Outside of Austin, Texas, off of an uneventful stretch of Highway 71, sits a U-turn worthy site for the squirrel worshiper in us all.

Standing at 14 feet tall, Ms. Pearl beckons passersby from the highway to have their picture taken with her. If you are wondering why she is clutching a pecan, it probably has something to do with the nearby Berdoll Pecan Candy & Gift Company, a family-owned business that includes a gift shop, a pecan orchard, and an adorable squirrel statue.

It was constructed in 2011 by Berdoll, Ms. Pearl received her name from a customer as part of a contest. In 2015, the statue received a facelift. She is available 24 hours a day and while the nearby gift shop has regular business hours, there is a vending machine outside the shop with fresh, full-sized pecan pies replenished daily for late night snacking.

IKEA Size Fact - IKEA uses 1 percent of the planet's lumber. That is about 530 million cubic feet of wood used to make IKEA furniture each year.

Paper Towels - Scott Paper Company capitalized on the demand for improved hygiene by essentially 'inventing' the market for toilet paper. Nearly a decade later, a manufacturing error at Scott's mills revolutionized the company by producing tissue that was too thick to use as toilet paper.

Remembering a story about a schoolteacher who cut up copy paper for her students to use as hand wipes (as opposed to a communal cloth that spread germs), company founder Arthur Scott set his sights on marketing the world's first disposable paper towel.

By perforating the thick, unusable paper so that it could be dispensed in individual sheets, Scott targeted his sales to railroad stations, hotels, industrial buildings, and schools under the name "Sani-Towels." By 1931, a paper manufacturer's mistake had become a successful household item throughout America.

Utility Blades - Many of us have those little utility knives with multiple snap off blade pieces, so we can break them when the blade gets dull. The problem is trying to snap a bit of blade with pliers, tapping with a hammer, using a rag or other protective material.

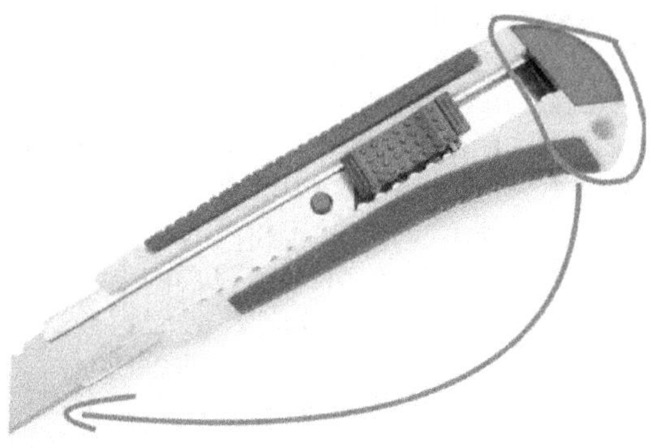

If you look close, a good number of those products have a removable tip at the other end that is to be used to snap off the blade. Pop off the tip, insert the blade into it and snap. Wow, easy.

NCIS Fact - NCIS during 2016 had about 18 minutes of ads for every 1 hour episode. During 2003 NCIS had about 16 minutes of ads per episode.

Those extra few minutes over a 23-episode season add up to an additional 46 minutes of ads. If you watched a typical 23-episode season of NCIS today you would watch about 414 minutes worth of ads or almost 7 hours.

Cold Weather Hack - We have not had much cold weather here lately, but I know some of you are dealing with it. When you are outside in cold weather, one of the first things to get cold is your feet. The reason is the body is protecting itself from the cold and trying to keep the core of your body, where all your internal organs are located, warm. That means blood flow to your hands and feet become limited, making them colder.

This is why it is important to have warm footwear when venturing outside in cold weather. A way to improve the warmth of even the cheapest boots is to go to a dollar store and buy a sun sheet, like the one you put in a car window to keep the sun out during summer. Remove shoe or boot insoles, place them face down on the sheet, trace the outside of them, and cut the sun sheet. Put the cut sun sheet in your boot and put your insole in over top of it. This will add insulation between you and the cold ground and it will also reflect your body heat back up into you.

Cosmetic Codes - There is a code on the back of a makeup container with a 6, 12, etc. Shelf life of cosmetics depends on the period after opening and production date. Some cosmetics should be used within a specified period of time after opening due to oxidation and microbiological factors. The packaging has a drawing of an open jar, inside it there is a number representing the number of months. In this example it is 6 months of use after opening.

Unused cosmetics also lose their freshness and become dry. According to EU law, the manufacturer must put the expiration date only on cosmetics whose shelf life is less than 30 months. The most common periods of suitability for use from date of manufacture:
Perfumes with alcohol - about 5 years,
Skin care - 3 years,
Makeup - 3 years (mascara) to more than 5 years (powders).
Expiration dates also may vary depending on the manufacturer.

Beer Yoga - Yes, it is a real thing. It is yoga that is done with beer. It first originated in places like Berlin and Burning Man, and is now becoming the biggest thing in Australia.

According to BierYoga founder Jhula, it is a marriage between two art forms, both of which are great for one's well-being. "BeerYoga is fun, but it is no joke," said Jhula. "We take the philosophies of yoga and pair it with the pleasure of beer-drinking to reach your highest level of consciousness."

Beer Can Origin - Prohibition was finally repealed during December 1933. During that same year, the first beer can patent was issued. After much testing and changing designs, the American Can Company finally was ready to sell its cans.

On January 24, 1935 the Krueger Brewing and Ale company began selling beer in cans for the first time. By the end of the year, 36 other brewers were also selling beer in cans.

A 'churchkey' type can opener was patented by another company that same year. One end was used for opening bottles and the other for puncturing the top of beer cans. They were usually given away for free. Young people will never be able to appreciate this handy device.

Incidentally, Churchkey Can Company is a brewery founded in 2012 by actor Adrian Grenier and former Nike designer Justin Hawkins in Seattle, USA. The brewery's name refers to its flagship beer, which must be opened using a can piercer, or 'church key'.

Horny Cows - First scientists have been trying to make dairy cows less flatulent, now they are trying to make them hornless. Dairy cows grow horns, but dairy cows in the US rarely have horns, because they are seared, cut, or chemically burned off. The purpose is to prevent injuries to other cows and handlers.

Recently, a company named Recombinetics took a hornless gene from a breed of beef cattle and inserted it into a breed of dairy cattle. The resulting cattle are hornless, good at producing milk, and still genetically 100 percent cattle. In the past, breeders could have crossed dairy cattle and hornless beef cattle to get hornless dairy cattle after many generations. *The good news for dairy farmers is that the cows are hornless, but not less horny, just confused.*

Falconry Terms - Some common terms we use come from falconry. For instance, the term, 'under your thumb' comes from the falconry way of holding the bird's talons under ones thumb to keep it from flying away.

A falcon is fitted with a small leather hood over the bird's eyes and head to keep it from being distracted. From this we get the term 'hoodwinked'.

Falconers regularly give their bird a small treat when landing on their hand. Each time the bird goes to find game, like rabbits, and returns it is given another treat. After a few sessions the bird is full and no longer wants to go hunt. It is said the bird is 'fed up'.

Free Art - The Metropolitan Museum of Art in New York City announced that 375,000 high resolution images of artworks in its collection are now under the Creative Commons Zero license. This means hundreds of thousands of artworks can now be accessed, downloaded, and used, without needing to ask for permission or being afraid of lawsuits.

> The Statue of Liberty seven spikes represent the seven oceans and seven continents.

Now you can download some real art, make it any size you like with your computer, go get a frame, and hang works from the masters on your wall for a fraction of the cost of an original.

Apple Museum - There is an Apple Museum in Prague, Czech Republic. Not sure why this place was chosen, but seems like a full fledged museum dedicated to rare Apple devices and Steve Jobs' memorabilia, and rare Apple souvenirs from private collectors.

The memorabilia in the museum dates from 1976 to 2012. The artifacts on display include mostly every printer, joystick, mouse, and PC, as well as software representations. One exhibit includes two long tables which showcase how the iPod and iPhone have evolved over time. The collections tell the story of Jobs along with the hardware.

Also included are high school yearbooks with Jobs and Steve Wozniak, the co-founder. Beyond Apple, it includes Pixar and NeXT items which are representative Jobs time with those companies. Next time you are in Prague, might be an interesting side trip.

Grass Art - Some things are as boring as watching grass grow. These artists take that idea to a whole new level. Heather Ackroyd and Dan Harvey make photographs using grass. They call it Chlorophyll Apparitions.

When grass is grown from seed on a vertical surface, it can record complex images much as photographic film does: Each germinating blade produces chlorophyll in proportion to the light that reaches it. Stronger light produces greener grass, and blades deprived of light grow, but produce no chlorophyll, leaving them yellow. "In a sense we have adapted the photographic art of producing pictures on a sensitive film to the light sensitivity of emergent blades of young grass."

They shine negatives of a picture through a projector to produce a light onto a canvas that has been coated with a growing medium and real grass seeds.

Michelin Stars - The first Michelin Guide for French drivers during 1900 included maps, listings of hotels, gas stations and mechanics, and helpful information for repairing tires. At the time there were only 3,000 automobiles in all of France. The forward-thinking Michelin brothers thought providing information for car travelers, would increase interest in French automobile tourism, which would in turn increase demand for cars and tires. The first US guide came during 2005.

During 1920, the guide started sending anonymous reviewers out to rate restaurants. A few years later, Michelin began ranking restaurants

using a rating system of one to three stars. Michelin stars are used to judge the quality of the food at a restaurant only, independent of any other aspects of the dining experience.
• One star = A very good restaurant in its category.
• Two stars = Excellent cooking, worth a detour.
• Three stars = Exceptional cuisine, worth a special journey.

Bibendum is the Michelin Man's nickname. He is also referred to as Bib or Bibelobis.

An additional designation of a small knife and fork, known as "couvert," describes other aspects of the restaurant's experience like comfort, venue décor, tabletop décor, and level of formality. A black fork and knife icon denotes a more basic experience, while a red icon indicates superior couvert.

Michelin inspectors, who have extensive training and experience in the field are required to hide their jobs from friends and even family members. They recruit dates to accompany them to romantic restaurants, so they do not stand out as solo diners. Some visit a restaurant multiple times to most accurately judge the quality and consistency of the experience.

Earliest Life on Earth - Scientists have recently discovered fossils of what look like red algae in Chitrakoot, India, which suggest that multicellular life arose several hundred million years earlier than previously believed.

Life can be traced as far back as 3.7 billion years or earlier, preserved in "mats" of fossilized single-celled microbes, but it took much longer for multicellular forms of life to emerge. Fossils appear to have been fairly common, beginning around 540 million years ago.

The new fossils, discovered by scientists from the Swedish Museum of Natural History, provide a clearer window into when advanced life began to form. Two types of fossils were found: one with a structure like thread, and the other with a more fleshy form. They are 400 million years older than the previously earliest known examples of red algae, making them the oldest plant-like fossils by a wide margin.

Movie Trailer Facts - The color of the background for movie rating cards is important. The rating for the film itself shows up in text, but is also indicated by the background color of the rating card splash screen.

There are three colors used - red, yellow, and green. The specific regulations surrounding what can be shown in the preview for each of these rating cards are set by the MPAA.

The most commonly seen one is the green rating card. Before April of 2009, a green background meant that the preview was approved for all audiences. Since April of 2009, the MPAA now states that the green card is for "appropriate audiences". This basically means it is appropriate for audiences in theaters, taking into account what movie the audience is about to watch.

A yellow rating card indicates the preview is for age-appropriate Internet viewers and is used on internet trailers only. The red rating card indicates that content in the preview is only appropriate for mature audiences. These previews can only be shown in theaters where the movie about to be watched is R-rated, NC-17-rated, or unrated.

Theatrical trailers must be less than two minutes and 30 seconds, as mandated by the MPAA (Motion Picture Association of America). The MPAA gives each movie studio one exception to this a year where they are allowed to show a trailer that is longer than 2 minutes and 30 seconds. Trailers shown online can be any length. The rating system itself is entirely voluntary on the part of studios. However, having a film rated tends to boost revenues significantly, so nearly all major studios submit all their films for rating.

Taxi Medallion Value - New York taxi medallions that are tightly regulated by the city and allow yellow cabs to legally pick up fares on the streets have drastically come down in value during the past three years. The tags sunk from about $1.05 million in 2014 to $241,000 for one sold during March 2017. The main cause is rivals Uber, Lyft, Via, and gett.

Also, during March, Philadelphia Parking Authority, which regulates the city's taxi industry, sold new medallions for $80,000 falling from last year with an initial asking price of $475,000, but received no bids. The value of taxi medallions in other cities, such as Boston and Chicago have also fallen sharply.

Tidbits - Charlie Chaplin died during 1977, the year Apple was founded.

The Wright brothers made their first flight during 1903, just 66 years before the first man stepped on the Moon during 1969.

Twelve million penguins in Antarctica celebrated World Penguin Day April 25, 2017. They consist of five species: Emperor, Adélie, Chinstrap, Gentoo, and Macaroni.

Five Time Tips for Success - Planning for success is necessary for achieving success. Remember the old adage, "Failure to plan means planning for failure." Here are a few tips that might help increase your chances for success.

Take time at the beginning of each day to plan your day. If you do not know what you are going to do, you will never know if you achieved it.

Create your ToDO list with A,B,C priorities, with A being most important to you. Spend Eighty percent of your time on A items, fifteen percent of your time on B items, and the remainder on C items. If you do this each day, you can satisfy your own needs as well as others, but with the proper priority for your own success.

Take time before every call and task to decide what result you desire. Define success and you can achieve it. When on the phone smile, it will do wonders for your attitude.

Do not answer the phone, email, or text just because they happen. I call this letting others steal your time. In order to be the most productive, schedule time to put phone in airline mode and shut down email and text. When you are ready for others, turn them back on and answer with your priorities, not others'.

Every day, compliment at least one person. Also, try to smile at people more often. An engaging smile is a precursor to success.

----

21 Gun Salute - The origin of gun salutes is usually attributed to soldiers or other armed types demonstrated peaceful intentions by placing their weapons in a position that rendered them ineffective. As cannons and small arms came into use, a good way to render them ineffective and demonstrating peaceful intentions, was to fire them, as reloading was a real pain. At sea, seven shots became the norm, probably because of superstition and mysticism about the number seven. On land, with a larger supply of gunpowder, they could fire three guns for every one shot from a ship, so a salute from a ship of seven guns would be answered by a salute from the shore batteries of 21 guns. When gunpowder technology and storage improved, ships at sea adopted the salute of 21 guns.

There is a complex protocol for salutes. Twenty one guns are only used to salute a national flag, the sovereign or chief of state of a foreign nation, a member of a reigning royal family, and anyone who has ever been elected President of the US. A vice-president, speaker of the house, American or foreign ambassador, a premier or prime minister (unless sovereign), chief justice, cabinet member, state governor, secretary or ranking general of a branch of the armed forces, and president pro tem of the senate all receive 19 gun salutes on entering. Generals, admirals, the assistant secretary of defense, and chairpersons of House committees receive 17. There are 15, 13, and 11 gun salutes for people of descending rank, both military and civilian.

For a full-honor funeral at Arlington, a President gets 21 guns. A secretary of defense, chairman of the Joint Chiefs of Staff, or other military officer given command over multiple branches of the service receives 19. Seventeen guns are fired for a four-star general, 15 for a three-star, 13 for a two-star, and 11 for a one-star.

Chocolate Diamonds - Another way jewelers have found to separate people from their money. Chocolate diamonds are brown diamonds. These are the most common diamonds, and up until the ad campaign, they were almost worthless. However, with a bit of rebranding, they are now being sold for the same price as other diamonds.

For every carat of diamond that is mined, 1,750 tons of rock needs to be mined and discarded.

Ten Interesting Tidbits of Knowledge -

The word 'ushers' contains five pronouns: us, she, he, her and hers.

By the time a glass of champagne goes flat, two million bubbles will have popped.

People suffering from superior canal dehiscence syndrome can hear their own eyeballs moving.

A Gongoozler is a person who stares for a long time at things happening on a canal.

Britons eat 97% of the world's baked beans.

By the time they leave high school American children will have eaten 1,500 peanut-butter-and-jelly sandwiches.

American bullfrogs' eyes have special retinas. The top half sees in daylight, the bottom sees into the water in infrared.

The act of snapping one's fingers is called a fillip.

Tyler, Texas, USA contains the world's largest rose garden: 22 acres with over 38,000 rose bushes and more than 500 varieties of rose.

The 2004 tsunami shifted the location of the geographic South Pole by a few centimeters.

Gift Card Tips - If you have a gift card with a balance of less than ten dollars, most states have laws that stores and restaurants are legally required to give you the balance in cash if you ask for it. Some states have a $5 or other lower limit. Most gift cards cannot contain an expiration date or a service fee.

Tip - wrap your receipt around the card to remember the balance.

Just Three American Cars Remain - Online car research site Cars.com, ranks the "most-American" cars and trucks and takes into account globalization of the supply chain. It found just three models qualified.

The definition of "Made in America" has been undergoing some changes, especially in the auto industry. Integrated supply chains and efforts to cut costs have made the auto industry's globalization "irreversible."

The criteria used: country of engine origin, country of transmission origin, US factory employment relative to the company's sales footprint, domestic parts content, and assembly location. The percentage of domestic parts that a car needs to be able to qualify is 60 percent.

The three "most-American" cars were Jeep Wrangler, Jeep Cherokee (made by Italian-American carmaker Fiat Chrysler Automobiles in Toledo, Ohio), and Ford Motor Co.'s Chicago-made Taurus.

Coral Bleaching - Newsmedia has been hyping the coral bleaching going on as a disaster, but it does not seem as dire as we are led to believe. The way it works is that coral polyps live as a symbiote with algae, which photosynthesize and produce carbohydrates for the polyps. When temperatures get too high, the algae starts to produce free oxygen radicals (which is harmful). The polyps have no choice but to expel the algae, which are responsible for the coral color, and to lose an important food source. This is known as coral bleaching.

Corals do not die from coral bleaching, but they are significantly weakened, but recover. They die out, then slowly grow back. Centuries do not mean much for a coral colony that exists for millenia.

Cleaning White Shoes - For major dirt stains, use 409 cleaner or any other all-purpose spray cleaner, an old toothbrush and a couple of paper towels.

Rub Whitening toothpaste into the shoe using an old toothbrush and let it sit for 10-15 minutes before wiping off.

Micellar water and cotton will help you clean the white shoe sole and rubber/leather toe bit of your shoes.

Magic erasers and vinegar are great for removing stains on white shoes as well.

To bring the white color of your canvas shoes back, use rubber gloves, mix one part of bleach and 5 parts water. Apply it with an old toothbrush to get rid of various stains and dark spots.

Chicken Facts - Here is something to cluck about. The UN's Food and Agriculture Organization concluded that, as of 2014, the world has about 21 billion chickens, which produce the 79 billion eggs eaten by Americans every year. As the human population grew by 80 percent between 1970 and 2008, the global chicken population grew by 262 percent. That makes three chickens for every human on earth.

Claddagh Rings - The Claddagh ring (Irish: fáinne Chladaigh) is a traditional Irish ring given which represents love, loyalty, and friendship. The hands represent friendship, the heart represents love, and the crown represents loyalty.

The design and customs associated with it originated in the Irish fishing village of Claddagh, located just outside the old city walls of Galway, now part of Galway City. The ring, as currently known, was first produced in the 17th century, but the name Claddagh ring was not used before the 1830s. In recent years it has been embellished with interlace designs and combined with other Celtic and Irish symbols.

The ring belongs to a group of European finger rings called "fede rings". The name "fede" derives from the Italian phrase mani in fede ("hands [joined] in faith" or "hands [joined] in loyalty"). These rings date from Roman times, when the gesture of clasped hands was a symbol of pledging vows, and they were used as engagement/wedding rings in medieval and Renaissance Europe.

Incidentally, "Top of the morning to you." "And the rest of the day to yourself." Both are Hollywood inventions and never used in Ireland.

Total Solar Eclipse - A total solar eclipse happened on August 21, 2017, and for the first time in nearly a hundred years, it was visible from much of the continental US. In the US, the eclipse appeared to move across the country from West to East, with the best view starting around 9:05 a.m. PDT in Lincoln Beach, Oregon, according to NASA, and moving southeast throughout the day to end around Charleston, South Carolina at 2:48 pm EDT.

It is true that you should not look directly at it with your naked eyes, because the sun delivers more power than our eyes are designed to handle, and it will damage your retinas. Not likely to make you blind, but could cause serious ongoing problems.

When the moon passes between Earth and the sun, and scores a bull's eye by completely blotting out the sunlight, that is a total solar eclipse. The moon casts a shadow on our planet. The total eclipse will last up to 2 minutes and 40 seconds in places. A partial eclipse will be visible along the periphery.

Ostrich Facts - Ostriches are the largest flightless bird living today, and also happen to lay the largest eggs of any living bird in existence today. In fact, the Guinness World Record for the largest egg laid by a bird was achieved during 2008 on a farm in Sweden – the egg weighed 5 pounds and 11.36 ounces. A typical ostrich egg is equivalent to about two dozen chicken eggs.

The shells of ostrich eggs are so thick that most people recommend getting into them by boring in with an electric drill. They usually take about two hours to cook, due to the thickness of the shell.

Ostriches sleep standing up. Ostriches are the fastest two-legged creature in the world. An ostrich when pushed or in danger can achieve speeds of up to 43 miles per hour, and can steadily keep up a pace of about 30 miles per hour for 10 miles at a time without needing to slow down or rest.

Ostriches are found naturally in Africa, but many are also found in southern Australia and some are farmed in the US.

Ostriches do not stick their head in sand when startled or threatened. They dig shallow holes in the dirt to use as nests for their eggs. Several times a day, a bird puts her head down and turns the eggs. It just looks like she is burying her head in the sand.

Nude Cartoons - Warner Brothers' Tweety Bird, was told to put some clothes on. In his first cartoon, Tweety was pink, but censors said he looked naked, so animator Bob Clampett said he was repainted yellow, so he appeared to have feathers.

Alphabet Facts - The word alphabet is derived from the first two letters of the Greek alphabet, alpha and beta. We owe our own alphabet to the Phoenicians. Their 22 letter alphabet had no vowels, but it was used as the basis of the ancient Greek alphabet, which in turn was adapted by the Romans, and is essentially the same as the one we use today.

A sentence that contains all 26 letters of the alphabet is called a pangram.

Ernest Vincent Wright's novel Gadsby: Champion of Youth (1939) - a story of more than 50,000 words in which the letter 'e' never appears. George Perec's novel La Disparition (1969) which does not contain the letter 'e'. Its English translation, A Void by Gilbert Adair, also avoids using the letter 'e' which is the most common letter in both languages.

Scissors Facts - Many people mistakenly give credit to Leonardo da Vinci for inventing scissors, but scissors were invented many years before him. Some believe scissors were invented in the Middle East over 3,000 years ago. The device consisted of two bronze blades connected by a spring-like mechanism that kept the blades apart until they were squeezed together.

Scissors longer than six inches are often referred to as shears.

A pair of scissors more like modern scissors with a cross-blade design was developed by the ancient Romans around 100 A.D.

Cross-blade scissors were made by hand for hundreds of years and were not mass-produced until 1761 when English manufacturer Robert Hinchliffe adapted the design so it could be manufactured in a factory. He was also the first to make scissors with steel.

Today, there are a wide variety of scissors with specific purposes. Children's or safety scissors have dull blades and rounded tips to ensure their safe use in school environments. Nail scissors were specially developed to cut fingernails and toenails. There are also specialty scissors used by hairdressers, seamstresses, doctors, and more.

Ig Nobel Awards 2017 - The Ig Nobel awards are given for achievements that first make people laugh, then make them think. On September 14, 2017 at the 27th First Annual Ig Nobel Prize Ceremony, at Harvard's Sanders Theatre, the following prizes were awarded.

Physics, Using fluid dynamics to probe the question "Can a Cat Be Both a Solid and a Liquid?"

Peace, Demonstrating that regular playing of a didgeridoo is an effective treatment for obstructive sleep apnoea (sic) and snoring.

Economics, Experiments to see how contact with a live crocodile affects a person's willingness to gamble.

Anatomy, medical research study "Why Do Old Men Have Big Ears?"

Biology, Discovery of a female penis, and a male vagina, in a cave insect.

Fluid Dynamics, Studying the dynamics of liquid-sloshing, to learn what happens when a person walks backward while carrying a cup of coffee.

Nutrition, First scientific report of human blood in the diet of the hairy-legged vampire bat.

Medicine, Using advanced brain-scanning technology to measure the extent to which some people are disgusted by cheese.

Gravity in Space - Contrary to common opinion, gravity is everywhere, even in space. Anything with mass creates gravity. The effect of gravity decreases as distance increases. At extreme distances, the gravity exerted on a particular object might be almost zero, but is never completely absent.

At the orbit of the International Space Station, Earth's gravitational pull is about 90% of what it is at Earth's surface.

Astronauts on spaceships in outer space are affected by gravity in the same way that their spaceships are. They are both orbiting Earth, which means they are falling sideways (in orbit) at the same time they are falling toward Earth.

On Earth, astronauts feel the force of gravity as weight, because the ground prevents them from falling. In outer space there is no ground to push against astronauts. As they orbit and fall toward Earth at the same rate as their spaceship, astronauts feel weightless, as if there were no gravity.

Einstein the Horse - Miniature horses were first developed in Europe during the 1600s, and by 1765, they were seen frequently as the pets of nobility. Miniature horse life span is 25 to 35 years, but often live longer, with the oldest known ones living 50 years of age.

The English began using small ponies in their mines. At the peak of this practice in 1913, there were 70,000 ponies underground in Britain. In later years, mechanical haulage was introduced on the main underground roads replacing the pony haulers. As of 1984, 55 ponies were still in use at the pit in Ellington, Northumberland. When Ellington closed in 1994, the last four pit ponies were brought out.

Einstein, who was born during 2010 in New Hampshire, US is a miniature pinto stallion and not a dwarf. This tiny steed is just 20 inches tall and weighs 47 pounds. His father and mother are 32 inches and 30 inches respectively and are national mini horse champions.

NUMBERS

Two Misconceptions of Judaism - Eating pork is prohibited for Jews who keep kosher. Other than pork, a kosher Jew cannot eat shellfish, hares, camels, and the hyrax, a small mammal closely related to the elephant and manatee. The Torah describes the types of meat that can be consumed as coming from a cloven hooved animal that chews the cud. This includes sheep, cows, and goats, among others. The pig, though cloven-hooved, does not chew its cud and is therefore forbidden.

In the United States, the highest population of Jews outside Israel, only about 21 percent of the 5.3 million Jews do so. Keeping kosher is a choice that not all Jews make. Even within Israel, only approximately 36 percent of secular Jews keep kosher.

Many people incorrectly believe that the Old Testament of the Christian Bible is the Jewish Bible. However, Jews follow the teachings of the Talmud and Tanakh, which are made up of the Torah, Nevi'im, and K'tuvim (Teaching, Prophets, and Writings).

It is true that many of these books are found in the Old Testament, but the Old Testament is only made up of parts of these books as a textual source. The Tanakh (Mikra) and Talmud offer guidance for the practices of Judaism and can be considered a compilation of sources that make up the Hebrew Bible.

Incidentally, there is no race of Jews, it is more of an ethnicity, with some shared DNA, but no single thread of genetics.

Four Rules of Three - The main point of the Rules of Three is that we need to concentrate on the most immediate problem first. People mainly think of these rules for being stranded in the wilderness, but they also apply in an urban setting, such as natural disaster, earthquake, flood, etc. In any extreme situation:

You can survive for 3 minutes without air (oxygen) or in icy water,
You can survive for 3 hours without shelter in a harsh environment (unless in icy water),
You can survive for 3 days without water (if sheltered from a harsh environment),
You can survive for 3 weeks without food (if you have water and shelter).

Some people have suggested a fifth rule and that is 3 months without hope.

Incidentally, if you have a stick, or knife, or any other object stuck in you, do not pull it out. The object restricts blood flow. Wrap the area around the wound and seek help as soon as possible.

Number Seven - I may be a day late, but seven is still a special number. The world was formed in seven days, there are seven wonders of the world, seven deadly sins, seven gifts of the Holy Spirit, seven hills of Rome, seventh heaven, etc.

Shabbat is the seventh day of the week. Shabbat connects the six days of the week. All of the other days revolve around it. It serves as the center for the three days before it and the three days after it.

Number 7 is the number of perfection, security, safety, and rest.

Number Seven contains the number three of the heavens and soul with the number four of the earth and body.

The Pythagoreans called the number 7 "the Septad".

Seven colors of the rainbow. Isaac Newton identified the seven colors of the rainbow as red, orange, yellow, green, blue, indigo, and violet.

There are seven days in a week.

Each airplane in Boeing's line of passenger jets is named with a 3-digit number beginning and ending in 7.

There are seven dwarfs.

As You Like It by William Shakespeare's contains Shakespeare's 7 Ages of Man theory.

There are seven notes to the diatonic scale.

Music has seven notes in an octave (the eighth is a repeat of the first): Do, Re, Mi, Fa, So, La Ti, Do.

There are seven letters in the Roman numeral system.

Seven circles form the symbol called "The Seed of Life". The Seed of Life symbolizes the six days of creation. The central circle symbolizes the day of rest.

- Number seven is the number of Neptune.
- In the Harry Potter series of novels by J.K. Rowling, seven is said to be the most powerfully magical number.

- Number seven is lucky for Cancer and Pisces.
- In the Tarot, seven is the card of the Chariot. The Chariot is symbolic of the need to focus.
- September means "the seventh month" in Latin.
- The British fifty pence coin is a heptagon (seven sided).
- Nitrogen (N) has the atomic number 7.
- Number 7 is the international country calling code for Russia.
- Lotus Seven was an open top, two-seater sports car.
- The opposite sides of a dice always equal the number seven when added.
- In Japan there are Seven Lucky Gods. They have a ship called Takarabune, the Treasure Ship. They arrive in town every New Year and give gifts to all worthy people.
- In Hindu weddings the bride and groom walk around the holy fire seven times during the wedding ceremony.
- Seven people have been beheaded privately on Tower Green within the walls of the Tower of London.
- There are seven continents – Asia, Africa, North America, South America, Antarctica, Europe, and Australia.

Lucky Seven - The number seven is seen as lucky in many cultures. According to biblestudy.org, the number gets 735 mentions in the Bible (860 if you count 'sevenfold' and 'seventh'). According to religious beliefs, it is the number of days it took God to create the universe, the number of miracles Jesus performed on the Sabbath, and the number of trumpets blown before the dead are resurrected in the Book of Revelation. There are also seven angels, seven churches, seven thunders, seven seals, and seven plagues.

Seven is also lucky in Japan, due to seven deities known as the Seven Lucky Gods. In China, seven is a lucky number, because it is pronounced "qi," which is the same as the Chinese words for 'arise' or 'life essence'. The seventh son of the seventh son always seems to get the kingdom.

The 'Seventh Son' is also a well known song (and one of my favorites) from Mose Allison, a legendary blues and jazz pianist, who passed away November 2016.

Top Ten Musician Sales - Amazing to see how many sales some of the new musicians are making vs. legends in the business. Units equals: sales of albums, singles, and music videos.

Mariah Carey — 131.9 million units
Led Zeppelin — 139.3 million units
Garth Brooks — 145 million units
Taylor Swift — 146.8 million units
Elton John — 166.9 million units
Madonna — 170 million units
Michael Jackson — 181.1 million units
Rihanna — 197.7 million units
Elvis Presley — 210.8 million units
The Beatles — 269.5 million units

Others of note: Celine Dion 123.7 million, Bruce Springsteen 100.2 million, Rolling Stones 95.3 million, Justin Bieber 88.9 million, Aerosmith 84.1 million, Bee Gees 67.3 million, Prince 63.7 million.

Origin of Unlucky Thirteen - Fear of the number 13, known as "triskaidekaphobia," has its origins in Norse mythology. In a well-known tale, 12 gods were invited to dine at Valhalla, a magnificent banquet hall in Asgard, the city of the gods. Loki, the god of strife and evil, crashed the party, raising the number of attendees to 13. The other gods tried to kick Loki out, and in the struggle that ensued, Balder, the favorite among them, was killed.

Scandinavian avoidance of 13-member dinner parties, and dislike of the number 13 itself, spread south to the rest of Europe. It was reinforced in the Christian era by the story of the Last Supper, at which Judas, the disciple who betrayed Jesus, was the thirteenth guest at the table.

Paraskevidekatriaphobia - That is the official name for fear of Friday the 13th. Therapist Dr. Donald Dossey, whose specialty is treating people with irrational fears, coined the term paraskevidekatriaphobia. It is also known as friggatriskaidekaphobia. The fear of the day is likely rooted in Christianity. Jesus was crucified on a Friday and ever since the day has been associated with general ill omen according to Michael Bailey, a history professor at Iowa State University who specializes in the origins of superstitions.

Weddings in the Middle Ages were not held on Fridays and it was not a day someone would start a journey. Thirteen guests are believed to have attended the Last Supper, the night before Jesus was killed, according to Stuart Vyse, a psychology professor at Connecticut

College. Judas Iscariot, the disciple who betrayed Jesus, is considered to have been the 13th guest, Vyse said.

It is unclear when Friday and number 13 became linked in the way we think of them today, according to Vyse and Bailey. There are no mentions of Friday the 13th before the 19th century.

Incidentally, Taylor Swift says her lucky number is 13. "I was born on the 13th. I turned 13 on Friday the 13th. My first album went gold in 13 weeks. My first #1 song had a 13-second intro." The performer was sued in 2014 by the clothing brand Lucky 13 for selling T-shirts on her online store with the phrase "Lucky 13" on them.

Quick Conversion - If you want to quickly convert between miles and kilometers, you can use the Fibonacci sequence to make a conversion with a good degree of accuracy. The Fibonacci sequence, which is the basis for the golden ratio (1.618), begins like this: 0, 1, 1, 2, 3, 5, 8, 13, 21, 34, 55, 89, 144.

Each number in the sequence after the first two is the sum of the previous two numbers. Look at any number in the sequence as a number of miles and the next number in the sequence is approximately that same distance in kilometers. For example, 55 miles equals about 89 kilometers. Conversely, 34 kilometers equals about 21 miles.

The conversion of miles to kilometers is 1.609. The small difference between that and 1.618 will cause higher numbers to not equal, but the numbers would need to be quite high to make a difference. When in your car, a quick way is to check the speedometer for comparison.

Alcohol Proof - The regulation to proof alcohol was simply to test and verify that the contents of a barrel of liquid was what it was claimed to be began in England during the 16th century to ensure that the King collected the proper amount of taxes on the sale of the product.

The first method involved soaking a gun pellet in the liquid, and then trying to light it on fire; if it burned, it was classified as a proof spirit. However, as alcohol's flammability is temperature dependent, the higher the temperature, the more vapors the alcohol infused solution will emit and therefore more flammable. Sometimes actual alcohol was passed off as something less and taxed at a lower rate.

Frequently the product would catch fire, and the authorities would know that the spirit was at least 57.15% alcohol by volume (ABV), which at that time was classified as being 100 proof.

As scientific skills improved during the early 19th century, a far more accurate test was developed which measured the liquid's specific gravity (the ratio of the density of a substance to a reference, in this case distilled water). Distilled water is actually denser than alcohol. In 1816 a test was developed using the fact that at 11°C (51°F), a 100 degree proof spirit (~57.15% ABV) would weigh 12/13 that of distilled water.

An IPA with an ABV of 6.9% in the UK would be 12.075 degrees of proof, while a 100% ABV pure alcohol would have a proof of 175 degrees.

In the US, proof is calculated by doubling the ABV. So alcohol with an ABV of 40%, is 80 proof. Nevada, US prohibits the sale of alcohol in excess of 80% ABV (160 proof), and California, US prohibits the sale of anything over 60% ABV (120 proof).

The US has singled out one alcohol in particular for regulation – absinthe (ABV 45-75%). It is infused with green anise, fennel, other herbs, and grand wormwood. During the early 1900s, a number of countries banned absinthe, due to a smear campaign conducted by the wine industry and the presumed presence of thujone, a chemical compound that is said to be poisonous in large amounts. It is now known that most absinthe has very little thujone and easily meets all regulatory requirements. Beginning in 2007, absinthe returned to the US as imports from Europe and with domestic producers.

Starbucks Sizes - A Venti iced size (24 ounces) at Starbucks is equal to two Tall (12 ounces). If you buy a Venti and split it with a friend you can save over a dollar each.

Incidentally, Short [8 fl. oz.], Tall [12 fl. oz.], Grande [16 fl. oz.], Venti Hot [20 fl. oz.], Venti Cold [24 fl. oz.] and Trenta Cold [31 fl. oz.]

MYTHS DEBUNKED

Blonde Myth Debunked - No, this is not an April fool's joke. The 'dumb blonde' stereotype is wrong, according to a new national study of young baby boomers. The Ohio State University study of 10,878 Americans found that white women who said their natural hair color was blonde had an average IQ score within 3 points of brunettes and those with red or black hair. The resulting findings showed that blonde-haired white women had an average IQ of 103.2, compared to 102.7 for those with brown hair, 101.2 for those with red hair and 100.5 for those with black hair. None of the differences are statistically significant.

The results for blond white men were similar. They also had IQs roughly equal to men with other hair colors. The study was published during March, 2016 in the journal Economics Bulletin.

> As an English noun, a blond is a fair-haired male, and a blonde is a fair-haired female.

Data from the study came from the National Longitudinal Survey of Youth 1979, a national survey of people who were between 14 and 21 years old when they were first interviewed in 1979. The NLSY79 was conducted for the U.S. Bureau of Labor Statistics. *Not sure why it took over thirty years to analyze the data or who paid for this wildly useless bit of old information. Further reading showed this article in close proximity to "Do unions reduce the wage penalty experienced by obese women?" Answer, yes.*

Cooking Steaks Myths - *Myth Searing steaks lock in juices.* Not true - it helps give a nice crunchy and flavorful snap when you take a bite and can have a nicer color on the outside. However, it does not lock in juices.

Myth Salting your steak before cooking will draw out the moisture and leave you with a tough cut of meat. Both true and not true - It is true, if you are going to salt-pack a steak for an extended period of time, the salt will draw out moisture. A good way to prepare a steak for grilling is to pat a solid coat of sea salt and crushed pepper on the exterior right before placing it over the heat. There is not enough time for the salt to draw out any moisture and you are left with a well-seasoned, great-tasting cut of meat.

Myth Only flip your steak once. Not true - It is simply a matter of personal preference. The effect on your steak's taste is negligible. It is more about how you prefer to grill, and where you are most comfortable. If you are regularly flipping your steak, chances are you have the hood open, which means you are letting out heat. This will affect the timeliness of your cook, but if you make an adjustment for the lower temperature by extending time, it will be fine. Some people prefer to flip their steaks often, because it helps prevent curling.

Myth Sizzling steaks hot of the grill taste best. - Not true - Resting your steak after cooking is not a misconception. Resting your steak for five minutes after coming off the grill will keep it juicier and more flavorful. Basically, there is much science that goes into this. When a steak comes hot off the grill the exterior is very hot, and there is little moisture. The center of the steak is considerably cooler and still has moisture. As a steak rests, the muscle fibers loosen and the juices will spread more evenly across the steak.

More About Cooking Steaks - When your steak hits a hot surface, the smell and color change from pink to brown is part of the Maillard reaction, named for scientist Louis Camille-Maillard, who discovered the principle.

Amino acids, the building blocks of proteins, and simple sugars rearrange themselves and produce thousands of molecules that result in smell and color changes, as well as flavor variation and intensification. This happens in all kinds of food, from baking bread to grilled shrimp. It is also what causes toast to smell so good and what turns beer brown.

For the ultimate in tender, juicy beef, slice it against the grain.

Having a dry surface encourages the Maillard reaction, which is why so many articles and recipes for steak tell you to let the meat air dry or to pat it with paper towels before cooking it. Drier food plus hot temperatures equals more reactive compounds in your steak. More Maillard reaction equals more flavor.

Serious Eats points out that flipping your steak several times during the cooking process lets the heat from one side disperse back into the meat, which rescues the outer edges from becoming tough and overcooked. Frequent flipping cooks the meat more even, and significantly faster. Flip every minute instead of once or twice and the meat will be done in a third less time.

This works because neither side has time to absorb much heat when facing the fire or lose too much heat when facing away. It also reduces the Maillard reaction.

To remove excess moisture, pat it dry with an absorbent kitchen towel or paper towel before you put it in a pan or on the grill.

You can salt steaks ahead of time and let them sit. The salt will add flavor and draw out surface moisture, all while slightly breaking down the proteins and improving the texture of the steak.

If you have any leftover uncooked steaks, freeze them properly for maximum flavor next time.

Grilling Tip - Cut a raw potato, rub it on your grill and the starch acts like a coating to keep food from sticking. Slice off the used edge and enjoy the rest of the potato.

Beer Myths Debunked - *False - If Cold Beer Gets Warm, Cooling It Again Will Make It Stale.* This is a myth brought on by marketers. The fact is, beer experiences substantial fluctuations in temperature during shipping. Of course, you do not want these changes to be drastic, and excessive heat will definitely ruin beer.

Maybe - The Color of the Bottle Affects Beer's Shelf Life.
It is not the color of the bottle so much as its translucence that affects beer's long-term quality. Clear and green bottles allow in significantly more UV light than brown ones. If you store green or clear bottles in complete darkness, there is no discernible difference in shelf life from that of a brown bottle in similar conditions.

True - Putting Beer in the Freezer Is an Easy Way to Quick Chill It.
This is true as long as you do not freeze it. Beer will explode when frozen. Placing a beer in the freezer for a short period should be fine. According to the American Homebrewers Association, freezing beer alters the molecular structure of the proteins in the beverage. It can also reduce the carbonation level and, in the case of bottle-conditioned brew, possibly kill the yeast.

True - Beer Should Be Stored Upright.
There are a few reasons why beer should not be placed on its side, and this applies to both corked and capped bottles. Yeast is critical to beer, but the sediment it leaves behind has a way of corrupting flavor. You want the yeast sediment to settle at the bottom of the beer. According to Beer Advocate, prolonged storage on the side will create a "yeast

ring" along the walls of the bottle. Upright storage slows the process of oxidation and prolongs the life of the beer.

False - Bottles Are Better Than Cans. This is a matter of personal taste. Canned beer has is often associated with mass-market. cheap beer and so the myth. It is not so much the receptacle, it is the beer that makes the taste. Many craft brewers have begun to can their beer. Some craft brew fanatics even swear by the distinctive flavor of canned brew. The Huffington Post conducted a blind taste test and found participants preferred the taste of canned beer to bottled three times out of four.

Water and Ice - Seventy percent of the Earth's surface is water. Of this, 98% is salt water, leaving 2% as fresh water. Of that two percent that is fresh, about 90% is frozen. This frozen water is locked up in the Arctic and Antarctic ice sheets, and glaciers on the Alps, etc. *I think the chance of us running out of water soon are slim.*

Banana Myths Debunked - There is an old wife's tale that you cannot store bananas in the refrigerator. There is a reason for this myth, bananas do get a dark and ugly skin in the refrigerator. However, this does not mean the fruit goes bad. Also, they do not produce gas or other toxins in the cold.

Once bananas are ripened, they can be kept in a fridge. A banana peel will turn dark brown, making it appear bad, but the part you eat inside actually stays quite good. Remove the ugly peel and you will see the flesh inside is as delicious as ever. You can let it sit out for a short time to return to room temperature, if desired before eating.

Bananas can typically be kept in the refrigerator for about a week, which is significantly longer than an optimally ripe banana will last at room temperature. A handy place to store them is in the crisper.

Banana companies Chiquita and Dole recommend you do this to make the banana last longer in its perfect ripeness stage. Once a banana reaches its optimal ripeness for your taste, stick it in the refrigerator to drastically slow the conversion of starch into sugars, almost to the point of stopping the ripening process.

It is important <u>not</u> to put the bananas in the refrigerator before they reach the level of ripeness you desire. Chiquita says, "If you place your unripe Chiquita bananas in the refrigerator, they may not be able to resume the ripening process even if they are returned to room temperature."

There are other ways to keep bananas fresh longer. For instance, you can slow the ripening process of a banana by keeping the banana away from other fruits, including separating a banana from the same hand it came from. Bananas put off large amounts of ethylene, relative to many other fruits. This triggers and quickens the ripening process significantly.

Incidentally, if you would like to speed up the ripening of some green bananas or other fruit or vegetables, put them in a paper bag together over night. The trapped ethylene will quickly ripen the fruit, and the paper bag will still let enough oxygen in to keep the ripening progress smoothly. Also, putting fresh bananas in the same container as an overripe banana will rapidly accelerate the ripening process of the fresh bananas.

Dairy and Healthy Bones Myth - Many people confuse "dairy" with "calcium," and assume they are the same thing. Most still believe that dairy is the best thing for healthy and strong bones. Dairy contains calcium, but so do dark-leafy greens. Milk is fortified with vitamin D, as are many other foods.

Bone health goes beyond calcium and vitamin D. Vitamin K is important for bone health, dark leafy greens have it, but dairy does not. Magnesium, which plays an important part of bone health, is present in foods like almonds, cashews, oatmeal, and potatoes, but missing in dairy products.

You should get enough calcium in your diet, and milk and cheese are good sources of it. However there are many other good sources. The Harvard School of Public Health and the University of Missouri point out that milk is not the best, or only source of calcium. If you are looking for good sources of calcium and Vitamin D, consider collard greens, mustard greens, kale, and bok choy instead of milk.

Water and Toxins Myth - There is a myth that says water flushes out toxins from our body. This popular misconception says drinking copious amounts of water will help magically cleanse our innards.

Drinking adequate amounts of water ensures our body's metabolism works correctly. Part of this is the natural detoxification process liver and kidneys conduct. They work fine as long as they are getting enough, but not too much liquid.

Additional water intake is not going to help. In fact, drinking too much water can actually prevent the detoxification process. It reduces the concentration of salt in our blood, which can damage kidneys and liver and prevent their normal functioning.

GMO Myth - Many headlines proclaim that GMO (Genetically Modified Organism) produced food is bad for us, however science debunks that myth. Sales of such GMO-free products are skyrocketing and they represent about $16 billion in annual sales. GMOs currently on the market provide ample cases of tangible benefit with relatively negligible risk. In the US, 70% of the food in US supermarkets contains GMO ingredients.

Organizations like the National Academy of Sciences, the American Association for the Advancement of Science, and the European Commission have publicly proclaimed GMO foods are safe to eat. A large 2013 study on GMOs found no "significant hazards directly connected with the use of genetically engineered crops."

In the US, 70% of food in supermarkets contains GMO ingredients.

Other experts cite the fact that practically all the food we eat today has been genetically modified in some way; everything from corn to watermelons have been selectively bred for thousands of years to give us the traits we find desirable, like large amounts of sweet, edible flesh, or small and fewer seeds.

It brings to mind the early ugly looking and untasty small kernel corn, tiny potatoes, tomatoes, and purple carrots. Thousands of years ago when people simply gathered wild fruits and vegetables for food, these plants were found naturally growing in the wild. Then, about 10,000 years ago, people began to domesticate these wild fruits and vegetables and eventually improve them.

For instance, potatoes were domesticated about 10,000 years ago. Following centuries of selective breeding, there are now over a thousand different types of potatoes. Over 99% of the presently cultivated potatoes worldwide descended from varieties that originated in the lowlands of south-central Chile.

Selective breeding is the process of developing a plant or animal based on selecting desirable characteristics of the parent. For example, saving seed for replanting from plants within a crop that have shown to be particularly robust; or breeding a white dog with a black patch over its eye via two parents that have the same trait. Selective breeding is a form of genetic modification which does not involve the addition of any foreign genetic material (DNA) into the organism. It is the conscious selection for desirable traits. GMO adds different genetic material into the organism, in order to create desirable traits.

Incidentally, during October 1995, the potato became the first vegetable to be grown in space. NASA and the University of Wisconsin, created the technology with the goal of feeding astronauts on long space voyages, and eventually, feeding future space colonies.

Cranberry Juice Myth - Contrary to popular belief, the cranberry juice commonly found on grocery store shelves is <u>not effective</u> at preventing urinary tract infections.

Cranberries do contain compounds that defend against bacterial infection in the bladder wall, which can help prevent UTIs, but cranberry juice does not have a high enough concentration of these compounds to do much good. In order for a noticeable reduction in bacterial adhesion, a person would have to consume at least 32 ounces of cranberry juice daily.

Gravity Myth - Many believe there is no gravity in space. Astronauts appear weightless in space, so there is an assumption that space is a place with zero gravity.

There is less gravity in space, but the idea that there is none is factually incorrect. There is gravity on Earth, on the moon, and on the sun. It all around us. The reason why space allows humans to appear weightless is because they are gravitating toward the Earth at the same rate as their ships.

Myth Busted: Never Eat Before Bed - It does not matter what time you eat. What matters is the amount of calories you consume.

It has long been a false belief that if you eat before going to sleep you will not be active enough to burn off those calories. What really matters is the total amount of calories you eat and not the time of day you eat them. If you consume the same amount of calories whether you eat them earlier or later, your body will digest those calories the same.

The reason some suggest an eating schedule is to prevent overeating. For example, if you skip meals you can become over hungry, which might lead to overeating when you finally do eat. The reason late night eating has been associated with weight gain is because it is often a late night snack in addition to a full day's worth of calories. So, eat whenever you like, just do not overeat and you will not gain weight.

Another myth, if you exercise on an empty stomach, you burn fat faster. When you exercise, you burn calories, whether they are from recently consumed food or fat. If you burn fat, then eat, the food is converted into fat again. So, food calories or fat calories, they are the same - more in and you gain weight, more out and you lose weight.

Fatty Food Myth - Low fat foods are always better for you is a myth that never seems to go away. In fact, Without fat, the human body is unable to absorb a large percentage of the nutrients needed to survive. The right fats in the proper amounts can actually aid in weight loss and cholesterol management.

Many products that are 'low-fat' are low in good fats as opposed to the bad ones, or substitute other ingredients like sugars and sodium that you do not need more of in your diet.

A good intake of healthful fats is beneficial for cardiovascular health. Prioritize mono-unsaturated fats (avocados, olives, almonds, peanuts) and omega-3 fatty acids (hemp seeds, chia seeds, sea vegetables, wild salmon). Virgin coconut oil and dark chocolate (80 per cent cocoa or higher) also offer healthful fatty acids.

Many low-fat diets are high in sugar and refined carbohydrates which are increasingly becoming linked to increased rates of heart disease.

GOVERNMENT AND GEOGRAPHY

Public Policy - A new analysis by the Center for Public Integrity found that between 2010 and 2014, there were six advocacy groups lobbying state legislatures for every single individual lawmaker.

National Flower - In 1985, the US Senate signed a bill declaring the rose America's national flower. President Ronald Reagan signed the bill into law during 1986

Price of Stamps - So, the agreement to raise the price of stamps by 3 cents for two years is complete and the Post Office is crying that the price of stamps set to drop by 2 cents, beginning April 10 will cost it money. It is still a penny ahead and Congress, true to style cannot let any tax end, no matter how little it is.

Traffic Cones - This sounds like another April Fool's Day joke, but it is not. Scotland spends $15,000 per year removing traffic cones from a statue's head.

The government is having a problem with revelers messing up a historic statue in the most hilarious way possible. In Glasgow, there is a statue of the Duke of Wellington. For the last several decades, this statue has been at the center of a bloodless battle between Glasgow City Council and the local drunkards, the latter of whom love nothing more than climbing the statue and placing a traffic cone on its head.

After years of being climbed, the statue has lost its sword and spurs. The cost of removing these cones is running up an annual bill of 10,000 GBP of taxpayer's money and the defaced statue is becoming a tourist attraction in itself.

As a result, Glasgow City Council planned to raise the statue's plinth (base) to such a height that the inebriated would not be able to reach anymore. However, thanks to a petition from local residents, the proposal was shot down.

German Pedestrian Red Light Assistance - Distracted smartphone users are alerted when it is safe to cross the road, after a pilot traffic light system was launched in a German city. It embedded rows of LEDs into the pavement. They flash red when the crossing is closed to pedestrians. According to German television station, it became necessary after a 15-year-old girl, who was wearing earbuds and looking at her smartphone, was killed when she stepped in front of a tram.

"We have the additional lamps installed on two crossings that are especially frequented by the relevant target group," said the city's spokesperson.

The first two pavement traffic lights have been installed near the local university. They are aimed particularly at young people and commuters, who tend to be too consumed by their smartphones to look up at the conventional traffic lights system.

US lawmakers take a different approach and seek to ban texting while walking, because distracted walking leads to falls, and nine percent "strike a motionless object."

Pumpkin Power - The US Energy Department claims pumpkins are responsible for adding to greenhouse gases in the atmosphere.

According to the department, most of the 1.3 billion pounds of pumpkins produced in the US end up in the trash, becoming part of the tons of municipal solid waste produced in the United States every year.

Municipal solid waste decomposes into methane, "a harmful greenhouse gas that plays a part in climate change, with more than 20 times the warming effect of carbon dioxide," according to the department. *We can all help by eating more pumpkin pie and munching pumpkin seeds.*

US Mail Photography - The USPS has been photographing letters and packages sent in the US for tracking and security reasons since at least 2013. Under a pilot program called "Informed Delivery," the USPS is emailing to people photographs of the front side of their mail every morning before it is delivered to their home (not business).

PO Box users are not currently targeted as participants in the pilot. PO Box customers in certain Post Offices nationwide can use the existing Real Mail Notification ® service to receive a text-only message without images, via email, or SMS message. You can check with your local Post Office for more details.

The free service will send up to 10 black-and-white photos of mail per day. People who get more than that will be able to check their mail online in the same place they track their packages, according to the USPS fact page.

In 2015 the service was available in the New York City metro area, including the following three digit ZIP Code locations: NY: 100-119; CT: 066, 069. The service has been available in select ZIP Code locations in Northern Virginia since 2014 starting with the following three digits: 201, 220, 221, 222, 223, 226, 227. Expansion to other areas is being considered.

Great for finding those mailings physically delivered to the wrong house.

Union Membership in US - The union membership rate, the percent of wage and salary workers who were members of unions, was 11.1 percent in 2015, unchanged from 2014, according to the US Bureau of Labor Statistics.

Workers in protective service occupations and in education, training, and library occupations had the highest unionization rates at 36.3 percent and 35.5 percent, respectively.

Private sector union membership rate, 24.2% in 1973, 6.6%: in 2014. Public sector rose sharply in the 1970s and has been relatively steady since 1980 at around 35 percent, more than five times higher than that of private-sector workers.

Overall union membership has fallen by about a half since 1983, according to the Bureau of Labor Statistics.

Stocks and Elections - According to research, the S&P 500 has correctly "predicted" the winner in 19 of the past 22 presidential elections. If stocks are higher during the three months before the vote, the incumbent party wins; if stocks fall during August through October, a new party wins the White House. *Hmmm, more stuff to watch.*

Gas Prices - According to Bloomberg, WTI oil is at $49.61 per barrel, and Brent is at $49.60 per barrel.

Memorial Day	Weekly Average Gasoline Price
29-May-00	$1.57
28-May-01	$1.74
27-May-02	$1.43
26-May-03	$1.53
31-May-04	$2.10
30-May-05	$2.17
29-May-06	$2.94
28-May-07	$3.25
26-May-08	$3.99
25-May-09	$2.49
31-May-10	$2.84
30-May-11	$3.90
28-May-12	$3.73
27-May-13	$3.70
26-May-14	$3.75
25-May-15	$2.75
29-May-16	$2.33

On Memorial Day 2015, Brent was at $65.37 per barrel, and two years before Brent was at $110.01.

GPS Alert - The US Federal Aviation Administration has warned that GPS signals could be unavailable or unreliable during 2016 on June 9, 21, 23, 28, and 30 across the west coast. The signals are most likely to be disturbed primarily around California, surrounding southwestern states. and the northern corner of Mexico. Although the disruptions will be more severe at higher altitudes, the signal could be scrambled as low as 15 meters (50 feet).

The FAA has advised pilots to avoid the areas at the mentioned times and instructed them to closely monitor their flight control systems.

According to the warning, the problem is something to do with "GPS Interference Testing." Other than that, the FAA remains quiet. The center point of the disturbances is the Naval Air Weapons Station China Lake in the Mojave Desert. This complex is the US Navy's largest installation, which is dedicated to researching, developing, and testing the majority of their weaponry and armaments.

European Union Origins, Changes - Many are aware of the recent headlines of the 'Brexit' or British secession from the European Union (EU), but are not aware of what the European Union is, how young it is, and how it began and changed over time. Here is a quick summary of the volatility, tenuousness, and fluidity of the EU.

During 1986 the *Single European Act* was signed. It is a treaty which provides the basis for a six-year program aimed at reducing problems with the free flow of trade across EU borders and creating a single market. In 1993 the Single Market was completed with the four freedoms of: movement of goods, services, people, and money.

During that time, there was major political upheaval when, during 1989 the Berlin Wall was pulled down and the border between East and West Germany was opened for the first time in 28 years, leading to the reunification of East and West Germany. The collapse of communism across central and eastern European brought Europeans closer together.

The *Maastricht Treaty* (formally, the Treaty on European Union) signed by the then 12 member nations, entered into force in 1993 with the goal of creating an economic and monetary union by 1999 for all EU states except the UK and Denmark. It aimed at unifying policies of defense, currency, and citizenship among the member nations. It has been amended by the treaties of Amsterdam, Nice, and Lisbon.

The euro was introduced to world financial markets as an accounting currency during January 1999 and in 2002 notes and coins began to circulate, with legacy currencies exchangeable at commercial banks in the currency's nation generally until 30 June 2002.

The *Treaty of Amsterdam*, which amended the Single European Act, other treaties establishing the European Communities, and certain related acts, was signed during 1997, and entered into force on 1 May 1999. It also made substantial changes to the Treaty of Maastricht.

"The recipe for perpetual ignorance is: Be satisfied with your opinions and content with your knowledge." *This is also the definition of a politician.*

Under the Treaty of Amsterdam, member states agreed to devolve certain powers from national governments to the European Parliament across diverse areas, including legislating on immigration, adopting civil and criminal laws, and enacting foreign and security policy, as well as implementing institutional changes for expansion as new member nations join the EU.

The *Treaty of Nice* came into force on 1 February 2003. It provided for an increase after enlargement of the number of seats in the European Parliament, which has ceremonial precedence over all authority at European level to 732 (currently 751), which exceeded the cap established by the Treaty of Amsterdam. It also provided for the creation of subsidiary courts below the European Court of Justice and the Court of First Instance to deal with special areas of law such as patents, among others. The treaty caused much consternation and debate among members.

The *Treaty of Lisbon* amends the two main treaties which formed the constitutional basis of the European Union. The Treaty of Lisbon was entered into force on 1 December 2009. The stated aim of the treaty was to "complete the process started by the Treaty of Amsterdam and by the Treaty of Nice with a view to enhancing the efficiency and democratic legitimacy of the Union and to improving the coherence of its action." It contained stronger powers for the European Parliament and a new role for national parliaments. One article called for "the word 'assent' shall be replaced by 'consent'".

The exact impact of the treaty on the functioning of the EU left many uncertainties which have led to calls for yet another new treaty to be drafted.

The European Union now consists of 28 countries, including Croatia, last to join the EU on July 1, 2013. *Stay tuned folks as this remains a very fluid situation.*

Why Donkeys and Elephants - Washington insiders considered Andrew Jackson as intemperate, vulgar, and stupid. Opponents called him a jackass. During the 1828 presidential campaign, he embraced the label and began including a jackass on his campaign posters. He became the first Democrat president.

Incidentally, donkeys are in the same family as horses. A male donkey is called a jackass.

During the 1870s, influential political cartoonist Thomas Nast helped popularize the donkey as a symbol for the entire Democrat Party. It first appeared in a cartoon in Harper's Weekly in 1870, and was supposed to represent an anti-Civil War faction. Nast drew a donkey clothed in lion's skin, scaring away all the animals at the zoo. By 1880 it had already become the unofficial symbol of the party.

Thomas Nast, in an 1874 Harper's Weekly cartoon portrayed various interest groups as animals, including an elephant labeled "The Republican Vote," which was shown standing at the edge of a pit. IIe employed the elephant to represent Republicans in additional cartoons during the 1870s, and by 1880 other cartoonists were using the creature to symbolize the party.

Democrats say the donkey is smart and brave and Republicans say the elephant is strong and dignified.

Motto of United States - The following is not meant to be political, but to remind what the Motto of the United States is. Contrary to what one of our candidates for president said during her recent acceptance speech, E Pluribus Unum was officially replaced as the motto of the US during 1956, by the US Congress passing an act making "In God We Trust" the official motto.

Incidentally, President Obama also made the same faux pas during another speech he made a few years ago.

Manhattan Border War - There is a small part of Manhattan that is physically part of the Bronx borough to the north. It is the neighborhood of Marble Hill. The two boroughs have been playing tug of war over this former island neighborhood for over a century.

The quarrel started with the building of the Harlem Ship Canal, which cut right through Manhattan's northernmost neighborhood, turning Marble Hill into an island. During 1914 the canal was filled in, making Marble Hill now physically part of the Bronx, but still legally part of Manhattan.

WWII is Not Over - There are a string of volcanic islands in the Pacific, known as the Kurils. A dispute between Russia and Japan, has prevented the two nations from signing a peace treaty to formally end World War II.

The islands are equidistant between the two countries and are rich in natural resources, including potentially large oil and natural gas reserves. Known in Japan as the Northern Territories and in Russia as the South Kurils, four of these islands are at the center of a dispute over ownership that continues. Many potential solutions to the conflict have been proposed, but talks between the countries have led to a stalemate and lack of war ending treaty.

WikiLeaks - WikiLeaks stays in the news and has for many years, but few of my friends have actually visited the website, or even know it exists. It is described as an international non-profit, journalistic organization that publishes secret information, news leaks, and classified media from anonymous sources. The published editorial policy says it accepts only documents that are "of political, diplomatic, historical, or ethical interest" and excludes "material that is already publicly available." Its website was initiated in 2006 in Iceland by the organization Sunshine Press. It no longer uses the 'wiki' method of user input and also is not related to Wikipedia.

WikiLeaks relies on volunteers and describes its founders as a mixture of Asian dissidents, journalists, mathematicians, and start-up company technologists from the United States, Taiwan, Europe, Australia, and South Africa. As of June 2009, the website had more than 1,200 registered volunteers and listed an advisory board, including Julian Assange and seven other people. It is entirely run on donations. Lawyers around the world provide pro bono assistance as needed.

Its leader, Julian Assange described himself in a private conversation as "the heart and soul of this organization, its founder, philosopher, spokesperson, original coder, organizer, financier, and all the rest."

World Population Statistics - These numbers may provide some perspective on how popular we think we might be: 104 million people are born each year, 57 million people die each year, 108 billion are estimated to have ever lived on earth, and there are over 7 billion people currently alive. *Next time someone tells you how great they are, ask them what percent of the seven billion people they can call friends.*

Point Roberts Double Currency - Point Roberts is a little tract of land attached to a suburb of Vancouver, British Columbia, Canada. It is officially part of Washington State, US, but inhabitants must cross through Canada to reach the rest of Washington State. Point Roberts has a small airport and a large marina for air and water access. These two point facilities allow the fourteen mile direct access to the rest of Washington State without the need to enter Canada.

Point Bob, as it is called, has a post office, with the ZIP code of 98281 had a population of 1,314 on the 2010 census. The US portion of the peninsula is about 2 miles (3 km) from north to south and about 3 miles (5 km) from east to west. It has a total area of 4.884 square miles (12.65 km2). From fourth grade on, American children must take a 40-minute ride through British Columbia, crossing back into the United States at Blaine, Washington.

It assumed its present political status in 1846, when the Oregon Treaty extended the 49th parallel as the boundary between American and British territory from the Rocky Mountains to Georgia Strait. Later, as the Boundary Commission was surveying the line, the British government realized that the peninsula of Point Roberts would be an isolated part of the United States.

Incidentally, The cash registers have two drawers in one. One side dispenses Canadian funds, the other side American. The registers are updated daily to properly calculate the current exchange rate.

Strange Flag - Nepal's flag is the only one in the world to not have four sides. It has a shape formed by two intersecting triangles. Its red color is Rhododendron, Nepal's national flower. The blue border around it symbolizes peace. The unusual shape of the flag was designed to show the Himalayan Mountains; a very important aspect of Nepal.

The sun within the lower triangle represents determination and a fierce resolve. The moon in the upper part stands for peace, tranquility, and harmony. Both of these elements stand together representing the hope that Nepal will be as everlasting as these two heavenly bodies.

It is also the only country whose flag design and construction are written into the Constitution. The previous flag of Nepal, prior to 1962, was of similar shape and somewhat more intricate design, and was in use for more than 2,000 years.

Incidentally, The flag of Libya is the only flag containing one color and consists solely of a solid green background. Green is the national color of Libya as well as a symbol of devotion to Islam. Green also represents Libyan President Muammar al Qaddafi's 'Green Revolution' - an intention to turn Libya into a wealthy agricultural nation.

California Cow Gas - It is true, California Air Resources Board (Senate Bill 1383) can now regulate cow flatulence. It looks for practical ways to reduce cows' belching and breaking wind.

"Although these gases do not linger in the atmosphere, they still make people sick and hasten global warming due to their heat-trapping ability", per Reuters. Governor Brown added, "We're protecting people's lungs and their health."

Perhaps the farmers will next be required to affix these to their livestock.

Argentina's National Institute of Agricultural Technology has come up with an innovative solution, the cow-fart-backpack to be used to fight climate change. The backpack captures the gases emitted through the cow's mouth or intestinal tract via a tube inserted through the cow's skin (which the researchers claim is painless). The gas is then condensed and ready to use to provide power for the farm.

Madrid Crosswalks - Here is a great idea. The crosswalks are livened up to promote awareness for both drivers and pedestrians.

There are a variety of colors and designs on different roads.

Electoral College - Much has been said during the past US election about wooing the electoral votes and the number needed to win. Both candidates even skipped visiting many states during the election season. States that typically vote for one party or the other have been ignored if they do not have enough electors to sway the vote. Those states are considered to have enough voters with party allegiance that it is not worth the time or expense to woo the people who actually vote.

The reason for this is when Americans go to the polls to vote for the next president of the United States, they are not actually voting for the president. Rather, they are casting a vote for a group of electors, who will then vote for the president as they choose. The presidential candidate that a given group of electors is pledged to vote for is put on the ballot instead.

Another common misconception about presidential voting in the United States is that the president is elected once the general public's votes are tallied up. Since the general public does not technically vote for a president, but rather Electoral College representatives, the president is not officially elected until the following January. Specifically, on January 6th the current vice president opens voting during a Joint Session of Congress. It is during this session that electoral votes are tallied.

There are many completely legal scenarios in which a different president may be chosen than the one who appears to have won after the general public has cast their ballots for electors.

Article II of the Constitution, which states that "no Senator or Representative, or Person holding an Office of Trust... shall be appointed an Elector." Other than that, that anyone can be an elector.

Each state's political parties nominate a group of electors who are extremely loyal to their respective parties. Their number is equal to the number of electoral votes the state has, which in turn is equal to the number of senators (two per state) and number of representatives (determined by population) the state has, or in the case of the District of Columbia, three electors.

An elector cannot vote for a vice president and president who both are from the elector's home state. This rule was meant to ensure an elector could not vote for two of their state's "favorite sons". This is obviously not an issue for anyone so long as the presidential candidate picks a vice presidential candidate from a state other than their own.

On election day, whichever political party's candidate wins the majority of the state's votes, that slate of electors get to vote for the president in their respective state. However, in Maine and Nebraska the state's popular majority is accounted for in some electors' votes, but others vote based on congressional district's popular majority within the state. This can potentially result in a splitting of the votes.

There are no federal laws or Constitutional provisions that require electors to cast their vote in accordance with the state's popular vote result. Just twenty nine states and the District of Columbia have laws that require the electors vote the way the popular vote has instructed them to, the rest allow electors to vote as they see fit, instead of how the general public directed them to vote.

Splitting States - The United States is strange for many reasons, not the least of which is separating states into two. For Instance, North and South Carolina's evolution from the colony to two separate colonies and then two states occurred back in the 1700s and was caused partly by messy beginnings of governance and poor leadership, and partly by the fact that the original land grant was too large.

West Virginia split from the eastern portion of Virginia in 1861, because the latter voted to secede from the United States in the lead-up to the Civil War.

North and South Dakota had at least two reasons to split. From the creation of the Dakota Territory in 1861 until 1883, Yankton was the capital, in the southeastern corner of the territory. It was a steamboat landing along the Missouri River. However, the landing was crushed by the breaking of an ice dam, in 1881, and the entire riverfront and downtown area were flooded.

Two years later, the northern region of the Dakota Territory declared Bismarck as the capital of the territory. The people living in the southern region planned to become a separate state from the northern territory, so that they could have their own capital. The government balked and said there were not enough people for two states. When North Dakota was finally populated enough to become a state, in 1889, there was a rivalry about which state would be admitted first.

Another, perhaps more important, reason for two separate states instead of one large state was four senators, instead of two, and more representatives. Since Dakotans from the north and the south routinely voted Republican, the admission of two Dakotas gave the

Republicans a majority in Congress. *I am surprised the residents of the various Hawaiian Islands have not thought of that tactic.*

A Different Election Perspective - Seems everyone likes to claim a victor as their own. The Buchan Observer, based in Aberdeenshire, Scotland, ran a presidential announcement with the headline: "Aberdeenshire Business Owner Wins Presidential Election."

Donald Trump owns the Trump International golf course in Balmedie, Aberdeenshire, which opened in 2011. He has visited the area several times, most recently during the 2016 election cycle. Trump is also half-Scottish. His mother, Mary Macleod, grew up on the Isle of Lewis.

Speaking after the result became official, Scottish First Minister Nicola Sturgeon congratulated Trump on his victory and said it's time for all those who share "progressive values" to speak up loudly together.

Great TP Tax - In New York, sales tax for toilet paper is 8.875 percent. Many New Yorkers are unaware of the taxation on a product that is a necessity of everyday life.

After discovering Florida's sales tax laws, Sun Sentinel columnist Michael Mayo launched a petition pleading for legislators to exempt toilet paper from taxation. His lone petition drew a mere 89 supporters.

New Jersey and Pennsylvania are the only two states that specifically exempt toilet paper from tax. during 2016, Costco in New Jersey was sued for charging toilet paper tax. Costco had the case dismissed. Target in Pennsylvania was also sued for charging tax on toilet paper.

All toilet papers today break down well in the septic system. However, thinner is better. One ply bath tissue will break down easier and is best in recreational vehicles and boats.

Incidentally, In 1996, President Clinton passed a "Toilet Paper Tax" of 6 cents per roll.

Berlin 1953 - 2016 - The Berlin Morning Post has developed a fascinating interactive map of Berlin during 1953 and updated as of 2016. The map is split in the middle and you can move cursor to slide the view from one side to the other interactively and can zoom in, as well as move north and south.

You can search for an addresses in the top left hand corner and see what the neighborhood looked like more than sixty years ago, before the Berlin Wall and while the city was still recovering from the Second World War. Berlin removed 75 million cubic metres of rubble in the years after the war. All names are in German.

Employment Facts - As of 1 October 2016, from a US population of 325 million, 113 million private sector workers support 32 million government workers and contractors, 94 million people who can work, but chose not to, 70 million who cannot work, and 16 million unemployed and underemployed.

That is 35% supporting 65%, including all of the government workers, which taxpayers pay for during working years and retirement until death.

Millennials overtake Baby Boomers - It finally happened, Millennials are now America's largest generation according to population estimates from the US Census Bureau. Millennials, those ages 18-34 in 2015, now number 75.4 million, surpassing the 74.9 million Baby Boomers, ages 51-69. Generation X, ages 35-50 in 2015 is projected to pass the Boomers in population by 2028.

> If you are over 45 years old, the world population has doubled within your lifetime.

The Millennial generation continues to grow as young immigrants expand its ranks. Boomers, whose generation was defined by the boom in US births following World War II are older and their numbers shrinking as their number of deaths exceeds the number of older immigrants arriving in the country. With immigration adding more numbers to its group than any other, the Millennial population is projected to peak in 2036 at 81.1 million.

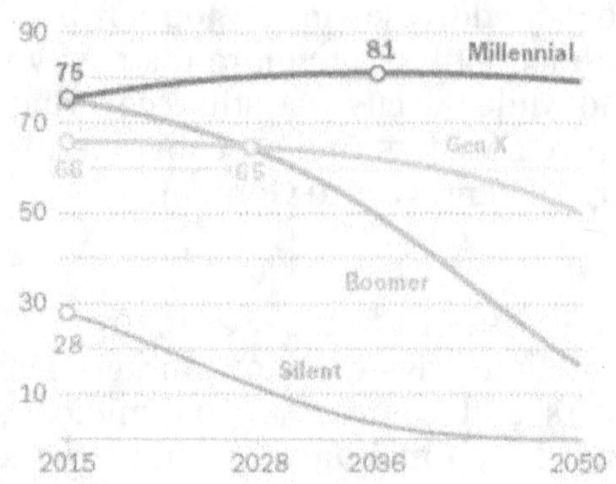

Pew Research Center established that the oldest Millennial was born in 1981 and the youngest Millennial was born in 1997.

Nazism, Fascism, Socialism, Communism - These terms are found in the media and social web sites much too often lately. However, it seems most are unaware of what each term means as they call anyone with a different point of view any of these words interchangeably.

Nazism - Nazi was formed from the first two syllables of the German pronunciation of the word 'national' (na-tsi̯-o-ˈnaːl). Its political and economic doctrines were put into effect by the Nazis in Germany from 1933 to 1945, including the totalitarian principle of government, predominance of Germanic groups assumed to be racially superior, and supremacy of the leader. It arose from attempts to create a nationalist redefinition of 'socialism' as an alternative to both socialism and free market capitalism. It is usually characterized as a form of fascism that incorporates scientific racism and anti-Semitism, developed from the influences of Pan-Germanism and the anti-communist movement. It aimed to overcome social divisions and create a homogeneous society, unified on the basis of racial purity.

Bottom line, Nazism is racist, anti-Semitist, anti democracy, anti capitalist, anti communist, and anti socialist.

Fascism - Originates from Italian fascismo, equivalent to fascio, meaning bundle or political group. The ideology originated in Italy and was established by Mussolini beginning during 1922 and is a governmental system led by a dictator having complete power, forcibly suppressing opposition and criticism, regimenting all industry, commerce, etc., and emphasizing an aggressive nationalism and often racism. He founded the National Fascist Party. His economic system intended to resolve class conflict through collaboration between the classes.

Bottom line, Fascism is militaristic, nationalistic, racist, anti democratic, anti liberal, anti Marxist, and organizes a country along hierarchical authoritarianism without ethical or legal restraints, and it is dedicated to increase its territory.

Socialism - Under Socialism, equality is the main focus. Instead of workers owning the facilities and tools for production, workers are paid and allowed to spend their wages as they choose, while the governing body owns and operates the means of production for the benefit of the working class. Each worker is provided with necessities so he is able to produce without worry for basic needs. Advancement and production are limited, because there is no incentive to achieve more. Without motivation to succeed, workers' human instincts prohibit drive and desire due to no incentives.

"Machines and other improvements must serve to ease the work of all and not to enable a few to grow rich at the expense of millions and tens of millions of people. This new and better society is called socialist society. The teachings about this society are called 'socialism'." ~ Vladimir Lenin

Socialism and Communism are structures that promote equality and seek to eliminate social classes. Sometimes, the two are used interchangeably, though they are different. *Communism is a political system, socialism is primarily an economic system.* Both espouse everyone doing their share and working together to provide for the greater good. Each utilizes a planned production schedule to ensure the needs of all community members are met. They are utopian economic structures that some countries have tried, but most have failed or became dictatorships. Socialist philosophy is "From each according to his ability, to each according to his contribution."

Bottom line, Socialism is mainly an economic system that espouses equality among the masses, dictated by leadership that owns all the resources. Two kinds of property: personal property, such as houses, clothing, etc. owned by the individual and public property including factories, and means of production are owned by the State, but with worker control.

Communism - From the French word communisme, a doctrine based on Marxian socialism and Leninism that was the official ideology of the U.S.S.R. It grew out of the Socialist movement and is a system of social organization based on the holding of all property in common, with actual ownership belonging to the community or the totalitarian state dominated by a single and self-perpetuating political party. The communist philosophy embraces a communal lifestyle to share all economic and material products between inhabitants of the commune, so that all may benefit from everybody's work. Communist philosophy is "From each according to his ability, to each according to his <u>needs</u>".

The Soviet Union was officially dissolved on December 26, 1991. Currently, countries controlled by Marxist–Leninist parties under a single-party system include the People's Republic of China, Cuba, Laos, Vietnam, and North Korea. Many other countries have Communist parties, that are not dominant.

Bottom line, Communism is totalitarian, anti individual ownership, and anti capitalist. It is equated with socialism and contrasted with democracy and capitalism. Communism is considered an extreme form of socialism. Private property is abolished. The concept of property is negated and replaced with the concept of commons and ownership with "usership".

Interesting to note that all four of these 'isms' promote equality, but all have a ruling class that is above the community and enjoys the riches denied to the masses.

Chesty Tax Deduction - Every now and then something I read is so completely crazy it tickles me. Thought I would share this IRS story. If you are an exotic dancer who needs the biggest assets possible to get the biggest tips, they might be deductible. The IRS initially denied the write off, which "Chesty Love" submitted for her (56-FF) breast augmentation. However, the Court allowed her 'stage props' as depreciable assets.

Political Correctness - I have always lacked my fair share of political correctness, mainly because it defies logic and common sense. Here are a few passages I have come across that describe it rather well.

The 2007 winning entry from an annual contest at Texas A&M University calling for the most appropriate definition of a contemporary term 'Political Correctness'. The winner wrote: "Political Correctness is a doctrine, fostered by a delusional, illogical minority, and rabidly promoted by an unscrupulous mainstream media, which holds forth the proposition that it is entirely possible to pick up a turd by the clean end."

"No one should ever underestimate the stupidity induced in bureaucrats by the procedures they are enjoined to follow."

"The perverse incentives that bureaucrats are often given nowadays are also worth a mention. On the false grounds that it is better to measure something than to measure nothing, the work of a bureaucracy (and therefore bureaucrats) is judged by some target or other plucked from the ether of political vacuity by their bosses."

Texas Obscenity Law, or Not - The Obscene Device Law is a Texas statute dealing with obscenity. In 1973, the Texas Legislature passed Section 43.21 of the Texas Penal Code which, in part, prohibited the sale or promotion of "Obscene device[s] mean[ing] a device including a dildo or artificial vagina, designed or marketed as useful primarily for the stimulation of human genital organs."

In an appeal from the United States District Court for the Western District of Texas, a three-judge panel of the 5th Circuit Court of Appeals overturned the statute on February 12, 2008, by a vote of 2–1, holding that "the statute has provisions that violate the Fourteenth Amendment of the U.S. Constitution".

On November 4, 2008, U.S. District Judge Lee Yeakel released a two-page document dated October 29, 2008, in which he stated that the Texas Attorney General's Office notified him that they would not file a writ of certiorari with the Supreme Court.

The following month, on November 13, Yeakel filed a "joint status report" that noted the parties had come to an agreement. "Texas Penal Code §§ 43.23, to the extent that it applies to "obscene devices" as defined in Texas Penal Code § 43.21(a)(7), is declared to be facially unconstitutional and unenforceable throughout the State of Texas," the report read.

British Slaves in America - Between 1718 and 1776, British authorities exiled approximately 50,000 male and female convicts to American colonies in a policy euphemistically known as 'transportation'. Once in America, the convicts fell under a life of servitude or outright slavery, underfed, and overworked.

They had to obey their masters or risk being imprisoned. In the early period of transportation, half of them died while in bondage. The Americans' demands for independence caused Britain to stop sending its convicts to America and forced the Brits to send them to Australia instead. The Australian convict trade was about three times as large as the American version.

Geography

Cradles of Civilization - Current scholarship generally identifies six sites where civilization emerged independently: Mesopotamia (Iraq, Syria, and Kuwait, including regions along the Turkish-Syrian and Iran–Iraq borders), the Nile River (Africa), the Indus River (Asia), the Yellow River (China), the Central Andes (southern Ecuador, Peru, western Bolivia, and northern and central Argentina, and Chile), and Mesoamerica (from central Mexico to Belize, Guatemala, El Salvador, Honduras, Nicaragua, and northern Costa Rica).

Historic times are separated from prehistoric times when records of the past begin to be kept for the benefit of future generations; that is, with the development of writing.

The earliest signs of a process leading to sedentary culture can be found in the Levant (from ISIL fame) to as early as 12,000 BC. The Levant is an approximate historical geographical term referring to a large area in the eastern Mediterranean, including all of the eastern Mediterranean with its islands, including all of the countries along the eastern Mediterranean shores, extending from Greece to Cyrenaica (Eastern Lybia).

Modern meaning includes Syria-Palestine or the region of Syria bounded by the Taurus Mountains of Turkey in the North, the Mediterranean Sea in the west, and the north Arabian Desert and Mesopotamia in the east. Today, Cyprus, Egypt, Iraq, Israel, Jordan, Lebanon, Palestine, Syria, and Turkey are sometimes considered Levant countries.

The first cities to house several tens of thousands were Memphis and Uruk, by 3000 BC.

Camels in Australia - Australia has camels and they were imported onto the continent during the 19th century from Arabia, India, and Afghanistan, because they were well suited to Australia's outback.

When the combustion engine came along, the camels were no longer needed, so they were released into the outback. Today it is a huge problem. In fact, there is one roaming flock that has 750,000 camels.

Australia exports camels to Saudi Arabia, a place you would think would be plentiful with camels. There are many camel farms in Saudi Arabia, but the camels are bred for domestic uses and racing. The camels from Australia are mostly used for meat, a delicacy for many countries in the Middle East.

More About Time Zones - Prior to standardization, there were thousands of local times around the world, generally based on the Sun's position at a given time. Even after clocks became somewhat commonplace, two cities a short distance apart sometimes had very different ideas about what time it was at any given moment. Usually, the accepted time for a given city was based on a well-known clock in the town, like a clock tower, which was often at least partially based on the Sun's position.

Once people began to travel, establishing a universal time became more important. During 1675 the GMT was invented at the Royal Observatory at Greenwich, England. As transportation and communication continued to advance, the need to have standard timekeeping became increasingly apparent. During 1840, the Great Western Railway in Great Britain adopted GMT (Greenwich Mean Time) as the standard for its schedule, and by 1847, all British rail companies were using GMT, which was also called Railway Time.

> **Q Quickie**
> Qatar is the only country that begins with a Q. Iraq is the only country that ends with Q.

The Royal Observatory began telegraphing time signals in 1852, and by 1855, 98% of the public clocks in Great Britain were displaying GMT, either alone or in conjunction with local time.

Sir Sandford Fleming was the instigator of a single, worldwide system of timekeeping. His basic idea of having a universal day beginning at Greenwich was ultimately adopted at the International Meridian Conference in 1884. The conferees decided that the line of longitude that passed through Greenwich would be the prime meridian where each universal day would begin at midnight.

As had once been the case in Europe, and for some semblance of standardization from town to town, railroad companies set their own times, which differed from company to company. William F. Allen's proposal was adopted by the US rail system on November 18, 1883. It was called the day of two noons, every railroad station clock was reset to reflect new time zones, which were designated Intercolonial, Eastern, Central, Mountain, and Pacific.

Less than one hundred years ago, the US Congress passed the Standard Time Act in 1918, which established a single, standard system of timekeeping for the entire country and designated its five time zones by reference to the Greenwich meridian.

Incidentally, it is called "Greenwich Mean Time," because the Earth's daily rotation time is slightly irregular, causing a variance of about plus or minus 16 minutes, so to be consistent, the mean time is used.

Daylight Saving - In the US, "Fast Time", as it was called then, was first introduced in 1918. The initiative was sparked by Robert Garland, a Pittsburgh industrialist.

Just seven months later, DST was repealed. However, some cities, including Pittsburgh, Boston, and New York, continued to use it.

During 1942, at the height of World War II, President Franklin D. Roosevelt reintroduced year-round Daylight Saving Time in the United States. Referred to as "War Time", DST was in force continuously from February 9, 1942 to September 30, 1945.

During 1972, Congress revised the law to provide that, if a state was in two or more time zones, the state could exempt the part of the state that was in one time zone while providing that the part of the state in a different time zone would observe Daylight Saving Time.

In spite of local and national political desires and aspirations to control time - observance of Daylight Saving Time around the world remains highly variable, with just 70 of the 195 countries observing some manner of daylight saving on varying days and times - and

----

Good Neighbors - The Canada–United States border officially known as the International Boundary, is the longest international border in the world between two countries. Eight Canadian provinces and territories and thirteen US states are located along the border.

At one point the border between Canada on the north and the US runs through the villages of Derby Line, Vermont, and Stanstead, Quebec - and though the middle of the town library.

It physically snakes through side streets, in and out of houses, through the public library, and straight down the middle of a main road that residents affectionately call "Canusa Avenue." An apartment building in town has two addresses, one for each country.

Incidentally, Canada borders are east, west, north, and south of the US. In Alaska, Canada is directly East. In many northern US continental states, Canada is directly North. In Maine, it is directly West and North. In Detroit, Michigan, Canada is directly South. Part of Washington State is both North and South of Canada.

Russia and US border - The news media usually fails to mention that Russia and the US share a border. There is no wall and not much traffic of refugees trying to pass illegally.

The Russia / United States maritime boundary follows the June 1, 1990 USA/USSR Maritime Boundary Agreement, but it has yet to be approved by the Russian parliament. The United States Senate gave its consent to ratification on September 16, 1991.

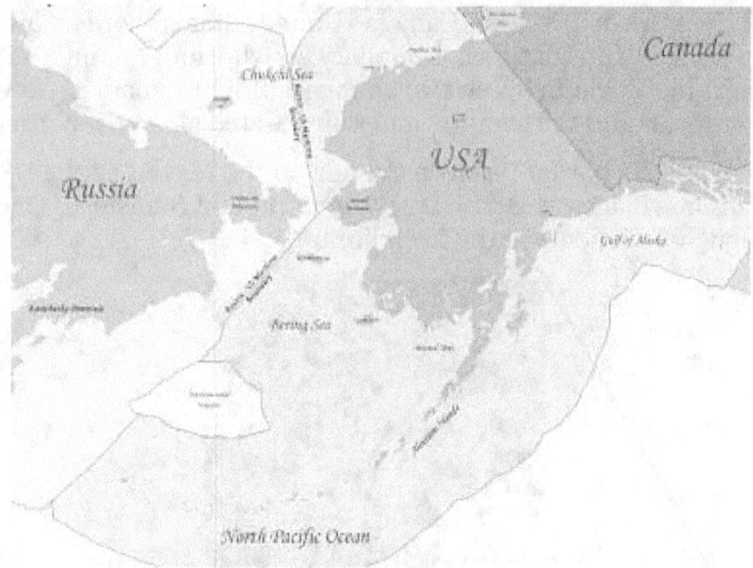

Two islands, Little Diomede, US and Big Diomede, Russia lie between Russia and the United States. The islands are only 35 km away from both Chukotka, Russia and Alaska, US. Because the international Date Line runs between them, the time difference between them is about 21 hours.

Incidentally, Russia's Eastern border is with China.

Funny Town Names - What started out as a temporary solution has become a point of pride for locals. In No Name, Colorado according to reports, a government official first marked a newly constructed exit off I-70 with a sign reading "No Name" as a placeholder. By the time officials got around to officially labeling it, "No Name" had the support of the community and it stuck. Visitors can find the spot near the No Name tunnels, No Name Creek, and the No Name hiking trail.

Saint Pierre and Miquelon - It is part of Appalachian Mountains, Canada, and France.

The Territorial Collectivity of Saint Pierre and Miquelon (French: Collectivité Territoriale de Saint-Pierre-et-Miquelon) is an overseas collectivity of France located in the North Atlantic Ocean about 30 kilometres (19 mi) south of the Canadian Island of Newfoundland. It comprises a group of small islands, the main ones being Saint Pierre and Miquelon located in the Gulf of Saint Lawrence and the center of the Grand Banks of Newfoundland in the North Atlantic, 25 kilometres (16 mi) southwest of Newfoundland.

The archipelago is composed of eight islands, totaling 242 square kilometres (93 sq mi), and of which only two are inhabited. The islands are bare and rocky, with steep coasts, and only a thin layer of peat to soften the hard landscape. It is geologically part of the northeastern end of the Appalachian Mountains along with Newfoundland.

Saint Pierre Island, whose area is smaller, 26 square kilometres (10 sq mi), is the most populous and the commercial and administrative center of the archipelago. Saint-Pierre Airport, has been in operation since 1999 and is capable of accommodating long-haul flights from France.

Miquelon-Langlade, the largest island, is composed of two islands, Miquelon Island (also called Grande Miquelon), 110 square kilometres (42 sq mi), connected to Langlade Island (Petite Miquelon), 91 square kilometres (35 sq mi), by the Dune de Langlade, a 10-kilometre (6.2 mi) long sandy split. A storm had severed them in the 18th century, separating the two islands for several decades, before currents reconstructed the isthmus. The waters between Langlade and Saint-Pierre were called "the Mouth of Hell" until about 1900, as more than 600 shipwrecks have been recorded in that point.

The official currency is the Euro, but the Canadian dollar is also widely accepted. The islands issue their own stamps. The inhabitants have French citizenship, speak French and their customs and traditions are similar to the ones found in metropolitan France.

The total population of the islands at the January 2011 census was 6,080, of which 5,456 lived in Saint-Pierre and 624 in Miquelon-Langlade.

French overseas collectivities like the French regions, are first-order administrative divisions of France. Other collectivities of France include, the Islands of Guadeloupe, Martinique, Saint-Martin, Saint-Barthélemy, (Atlantic Ocean) Reunion island, Mayotte, the French Southern, and Antarctic Lands (Indian Ocean) French Polynesia, New Caledonia, Wallis and Futuna (Pacific Ocean).

The Island of Discussion - The island in Glencoe, Scotland was a place to settle disputes and resolve differences. Officially named Eilean a' Chomhraidh, the Island of Discussion is small and alone.

This island served a noble purpose for many years. During more than 1,500 years, when clansman had a disagreement, this is the place they went to work it out. When there were quarrels or arguments, the feuding parties where taken to the island and left alone with whiskey, cheese, and oat cakes. They did not leave the island until the dispute was settled. The result, in over 1,500 years, only one recorded murder in the area.

Europe in Africa - Ceuta and Melilla are fragments of Europe on north Africa's Mediterranean coast. They came under Spanish control about 500 years ago. Madrid says they are integral parts of Spain. On three sides they are surrounded by Morocco. For both, the currency used is the Euro.

Ceuta is an 18.5-square-kilometre (7.1 sq mi) Spanish autonomous city located on the north coast of Africa, separated by 14 kilometers from Cadiz province on the Spanish mainland by the Strait of Gibraltar and sharing a 6.4 kilometer land border in the Kingdom of Morocco. It lies along the boundary between the Mediterranean Sea and the Atlantic Ocean and is one of nine populated Spanish territories in Africa and, along with Melilla, one of two populated territories on mainland Africa. It was part of Cádiz province until 14 March 1995 when the city's Statute of Autonomy was passed.

Melilla is a Spanish autonomous city located on the north coast of Africa, sharing a border with Morocco with an area of 12.3 square kilometres (4.7 sq mi). Melilla is one of two permanently inhabited Spanish cities in mainland Africa. It was part of Málaga province until 14 March 1995 when the city's Statute of Autonomy was passed.

Melilla, like Ceuta, was a free port before Spain joined the European Union. As of 2011, it had a population of 78,476 made up of ethnic Spaniards, ethnic Riffian Berbers, and a small number of Sephardic Jews, and Sindhi Hindus. Both Spanish and Riffian-Berber are the two most widely spoken languages, with Spanish as the only official language.

This year, migrants were attempting to reach Ceuta to get to the rest of Europe. Only two were successful, but both were injured scaling the six-metre (20 ft) surrounding fence and needed hospital treatment. The attempt comes after more than 400 migrants succeeded in breaching Ceuta's fence in December. Hundreds of sub-Saharan African migrants living illegally in Morocco try to enter Ceuta and Melilla each year in hope of getting to Europe.

The Great Lakes — Lakes Superior, Huron, Michigan, Ontario and Erie make up the largest body of fresh water on Earth, accounting for one-fifth of the freshwater surface on the planet with 6 quadrillion gallons.

The area of all the Great Lakes is 95,160 square miles (246,463 square kilometers) and span 750 miles (1,200 km) from west to east. The square mileage is larger than the state of Texas.

The lakes are on the US and Canadian border, touching Ontario in Canada and Michigan, Wisconsin, Minnesota, Illinois, Indiana, Ohio, Pennsylvania, and New York in the United States. The St. Lawrence River connects Lake Ontario to the Gulf of St. Lawrence, which leads out to the Atlantic Ocean.

As of 2017, more than 30 million people live in the Great Lakes basin, according to the US Environmental Protection Agency. This equates to about 10 percent of US residents and 30 percent of Canadian residents. More than 3,500 species of plants and animals inhabit the Great Lakes basin, as well as more than 170 species of fish.

Tree Growth - In the United States, which contains eight percent of the world's forests, there are more trees than there were a hundred years ago. According to the Food and Agriculture Organization, "Forest growth nationally has exceeded harvest since the 1940s. By 1997, forest growth exceeded harvest by 42 percent and the volume of forest growth was 380 percent greater than it had been in 1920."

The US had 319 million people in 2014 and 228 billion trees. The greatest gains have been seen on the East Coast, with average volumes of wood per acre almost doubling since the 1950s. Over 75 percent of the productive commercial forest land in the US is privately owned.

In a study released during 2015 in Nature, a team of 38 scientists found that the planet is home to 3.04 trillion trees, far surpassing the previously estimate of 400 billion. The researchers estimated there are 422 trees for every person on Earth.

Incidentally, the US federal government owns 28% of all US land.

Deserts and Sand and Ice - The two biggest deserts are the Antarctic and the Arctic. Even though they are covered with ice, they are dry enough to be considered deserts.

The Sahara, spanning an area of 8.5 million square kilometers (covers 29.6% of Africa) is the world's hottest desert and third in size. The Sahara is only twenty percent sand, the rest of it is mostly made up of bare rock, gravel, and pebbles.

Hottest Planet - Even though it is not closest to the sun (Mercury is), the hottest planet in our Solar system is Venus, second closest. The average temperature on the Venus does not go below 462 degrees while that of Mercury reaches only up to 420 degrees.

Oolitic Sand and Brine Shrimp - Oolitic sand is pill-shaped sand prevalent on the bottom of Great Salt Lake and several beaches. It is soft, smooth and round unlike regular sand that is jagged-edged. A grain of oolitic sand begins as a brine shrimp fecal pellet or other small bit of debris. Calcium and magnesium carbonate particles build up around it, creating oolitic sand and separating brine shrimp waste from the rest of the water. In this way, oolitic sand functions as a filter for Great Salt Lake.

Brine shrimp are the most populous animal in Great Salt Lake. These tiny crustaceans live in salt water around the world, but only one species, Artemia franciscana lives in Great Salt Lake. They measure up to 0.5 inches (1.37 centimeters) long and can live in water with up to 33 percent salinity, according to Great Salt Lake Ecosystem Program. They can control how much salt gets into their body tissues better than any other organism on Earth, due to skin lining their stomachs and gills.

Incidentally, a massive brine shrimp harvest occurs every Autumn. The brine shrimp are primarily sent to Asia and South America where they are used as feeders for commercially grown prawn and fish.

Food Facts

FUN FOOD FACTS

Looking Back to 1932 - Elmer Doolin purchased a corn chip recipe during the early 1930s and started mass producing his corn chips in 1932. He also invented Cheetos.

Lay's introduced its classic potato chip in 1932.

Girl Scout Cookies - Girl Scout cookies trace their roots back to 1917, when an Oklahoma scout troop sold cookies as a fundraiser at their local high school.

> **Sticky Things**
> When measuring ingredients for cooking, like peanut butter, honey, etc. Spray the measuring cup with cooking spray first. It will make cleanup much easier.

The cookies are produced by two bakeries: ABC Bakers (a subsidiary of Interbake Foods) and Little Brownie Bakers (owned by Keebler/Kellogg's). There are some major differences between the cookies they produce, but the core five cookies are the same, although with different names: Thin Mints, Trefoils or Shortbread, Samoas or Caramel deLites, Tagalongs or Peanut Butter Patties, and Do-si-dos or Peanut Butter Sandwiches.

Samoas, Tagalongs, Trefoils, and Do-si-dos, are produced by Little Brownie. Shortbread, Caramel deLites, Peanut Butter Patties, and Peanut Butter Sandwiches are produced by ABC. The only cookie name shared by both companies is Thin Mints.

Other, newer names cater to specific audiences. Both Little Brownie's Toffee-Tastic and ABC's Trios are gluten-free. Little Brownie's Thin Mints and ABC's Lemonades, Thanks-A-Lots, Thin Mints, and Peanut Butter Patties are vegan.

About 25 percent of all Girl Scout cookies sold are Thin Mints. Samoas or Caramel deLites are second with 19 percent of sales. Once the cost of the cookies is repaid to the bakery, all of the net revenue raised through Girl Scout Cookie sales stays with the local councils and troops. *Am waiting for a new flavor, bacon peanut butter sammie.*

Asparagus - I read an email touting the cancer killing properties of asparagus last week. After looking on the web, found that it originated in 2006 and has been long since debunked, but still keeps floating around. Below are a true facts about cancer and asparagus.

According to Johns Hopkins Kimmel Cancer Center, "There is no evidence that certain foods alter the environment of an existing cancer, at the cellular level, and cause it to either die or grow."

The odor causing ingredient in asparagus has long been known. Benjamin Franklin stated in a 1781 letter to the Royal Academy of Brussels, "A few stems of asparagus eaten, shall give our urine a disagreable odour (sic)."

According to Carolyn O'Neil on Web MD, "Researchers believe that, during digestion, the vegetable's sulfurous amino acids break down into smelly chemical components in all people." Within 15 to 30 minutes of eating asparagus, the odor can be present.

In 2010, the genetic sequencing company 23andMe conducted a study in which they asked nearly 10,000 customers if they noticed any scent in their urine after eating asparagus, and looked for genetic similarities among those who could not. This stems from a single genetic mutation, a switched base-pair among a cluster of 50 different genes that code for olfactory (sense of smell) receptors.

On a positive note of the benefits, women have long known that asparagus is a wonderful natural diuretic.

An easy way to oven-roast, preheat the oven to 450, mix trimmed asparagus with olive oil, salt, and pepper. Roast in a single layer in a pan, or on aluminum foil for 10 – 15 minutes. I prefer foil, as it is easy to roll up and toss, no washing necessary.

Salty Tip
Before frying, put a pinch of salt in the pan.
It should keep the oil from spattering so much.

It is best to store the stalks whole and unwashed, in a standing glass of water and place the glass on a refrigerator shelf with the tips sticking out. You can place the vegetable in a sealed plastic bag in fridge vegetable drawer if you will be using quickly. It is usually good for about five to seven days.

For a longer term option, asparagus may be frozen for 6-8 months, but should be cooked or blanched first and placed in freezer safe containers.

Olive Oil Facts - Generally speaking, olive oils fall into one of two broad categories: unrefined (virgin and extra virgin), and refined (pure and light).

Olives used to make the two virgin, unrefined oils are cold pressed and not treated with heat or chemicals. The olives are simply pressed and squeezed to get the oil out. Olives that produce the highest quality oil in terms of rich taste and acidity make extra virgin olive oil. Slightly riper olives, that are also just pressed, produce virgin olive oil.

To be graded extra virgin, the olive oil must have an oleic acid content of less than 0.8%, while virgin olive oil can have as much as 2.0%, or 1.5% under International Olive Council standards.

Extra virgin olive oil is generally preferred for things like dressing and dips, where a flavorful oil is preferable and the oil is not going to be subjected to high heats that would rapidly degrade it.

The refined oils are generally made from oils that would be relatively unpalatable if bottled without further processing. They are treated with solvents and high heat to remove undesirable odors and flavors. The process leaves a relatively neutral-tasting, light color olive oil. Sometimes, in order to make light oils taste a bit like the more expensive grades, a small percentage of virgin olive oil is blended into the refined oil. Some labeled light olive oils are blended with other oils such as canola.

While the refined olive oils are less nutritious, they are also less affected by high temperatures when compared with the virgin oils. For comparison, the smoke point of extra virgin olive oil is approximately 320°F (160°C), virgin at approximately 420°F (215°C), and light at approximately 465°F (240°C). As such, it is typical to use light olive oil for baking, grilling, frying, and sautéing, essentially where high temperatures are required.

During 2015, Italian authorities discovered that 9 out of every 20 bottles of olive oil sold by its top exporters were tainted with other types of oil. Among the companies allegedly selling lesser-quality oils as "extra virgin" were Bertolli, Carapelli and Primadonna.

To get around the problem of mislabeling, in the US the California Olive Oil Council provides olive oil grade certification, with its seal appearing on certified bottles. Beyond looking for these certifications, it is also important to avoid olive oils that lack a harvest date on the label, as extra virgin olive oil's shelf life is generally only in the range of 18-24 months and a lack of such data could possibly indicate older oil being sold. Choosing oils that include their harvest date on the label ensures fresher oil.

It is best to store olive oil away from light and heat, as well as to limit exposure to air as these factors will rapidly degrade the quality of the oil.

Mustard Facts - People have been eating mustard since biblical times.

Mustard's variety is staggering, but it all comes down to one plant in the Brassica family and three types of seeds it produces: white, also referred to as yellow, because it is light yellow in color; brown, and black. The majority of commercial mustard is made with white or brown mustard seeds, or a mix of the two.

Black seeds are rarely used for mustard. They are sold whole at Indian markets and are common in Indian cooking.

Prepared mustard in a jar is: dried mustard seeds mixed with water and some other liquid, typically vinegar to get that chemical reaction going. Dry mustard or mustard flour is the dried seeds ground to a fine powder.

Brown seeds carry more pronounced heat than white seeds. The addition of other ingredients, such as wine or beer instead of vinegar, spices, herbs and the degree to which the seeds are milled give prepared mustard its personality and flavor.

Yellow or American ballpark - The classic hot dog condiment gets its bright hue from turmeric, not from the ground white seeds from which it's made. It is acidic, but not spicy hot.

> There is a National Mustard Museum in Middleton, Wisconsin, US.

Dijon - A silky smooth mustard made with brown seeds. Dijon is made in Dijon, France and must adhere to strict standards as defined by the government, but no such US standards exist. What is sold in the US as 'Dijon-style' mustard is less flavorful than the original.

Deli or American brown - This deli staple made from brown seeds is mildly spicy and not as tart as yellow mustard.

Chinese - Hot dry mustard is ground brown seeds mixed with water. The mustard that comes with egg rolls at a Chinese restaurant is in this category.

English - This mustard is made from white and brown seeds. It is most often seen in powdered form, but also sold in jars.

German - These mustards range in flavor, texture, and heat, but the two most popular styles, both made primarily with the brown seed, are hot and smooth. Bavarian-style, is coarser, milder, and sweeter.

Whole or coarse grain - This is made from a mix of whole and ground seeds, usually the brown.

Mustard, whole mustard seeds, and dry mustard retain their flavor for years. Keep both in a dark, cool spot. Jar mustard, even flavored ones can last for well over a year, but may lose its zing over time. The best way to keep jar mustard fresh is to refrigerate before opening.

Regrowing Herbs at Home - For a fun organic money saver, you can grow your own herbs with leftovers. Below are a few favorites.

Mint is an easy-to-grow perennial herb. Snip a stem off the plant so it measures about 2-3 inches lengthwise just below the leaf node (where the leaves begin to grow). Remove the lower leaves for use in your recipe, but leave a few at the top. Place the stem in a glass of water on a windowsill that receives sunshine. The mint will develop roots within a few weeks. Change the water when it starts to look murky. About a week after roots appear, plant in a pot with soil and continue to water as necessary. Keep it contained, as it develops runners and spreads quickly in a garden.

Rosemary is a great addition to pork chops, roasted meats, fish, and vegetables. Snip a few sprigs of rosemary from 2-3 inches off the top of the plant and pull away the lowest leaves, leaving a few at the top. Place the sprigs in a small glass with the stem fully immersed in water on a windowsill. Change the water every few days. Rosemary is slow to produce new roots and can take two months or longer before you see progress. About a week after roots appear, transfer the plant to soil.

Lemon Balm, Oregano, Sage, Thyme - The process for regrowing these is identical to regrowing rosemary or mint. You can even combine all in the same glass to save space, but do not pack too close as the roots will tangle.

Parsley only grows for two gardening seasons and then dies. In its first year it produces the delicious leaves that are commonly used for sauces and the second year it goes to seed. A benefit of its final year are its edible roots, which are considered the most flavorful part of the plant. The process for regrowing parsley is identical to the others above.

Fennel is slightly sweet and licorice-flavored in taste and great for poultry. I use dried fennel on pizza. The directions for growing this is different from the others. Cut off the fennel stalks and place the fennel bulb fully submerged in a bowl of water. Place in direct sunlight and change the water every few days. New fennel stems will grow within a few days.

Peanut Butter and Jelly Sandwiches - The peanut butter and jelly sandwich is such a staple of American childhood that it seems like it has been around forever. However, there are people alive today in America who grew up in a world when the PB&J sandwich was not well-known. The first known reference to a peanut butter and jelly sandwich was in a 1901 cookbook.

The first reference of peanut butter dates back to about 1000 BC with the Ancient Incas. Records show both Africans and Chinese grinding peanuts into a paste early in the 15th century. Marcellus Gilmore Edson of Montreal, Quebec was the first person to patent peanut butter. He was issued with US patent #306727 in 1884. J.H. Kellogg of cereal fame, secured US patent #580787 in 1897 for his 'Process of Preparing Nutmeal', which produced a "pasty adhesive substance" that Kellogg called 'nut-butter.' George Washington Carver was born only a few years before Edson's patent was issued and he did develop a number of uses for the peanut, but he did not invent peanut butter.

US law dictates that any product labeled "peanut butter" in the United States must be at least 90 percent peanut. Eighty percent of the peanut butter sold in the U.S. is creamy, while seventeen percent is crunchy. The rest is mixed.

The jelly part of the sandwich could mean jelly, jam, or other fruit preserves. It has also been around for a long time, going all the way back to at least the first century, mentioned in 'Of Culinary Matters' by Marcus Gavius Apicius.

Mr. Welch developed Grapelade from Concord grapes in 1918, which proved to be extremely popular among the troops during World War I. When they got back from the war, they spread the practice of using it on bread. *I just enjoyed a PB&J on a toasted English Muffin.*

Six More Peanut Butter Facts - Peanut butter may have long-term health benefits. One recent study showed that girls between the ages of 9 and 15 who regularly ate peanut butter were 39 percent less likely to develop benign breast disease by age 30.

Peanut butter is loaded with potassium, which is shown to help counteract the effects of a high-sodium diet by relaxing the blood vessels. This is especially helpful when pairing peanut butter with bacon.

> Animal trainers for movies and TV achieved a 'talking horse' effect by feeding them sticky peanut butter and letting them flap their jaws.

Thomas Jefferson did peanut farming before becoming president.

Peanut butter and jelly sandwiches are considered the all-American school lunch food, but Canadians and the Dutch consume more peanut butter per capita than Americans do.

The peanuts in peanut butter today are a different variety than the ones used 50 years ago. During the 1960s, peanut butter was made with a combination of Spanish peanuts and Virginia peanuts. Now the less expensive runner peanuts are used.

Peanut Butter Nutrition - According to the National Peanut Board, the average American eats about three pounds of peanut butter each year, totaling about 800 million pounds nation-wide. The good news is that peanut butter is more than just a tasty sidekick for jam and bread.

Nutritionally speaking, it is a great source of unsaturated fats and vegetarian protein. Over 80 percent of the fats found in peanut butter are unsaturated, 50 percent being monounsaturated fats that can help cut bad cholesterol (LDL). Also, peanuts contain important B vitamins, potassium and resveratrol, a powerful antioxidant known to have cancer fighting properties.

Cheddar Cheese - Cheddar cheese has been around since at least the 12th century and takes its name from the English village of Cheddar. The nearby Cheddar Gorge is full of caves that offer ideal conditions for aging cheese, so dairy farmers began using their surplus milk to make a new kind of cheese. Unlike other cheeses with geographically protected names, modern cheddar can come from anywhere, not just the area around Cheddar.

Cheddar cheese eventually became one of England's most popular snacks. In 1170, King Henry II bought over five tons of the cheese for the bargain price of just a little over £10. By the time Charles I took over the throne in 1625, demand for the cheese had grown so high that the only place one could find it was at the king's court.

Holey Swiss Cheese - The majority of holes in Swiss cheese, by USDA regulation, must measure between 11/16 and 13/16 of an inch in diameter.

Armies of microbes consume lactic acid excreted by other bacteria. They belch and otherwise exude carbon dioxide gas. This produces the familiar Swiss cheese holes. These big holes are tough on current cheese slicing machines, so the industry is asking that the regulations for Grade A Swiss be revised to make the average hole 6/16 of an inch in diameter. Many are upset that the government even bothers to regulate Swiss cheese hole size.

Six Cheesy Names - *Monterey Jack* takes half of its name from a place where Franciscan friars around Monterey, CA, crafted a mild white cheese throughout the 19th century. The second part comes from Scottish immigrant David Jack, who started marketing his own version of the cheese.

When Jack first came to the US in 1841, he worked as an army contractor, and he eventually became so successful that he owned most of the real estate in Monterey County. The rapid expansion of his land holdings left him owning shares in a number of dairies and he began mass-marketing the friars' cheese recipe, first under the name Jack's cheese and later as Monterey Jack.

Colby cheese is another American invention. In 1885 Wisconsin cheese maker Joseph F. Steinwand started varying his production process for cheddar by washing the curds with cold water. The washing process cut down on the acidity of the cheese and gave it a milder flavor than regular cheddar. Steinwand named his creation after the nearby town of Colby, WI. *Longhorn Colby* refers to the size and cylindrical shape of the block the cheese comes in.

Pecorino comes from Pecora, the Italian word for sheep and this family of hard Italian sheep milk cheeses derives from it.

Hanne Nielson created *Havarti* cheese at her family's farm in Øverød, just north of Copenhagen, during the mid-19th century. Nielson decided to create a Danish equivalent to Switzerland's tasty cheeses and the buttery Havarti was the result of her experimentation. She named the cheese after the family's farm, which was known as Havarthigaard.

Mozzarella takes its name from the diminutive of the word mozza, which in Neapolitan dialect means cut. Mozza, in turn derives from the verb mozzare, which means to cut off. It refers to how the cheese is produced by cutting the curds and shaping them into the familiar ball shape.

American cheese gets its name from the British. When British colonists first came to North America, they brought their knowledge of cheddar production with them and began making cheese cheaply and in great volume. Colonists would ship the cheese back across the pond and sell it at discount prices. British shoppers did not love the quality of this 'Yankee cheddar' or 'American cheese', but since it was cheap, it sold well. By 1878, Americans were sending over 300 million pounds of cheese back to England every year.

Americans called it either yellow cheese or store cheese. During 1916, James L. Kraft patented a pasteurization process that stabilized cheese to allow for easy transport over long distances. The name American cheese stuck to Kraft's processed cheeses.

Sweet Watermelon - True. If you want to make your watermelon sweeter, sprinkle a bit of salt on it.

T-Bone, Club, and Porterhouse - T-Bone steaks, Club steaks, and Porterhouse steaks are the same. T-Bone Steak must be at least 0.25" thick. Any smaller, it would be called a Club Steak. The filet portion of a Porterhouse must be at least 1.25" thick at its widest point.

A center T-shaped bone divides two sides of the steak. On one side is a tenderloin Filet and the other is a top loin, better known as the New York Strip Steak. If you cut the bone out, you get a Filet and a New York Strip. If you leave one side on the bone, you get either a bone-in Filet or a bone-in New York Strip.

So, all T-bones contain a filet and a New York Strip and all Porterhouses are T-bones, but not all T-bones are Porterhouses.

Incidentally, Ribeye and Rib Steak are the same. The Ribeye is boneless and the Rib Steak includes the rib bone, and is often called a Bone-In Rib Eye Steak. In Australia, when the bone is removed, it is often called a "Scotch Filet". Other names include: Beauty Steak, Market Steak, Delmonico Steak, and Spencer Steak.

Baking Soda - You likely have one or more boxes of baking soda in your home. Baking soda can be used for many purposes. It cleans homes, deodorizes furniture, exfoliates skin, kills mold, polishes silver, and more. You can use it to wash your hair, to make deodorant, and to take the stink out of sweaty clothes.

Baking soda comes out of the ground in the form of minerals nahcolite and trona, which are refined into soda ash (calcium carbonate), then turned into baking soda (sodium bicarbonate), among other things. Most of it comes from the United States, which contains the world's largest trona deposit. Nahcolite, a naturally occurring sodium bicarbonate, is often found in evaporated lake basins. It is also mined in Botswana, Kenya, Uganda, Turkey, and Mexico.

Glass-making consumes about half of the soda ash and the chemical industry uses about a quarter of the output. Other uses include soap, paper manufacturing, and water treatment.

Caffeine Facts - The Mayo Clinic says most healthy adults can safely consume up to 400 mg of caffeine each day (about four 12oz. cups).

Caffeine is a central nervous system stimulant that makes us feel alert. It can also improve our mood and is associated with a reduced risk of depression. It can also increase our adrenaline level, which can leave us more irritable, anxious, and far more emotionally-charged. Caffeine has been shown to improve certain types of memory in some, but not all studies. Controlled amounts of caffeine can boost notable performance gains for athletes. Some studies also indicate caffeine is effective to increase long term memories. Although ingesting too much caffeine makes it difficult to focus on anything.

There is some evidence that caffeine, when combined with certain pain-relieving medications like acetaminophen, the main active ingredient in Tylenol, and aspirin, helps those medications take effect quicker, last longer, and increases their effects. Excedrin contains caffeine.

Here are a few common sources of caffeine:

Most 12-ounce cups of coffee contain 90 to 120 mg of caffeine,
One 12-ounce cup of Starbucks contains about 260 mg,
Dunkin Donuts has 215 mg,

<table>
<tr><td>Latte is espresso plus steamed milk
Cappuccino is espresso plus milk and foam</td><td>One 2-ounce shot of 5 hour energy contains about 215 mg,
One 12-ounce cup of McDonald's coffee has about 109 mg,
One 8-ounce can of Red Bull contains 80 mg,
One cup of brewed black tea contains about 67 mg,
One shot of espresso contains about 71 mg,</td></tr>
</table>

One 12-ounce can of diet Coke has 46 grams of caffeine,
One 12-ounce can of regular Coke has 34 grams of caffeine.

Pumpkin Reuse - Now that Halloween is over and you want to preserve the feeling a while longer, here are a few things you can do.

Use some WD40. The main ingredient in WD-40 is mineral oil—the same stuff in Vaseline It will keep your pumpkins hydrated, protected from moisture, and fresh looking. It also contains several alkanes that are water-repellant and freeze-resistant. So go forth and use it to preserve both carved and uncarved pumpkins.

Spray all over your uncarved pumpkin to keep it looking shiny and new. For carved pumpkins, spray inside and outside making sure every part is saturated. Keep in mind that mineral oil is flammable, so you may want to be cautious about putting a lit candle inside.

Another idea. Get three pumpkins of varying sizes, small, medium, and large. Paint them white. Then stack them up like a snowman. add a hat, scarf or other typical snowman clothes. The paint will help preserve the pumpkins and you can enjoy them for months as wintry guests on the front porch.

Affogato - In Italian, the word affogato means 'drowned'. For those of you not in the know, affogato is a coffee-based treat usually consisting of a scoop of vanilla gelato or ice cream drowned in a shot of espresso. Sometimes there are even additions like Grand Marnier, Amaretto, or whipped cream. It is difficult to decide whether this is a drink or a desert. Either way, it is easy to put together and will make your guests happy.

Freeze ice cream in ice cube trays, then top your ice cream cubes with room temperature coffee, they will naturally float to the top. If you like, add a shot of liqueur, a dollop of whipped cream, berries, or some ground coffee beans on top.

Diet Drink, Coffee with Butter - Some people have only coffee for breakfast, thinking it can help them lose weight, because caffeine does suppress appetite. Butter makes plain coffee considerably thicker, which makes you feel more physically full.

You can take a tip from paleo dieters and add real butter to your cup of Joe. Adding butter, which is higher in fat than cream or whole milk, will slow down the digestive process and maximize the beneficial effects of caffeine. Drop two tablespoons of melted, unsalted butter into your coffee.

One product on the market is called Bulletproof Coffee. It combines coffee beans, butter, and a few teaspoons of coconut oil to combat hunger and help your body burn fat throughout the day. This beneficial fat is a key reason the drink has taken off among paleo dieters. Ingesting butter provides nutrients that frequent breakfast-skippers miss out on.

According to dietitian Tanya Zuckerbrot, butter's fat content is key to keeping your caffeine buzz, because fat slows down the digestion process, it takes longer for your body to absorb coffee's caffeine. Rather than running through the energy boost quickly, butter helps prolong coffee's effects.

The traditional coffee additives of cream and sugar can't match butter's meal-like effects. Real butter contains the best benefits. Spreads won't offer the same texture and are made of different ingredients.

Of course, adding butter to your coffee also affects the taste. Many Bulletproof drinkers love the creamy, smooth feel of the drink, and it is often compared to the taste of a latte.

Bottled Water Sources - Companies are not required to publicly disclose exactly where their sources of collection are. Ironically, most US bottled water comes from (drought stricken) California. Almost all US tap water is better regulated and monitored than bottled water is.

Purified water is a different story. It is usually produced by distillation, de-ionization or reverse osmosis. This water can originate from either the tap or from ground water. Often labeled "purified" or "drinking water," this processed water often has minerals added to it to give it taste.

There are more than 3,600 brands of bottled water available. Many now come packed with vitamins, minerals, probiotics, flavors, and natural and artificial sweeteners.

The various types of bottled water are sourced from:

Well water (water found underground that is trapped by rocks or sand)

Spring water (collected at the source of a spring)

Groundwater (mineral water contains natural minerals dissolved from the source)

Distilled water (collected from the steam of boiled water)

Purified water (water from anywhere, but it is treated to remove chemicals).

About 55 percent of bottled water in the United States is spring water, including Crystal Geyser and Arrowhead.

Evian, Perrier, and Vittel come from natural springs in France. FIJI Water comes from a source in the Yaqara Valley of Viti Levu, one of Fiji's two principal islands, and is now the number one imported bottled water in the United States. San Pellegrino comes from mountain springs in Italy. Mountain Valley Spring Water comes from Arkansas. Saratoga Springs comes from New York and is injected with additional carbonation during bottling. Everest water comes from Texas, Glacier Mountain comes from Ohio, and only about a third of Poland Springs water comes from the actual Poland Spring, in Maine.

Aquafina and Dasani use tap water and treat it. In fact, Aquafina, was recently forced to change their labels to reflect the true source of their water: Public Water Source, in other words, tap water. Coca-Cola bottling plants, which produce Dasani, use 1.63 liters of water for every liter of beverage produced in California.

The following are bottled water brands who refuse to release the location of their water source.

    Big Y Natural Spring Water
    Cool Springs Purified Drinking Water
    Crystal Clear Bottled Water Purified Drinking Water
    Deja Blue Purified Drinking Water

Floravita 2000 Super Aqua Ultrapure Premium Water
H2om Natural Spring Water
Kroger Distilled Water
Nursery Purified Water
Publix Drinking Water
Simply H2o
Smart Sense Purified Water
Sunnyside Farms Purified Water
Trader Joe's Electrolyte Enhanced Water
Vintage Natural Spring Water
Voss Artisian Water
Whole Foods Italian Still Mineral Water
365 Everyday Value Spring Water.

The International Bottled Water Association lists more than 20 brands of bottled water that contain fluoride. A few of the brands are Arrowhead, Deer Park, Hinkley Springs, Nursery Water, Ozarka, and more. DS Services and Nestle Waters North America are the most common manufacturers listed.

A new type, Alkaline water, also called ionized water has claimed health benefits. However, researchers have not yet verified claims that alkaline water can cure illnesses or prevent certain conditions. Most doctors agree more studies are needed.

> *Whole milk has just 3.25 per cent fat content vs. 2 percent and 1 percent milk.*

The consensus between the two main water quality regulating groups EPA and EWG, and health research is that bottled water is inferior in quality to tap water. This is due to the extreme filtering process and type of disinfection used.

Whole Fat Milk - Contrary to current publicity, children who drink whole milk are leaner and have higher vitamin D levels than those who drink low-fat or skim milk, according to a recent study at St. Michael's Hospital, Toronto, Canada.

Another interesting fact to back up that study, childhood obesity has tripled in the past 30 years while consumption of whole milk has halved over the same period.

Birthday Cakes and Candles - The Ancient Greeks served some form of cake with candles to honor Artemis, the goddess who, among other things, had dominion over the Moon. As such, people offered cakes that were not only shaped like the celestial object, but decorated with lit candles, presumably to make it glow. It has also been reported that smoke from the candles was thought to help the goddess hear an individual's prayers as it ascends to the heavens.

Persians and Romans are known to have celebrated the birthdays of at least some 'commoners', although it does not appear that the custom was as ubiquitous as it is today. Rather, when a wealthy person reached a major milestone like 50, family and friends might throw the person a party and serve a special cake. However, it does not appear that they put candles on the birthday cakes.

The Chinese have long had birthday celebrations, though eating cake on that day has only been a recent practice, adopted from the Western world. In China it is traditional to eat longevity noodles on one's birthday.

German bakers during the 15th century, began marketing single-layer cakes for birthdays. By the end of the 18th century, the practice became common in the west. The Germans were also adding candles on the birthday cakes, numbering at least the years the child had been alive plus often more in the hope of a long life to come.

During 1746 Count Nikolaus Ludwig von Zinzendorf had "a cake as large as any oven could be found to bake it, and holes made in the cake according to the years of his age, every one having a candle stuck into it, and one in the middle."

It was not until the end of the 19th century that ordinary people had sufficient funds and ingredients were cheap enough, that the masses began incorporating enriched, frosted birthday cakes as part of a birthday celebration.

Fluffly Eggs - A friend of mine, Jeff Flanagan passed along this quick scrambled egg tip. Instead of butter or spray for a pan coating, use a little olive oil. Much fluffier eggs. I verified this and it works.

Chalaza - When you crack an egg, there is the white albumen, the yolk, and that strange white string. It is called the chalaza, and its job is to hold the yolk in place in the center of the white. It is completely edible, but is sometimes removed during baking for aesthetic reasons.

Hot Cheese - Sometimes new products come around that just tickle me. The Fondoodler, a hot glue gun for cheese, is one of them and it is a big seller.

It can be described as a culinary caulking gun that dispenses hot, coagulated cheese over your bacon, nachos, crackers, or tongue.

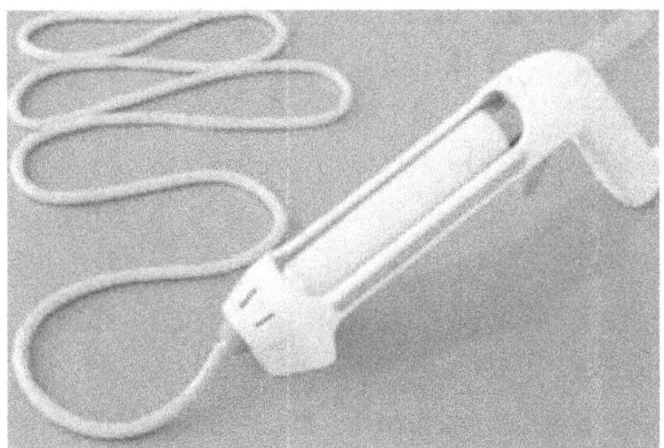

Load up the canister with whatever cheese you see fit, let it heat up for three minutes, wave goodbye to any semblance of shame you may have once had, and cover everything with pure, melty cheesiness. Of course, you can just drizzle it directly into your open mouth.

Every piece of the Fondoodler can be washed in a dishwasher. The Fondoodler costs $25.

More Egg Tidbits - To clean a dropped egg up off the floor cover it in salt to help it congeal, then clean.

The older the hen, the bigger the egg.

Eggs can stay good in the refrigerator for up to a month after the sell-by date on the carton.

Seven More Peanut Butter Facts - Peanut butter more or less as we know it today was popularized at the 1893 World Fair. In the early 1900s, peanut butter made frequent appearances in tea rooms across the nation where it was billed as a dish for rich people. Back then, it was paired with items, such as cucumbers, cheese, celery, and crackers. At that point, peanut butter was still considered a "high end" food and peanut butter and jelly sandwiches were not a commonly eaten food item.

Peanut butter spread to the masses during the 1920s and 1930s, shortly after pre-sliced bread came into existence. At that time commercial brands Skippy and Peter Pan began.

With the Great Depression, peanut butter on bread became a staple in many American households, because it provided a hearty, filling meal with a cheaper-than-meat substitute for protein.

During WWII the peanut butter and jelly sandwich became a popular meal among United States soldiers. When soldiers arrived home from the war, peanut butter and jelly sales skyrocketed.

The PB&J is a bigger hit in the United States than in most other countries.

The average American will eat around 1,500 peanut butter and jelly sandwiches by the time they turn 18.

Incidentally, peanuts are not nuts, they are legumes (a type of plant with seeds that grow inside pods like peas or beans). Nuts are grown on trees, peanuts grow underground. March is National Peanut Month.

Pemmican - It is a concentrated mixture of fat and protein used as nutritious food. The word comes from the Cree root word pimî, "fat or grease". It was invented by the natives of North America. It is often called the ultimate survival food and is still used today.

"If God did not intend for us to eat animals, then why did he make them out of meat?" ~John Cleese

Specific ingredients used for pemmican were usually whatever was available. The meat was often buffalo, deer, elk, or moose. Fruits such as cranberries, choke cherries, blueberries, and saskatoon berries were sometimes added. Now, honey, maple syrup or peanut butter are also added.

The meat, with fat removed was cut in thin slices and dried, either over a slow fire or in the hot sun, until it was hard and brittle. About 5 pounds (2,300 g) of meat are required to make 1 pound (450 g) of dried meat suitable for pemmican. Then the meat and berries were pounded into almost powder-like in consistency, using stones. The pounded meat was mixed with melted fat in an approximate 1:1 ratio. Now it is made using food processors or blenders.

Pemmican was widely adopted as a high-energy food by Europeans involved in the fur trade and later by Arctic and Antarctic explorers. The resulting mixture was usually packed into rawhide bags for storage. It can be safely stored for many decades. It is usually served raw, boiled in a stew, or fried. Pemmican beef jerky and pemmican energy bars are still sold in the US and Canada.

Incidentally, During the Second Boer War (1899–1902), British troops were given an iron ration made of four ounces of pemmican and four ounces of chocolate and sugar.

Banana Facts - The wonderful banana probably first grew in Southeast Asia, and did not make a big impact elsewhere until the early Islamic period when it was brought from India to the Middle East, and on to Africa. The banana turned up in Europe before that, but only as an exotic rarity. In ancient Rome, it had to make do with borrowing the name of the fig (a notion which lived on in the early French term for 'banana', figue du paradis).

Spanish and Portuguese colonists took the banana with them across the Atlantic from Africa to the Americas, and along with it they brought its African name, banana, apparently a word from one of the languages of the Congo area (it has been speculated that it derives ultimately from Arabic banana 'finger, toe', an origin which would be echoed in the English term 'hand' for a bunch of bananas, and serves as a reminder that many varieties of banana are quite small, not like the large sizes imported into Britain).

Since the end of the nineteenth century Bananaland has been used by Australians as a colloquial and not completely complimentary name for Queensland, a state where the banana is a key crop. Even less complimentary is banana republic, a term coined in the 1930s for small volatile states of the South American tropics (from their economic dependence on the export of bananas).

Butter Types - The three main types are uncultured, cultured, and European-style.

Uncultured or sweet cream butter, churned from pasteurized cream is the supermarket standard.

Cultured butter is made from cream that has been fermented with 'good bacteria', and it is churned longer and slower, according to the American Butter Institute.

European-style butter is made similarly, but not all European-style butters are cultured.

Both cultured and European-style butter have less water, more butterfat (from 82 to 87 percent) and a tangier, deeper flavor than mellow, sweet cream butter. There are salted and unsalted versions of each.

There are other variations of butter, such as 'light' butter, which has more water and about half the fat and calories than regular butter, but because it is made to be spreadable, it also contains preservatives and emulsifiers. Whipped butter gets its light, spreadable texture from nitrogen whipped into it after churning. USDA-certified organic butter comes from cows raised on organic, pesticide-free feed, without antibiotics or growth hormones.

Salt adds flavor and extends the shelf life of butter. According to the US Butter Institute, unsalted butter has a two-week refrigerator shelf life and salted butter two months. The USDA is a bit more generous, giving a range of one to three months. What you buy from the store has probably been in cold storage for longer than that. If you are not using your butter quickly, it will stay fresher if you store it in the freezer, where it will keep for up to nine months.

Texas Rangers Food - It is baseball season and the Texas Rangers are changing their famous "Boomstick" and taking it up a notch for the 2017 season.

Here is the "Most Valuable Tamale", a 2-foot tamale filled with the Rangers' 24-inch "Boomstick" hot dog and covered with all sorts of foodie goodies.

Taco Bell Beef - Taco Bell 'meat' is made up of 36 percent beef. The other 64 percent includes: water, isolated oat product, wheat oats, soy lecithin, maltodrextrin, anti-dusting agent, autolyzed yeast extract, modified corn starch and sodium phosphate, as well as beef and seasonings.

Banana, Herb or Fruit - The banana plant is a hybrid, originating from pairing two South Asian wild plant species. Every Cavendish banana, the most widely known in the world, is genetically identical.

They are cultivated from cuttings under the ground. A banana (the yellow thing you peel and eat) is a fruit, containing the seeds of the plant. However, commercially grown banana plants are sterile and the seeds are reduced to little specks. The banana plant is called a 'banana tree' in popular use, but it is technically regarded as a herbaceous plant or herb, not a tree, because the stem does not contain true woody tissue.

> A banana is both a fruit and herb.

Natural Foods - Natural is a broad term used to describe products that are minimally processed, and free of synthetic dyes, coloring, flavorings and preservatives. Products labeled "natural" can still contain fructose corn syrup and GMOs. The term is largely unregulated by the USDA. Even meat, poultry, and egg products can still have antibiotics and growth hormones, and can be fed on GMO feed. The US FDA has not developed a definition for use of the term natural or its derivatives.

The USDA says, claims indicating that a product is natural food, such as "natural chili" or "chili - a natural product" would be unacceptable for a product containing beet powder which artificially colors the finished product. However, "all natural ingredients" might be an acceptable claim for such a product.

The UK FSA guidance states: "The term 'natural' without qualification should be used ... to describe single foods, of a traditional nature, to which nothing has been added and which have been subjected only to such processing as to render them suitable for human consumption."

Natural or all natural labels are more marketing than fact based. Naturally, this is all unnatural label mumbo jumbo that means little, but makes us feel good.

Organic Food - Multi-ingredient agricultural products in the US "Made with organic" category must contain at least 70 percent certified organic ingredients (not including salt or water). These products may contain up to 30 percent of allowed non-organic ingredients. All ingredients – including the 30 percent non-organic ingredients – must be produced without GMOs.

Tomato Preservation Tips - Keep your tomatoes at room temperature, ideally in a single layer out of direct sunlight. To keep them fresher longer, store them stem side down. If they do not lay flat, peel more of the stem off, until they can lay flat on a counter or plate. Also, it is OK to store in the refrigerator if you will use them within a few days. Last, you do not need to keep them in a brown paper bag, unless there are flies in the area.

Keep Fruit Fresh - One way to keep your fruits and veggies fresh longer is with an inexpensive ethylene gas absorber. It can extend the life of fruits and veggies by weeks or more vs. using nothing. Ethylene is a harmless, odorless, and colorless gas that is given off naturally by fruits and vegetables as a signaling mechanism for produce to ripen faster. Many growers add extra ethylene or absorbers to their delivery trucks to hasten or reduce ripening during fruit's trip to the store.

These are relatively cheap and come in various guises, such as food storage tray liners for fridge, plastic apples filled with absorber, 'stayfresh' bags, and sachet type packets. Some of them use a coated zeolite, which has a honeycomb like structure which absorbs odor and ethylene. Depending on type, the absorbers last about three months to a year in constant use. When not in use, they can be stored in an airtight container almost indefinitely, for later use.

Odor produced by:	Will be absorbed by:
apples	cabbage, carrots, celery, figs, onions, meat, eggs, dairy products
avocados	pineapples
carrots	celery
citrus fruit	meat, eggs, dairy products
ginger root	eggplant
grapes fumigated w/sulfur dioxide	other fruits and vegetables
leeks	figs, grapes
onions, dry	apples, celery, pears
onions, green	corn, figs, grapes, mushrooms, rhubarb
pears	cabbage, carrots, celery, onions, potatoes
potatoes	apples, pears
peppers, green	pineapples
Herbs	citrus fruit

There is scientific evidence that absorbers are effective and growers would not waste money on technology that does not work. A US Navy test showed a 245% improved shelf life for tomatoes, 88% for lettuce, and 10% for cucumbers. All indications are that they work best in closed area, rather than simply putting an absorber on a counter next to fruit. They can be purchased online and at Walmart, Bed Bath, etc. I read many comments from users and they appear to work as advertised, which is a pleasant change these days.

More Egg Facts - Most eggs are not egg-shaped. Hummingbirds lay eggs that look like Tic Tacs, owls lay almost perfect spheres, and sandpipers lay almost conical eggs that end in a rounded point. Swift eggs are pointed, more like pine nuts than Tic Tacs. The most common shape, exemplified by a songbird called the graceful prinia, is more pointed than a chicken's. Eggs of 1,400 bird species had measurements extracted from 50,000 photos. It revealed the left-field nature of chicken eggs.

Incidentally, if you dissolve an egg shell in acid, the naked egg will still retain its original shape due to the internal membranes.

Vanilla vs. French Vanilla Ice Cream - Both are made with vanilla beans for flavor. Vanilla ice cream is more white and French vanilla ice cream tends to have a slightly yellow coloring.

The name French vanilla is derived from the classic French way of making ice cream using an egg custard base. French vanilla ice cream has egg yolks, which give it a smoother consistency and its distinctive yellow hue. The taste is a bit richer and a bit more complex than a regular vanilla, which is made with just milk and cream.

Burger and Booze Home Delivery - Saw an ad that shows Friday's is starting home delivery of booze along with food. It claims to be first to home deliver this combination and is rolling out in Dallas and Houston, Texas, then nationwide during 2018. The liquor and mix come separate and you need to mix it yourself. It will be interesting to see how this will work with so many unique local liquor laws around the country.

Spaghetti Scooper - Have you ever wondered what the hole in the middle of the scooper is for? It is to measure one serving of spaghetti, it also helps drain water after cooking. *Now you know.*

Bacon Facts

Three Kinds of Bacon - They are: smoky, sweet, and funky.

Funky bacon is funky, because it is not necessarily made of pork, or it is cured or seasoned in a prominent way. Funky bacon can also be sweet or smoky.

A smoky bacon can be sweet, but a sweet bacon is qualified by its sweetness and has a lack of overall smokiness.

All bacon should be salty, without allowing the salt to overpower and should be cut in a way that is appropriate to its use and the bacon's own fat-to-meat ratio.

The fat-to-meat ratio should be a one-to-one balance of fat to meat, one that errs on the fatty side. A 60 percent fat to 40 percent meat ratio is the limit of acceptability for a standard bacon slice (cut from 1/16 to 1/8 inch thick).

Bacon Cures - Cured bacon cures disease. Not a joke. Dr. Jennifer Gunter found that bacon has historically been used to stop severe nosebleeds, which can potentially be extremely hazardous, by stuffing it up your nostrils (the saltiness of the meat constricts blood vessels).

Bacon can also be used to expedite the removal of harmful Dermatobia hominis parasites by using it as bait (they like bacon, too).

Bacon can also treat scabies, by rubbing rendered bacon fat on yourself, which is apparently 88% effective compared to actual medicine.

Bonus, bacon can also reduce hunger and boredom.

Candied Bacon - If you love maple syrup and if you love bacon, Bob Evans should be on your breakfast list of places to visit. It is now serving a candied bacon appetizer.

"It's so crunchy, it doesn't even feel like meat, but it tastes like meat," said one taster. "It's sweet and savory and it's still crisp," said another satisfied taster. "It's God's food," said another of the pulcritudunous porcine product.

Healthy Bacon - Health concerns, at least when it comes to bacon may not be much of a concern for the average American. According to the National Pork Board, ten pounds of bacon is sold annually per person, demonstrating the continuous popularity of pork.

The sweet and salt combo will the spot for breakfast, lunch, brunch, or dinner and every snack in between.

Incidentally, recently, a British man legally changed his name to Bacon Double Cheeseburger.

Bacon Bow - Here is something completely different. Japanese girls have begun wearing plastic food as head decorations. I really appreciate this tasty looking bacon bow.

Stone Age Bacon - Oetzi the famous "iceman" mummy of the Alps appears to have enjoyed a fine slice or two of Stone Age bacon before he was killed by an arrow some 5,300 years ago. His last meal was most likely dried goat meat, according to scientists who recently managed to dissect the contents of Oetzi's stomach.

"We've analyzed the meat's nanostructure and it looks like he ate very fatty, dried meat, most likely bacon," German mummy expert Albert Zink said at a talk in Vienna.

More specifically, the tasty snack is thought to have come from a wild goat in South Tyrol, the northern Italian region where Oetzi roamed around and where his remains were found in September 1991.

Tilapia vs. Bacon - Nutritionists have referenced a study that implies eating tilapia is worse than eating bacon. Dr. Floyd Chilton, professor of physiology and pharmacology who directed the Wake Forest study, says the comparison of tilapia to bacon was taken out of context.

A 4-ounce serving of tilapia has about 29 grams of protein and about 200 mg of omega-3. By comparison, a 4-ounce serving of bacon has 40 grams of protein and 228 mg of omega-3.

The report said the, "inflammatory potential of hamburger and bacon is lower than the average serving of farmed tilapia (100 g)." The fish currently tests in the "red zone" for the presence of banned or illegal chemicals such as antibiotics, malachite green, and methyl testosterone hormones used in Chinese tilapia production.

Incidentally, the USDA does not currently have guidelines for classifying seafood as organic.

First Moon Meal - The first full meal eaten on the Moon consisted of bacon, cookies, and coffee, along with some peaches, and a glass of grapefruit juice. However, this is not the first food consumed on the moon.

When Buzz Aldrin set off on the Apollo 11 mission, he took with him a small communion kit given to him by Rev Dean Woodruff, so that he could symbolically take part in the ceremony with the other members of his Presbyterian church. This kit contained a small piece of communion bread and a small vial of wine, both of which Aldrin consumed after saying a prayer during the Apollo 11 radio blackout. This was also, unsurprisingly, the first religious service held on the Moon. *Of course moon meal, another first for beloved bacon. It proves bacon is out of this world goodness.*

Bacon and Nose Bleeds - According to a study conducted by the Detroit Medical Center, bacon can quickly and effectively treat a nosebleed by serving as a nasal tampon. For this bizarre method to work, one must plug the bleeding nostril with a piece of cured uncooked pork. (see bacon cures back a page)

The team tested their bacon hypothesis on a girl who had Glanzmann thrombasthenia, a rare hereditary disease that causes prolonged bleeding. After sticking a piece of cured pork inside the girl's bloody nose, the bleeding stopped immediately.

The results of this scientific research were published in the Annals of Otology, Rhinology, and Laryngology. The researchers acknowledged that doctors had used cured pork to treat nosebleeds in the past. However, the practice was discontinued.

The researchers speculated that the high risk of acquiring parasitic and bacterial complications from stuffing one's nose with cured pork caused the unconventional treatment to be abandoned.

Calendar and Holiday Facts

National Days to Celebrate - January 19 was National Popcorn Day, January 20 is National Cheese Day and January 21 is National Hug Day. Followed on January 24 with Global Belly Laugh Day. *What a week, popcorn and cheese followed by hugs and topped off with a great big belly laugh to be heard 'round the globe.*

World Cancer Day - Saturday, February 4 is World Cancer Day 2017. The day is celebrated to raise awareness of all types of cancer and to encourage the prevention and treatment of cancer. The idea is to become aware and push for actions that will reduce premature deaths, improve quality of life, and increase cancer survival rates.

National Lame Duck Day - On February 6 National Lame Duck Day recognizes the ratification of the 20th Amendment on February 6, 1933 to the United States Constitution, or the Lame Duck Amendment.

The term 'lame duck' originated as a description of stock brokers in 1700s England who could not pay off their debts. The term later carried over to businessmen who, while known to be bankrupt, would continue to do business.

The official record of the United States Congress of January 14, 1863 read, "In no event ... could [the Court of Claims] be justly obnoxious to the charge of being a receptacle of 'lame ducks' or broken down politicians." In politics a lame duck is a person currently holding a political office who has either: lost a re-election bid, chose not to seek another term, was prevented from running for re-election due to a term limit, or the office held has been eliminated.

Prior to the ratification of the 20th Amendment to the United States Constitution there was, for Congress a 13 month delay between election day and the day the newly elected officials took office. In the case of a lame duck, this was a 13 month notice his or her job was terminating, crippling his or her influence. Hence the lame or injured duck. The 20th Amendment shortened this period from 13 months to 2 months and changed the dates for the beginning of the new Congress to January 3 and when the newly elected president took office from March 4th to January 20th.

During a lame duck session, members of Congress are no longer accountable to their constituents. It is possible for their focus to switch to more personal gain instead of acting on behalf of their constituents with an eye toward re-election. Lame duck Congresses have declared war, impeached a president, censured a senator, and passed the Homeland Security Act among other actions. Lame duck Presidents have pardoned many criminals, issued executive orders, confiscated land to create national parks, declared areas to be newly opened or newly restricted from drilling for oil, created additional federal judges, provided executive clemency for family members, and more.

Jimmy Carter's administration published more than 10,000 pages of new rules between Election Day and Ronald Reagan's Inauguration Day. When President George W. Bush took office in 2001, his administration acted to block the implementation of 90 final rules that were issued in the final months of the Clinton administration, but that had not yet gone into effect.

Incidentally, unlike the United States Congress, there is no 'lame duck' session of Parliament in most Commonwealth countries between the general election and swearing in of elected officials.

Happy National I Want You to be Happy Day - Celebrated March 3. This day was created as a day encouraging us to do something to make others happy. Putting a smile on someone's face tends to put one on yours, too.

Pancake Day - Pancake Day is celebrated primarily in the UK, Ireland, Canada, and Australia. It is also known as Shrove Tuesday, Pancake Day is the day before Ash Wednesday, which is the first day of Lent.

Pancake Day was originally a pagan celebration of the changing of seasons, a sort of recognition of the maddening battle this time of year between very cold and beginnings of Spring. Pancakes, in their roundness and warmth, symbolized the sun.

Incidentally, a Bristol-based design firm called Kinneir Dufort has come up with a 3-D printing machine that uses facial recognition technology to print your likeness on a pancake. The system utilizes both the high-tech and the low-tech to mirror your face, combining complex face-recognition and tracking software with the practice of layering strokes of pancake batter onto a hot plate to result in color gradation caused by the varied cooking times of different parts.

IHOP National Pancake Day - Unlike the worldwide pancake day, IHOP has its own. It began as a charitable event during 2006. Head over to IHOP on Tuesday March 7 for a free short stack of pancakes. IHOP encourages a donation for its charities supporting children battling critical illnesses.

Daylight Saving - March 11, 2017, 2am was the time to change your clocks and the batteries in smoke and fire detectors. This time of year we again tear the bottom off the blanket and sew it on the top as we heed the political call to control time and change our clocks to Spring Forward. Lots of fun as we continue the semi-annual game to convince ourselves that we are indeed the masters of time. Meanwhile the birds and bees happily continue to forage, blissfully ignorant of our plight.

Happy National Pi and Potato Chip Day - Not sure how it happened these two are celebrated on the same day, March 14. Especially because Pi is infinite without repetition and eating potato chips is infinite with repetition. Regardless, I bet you cannot eat just 3.14 potato chips, especially if they are Better Made brand.

Happy Easter - Here are a few events that take place around the world leading up to and on Easter.

Semana Santa is held within cities across Spain and Mexico. It means Holy Week, the period leading up to Easter Sunday. All shops and stores except restaurants close and the entire city is transformed. Fifty five different churches take part in the festival, parading large floats that resemble Jesus in some way. The floats make their way from their church of origin to the cathedral, and then back again. It draws tourists from all over the world.

The *Epitáphios Threnos* is a tradition in Greek Orthodox religions that is held on Good Friday. It means Lamentation at the Tomb, and is in essence a funeral service to respect the death of Jesus by re-enacting the way he was buried after his crucifixion. It takes place in churches, where an epitaphios is placed atop something representing the tomb of Christ. The epitaphios is a highly-adorned piece of cloth that represents the shroud Jesus was wrapped in. The tomb is decorated with flower petals and rosewater. Interactions with this tomb vary depending on tradition. Some will hold it over the church entrance so that believers pass under it, a symbol of entering the grave alongside Christ.

The *Easter Ham* story states that a wicked queen named Ishtar (became root of Easter) gave birth to a son called Tammuz. This son would become a hunter, but his career was cut short when he was killed by a wild pig. Ishtar then designated a forty day period (the source of Lent) to mark the anniversary of Tammuz's death. During this time, no meat was to be eaten. Every year, on the first Sunday after the first full moon after the spring equinox, a celebration was made. Ishtar also proclaimed that because a pig killed Tammuz, that a pig must be eaten on that Sunday.

Another theory states that, while lamb was usually the go-to dish for its symbolism with Passover, ham would be used because pigs were considered a symbol of good luck. Another source gives a more practical approach. Before the invention of refrigeration, pigs were slaughtered in the fall and preserved during winter. Should some of the meat not be consumed during the winter months, it would be cured so it could be eaten during springtime around Easter, making it an ideal dish for the season.

In the United Kingdom, a select few people are given money the day before Good Friday. These coins, known as *Maundy Money*, have a long history. It began when Jesus gave the command, "That ye love one another" after he washed the feet of his disciples. This became a fourth century tradition where the poor have their feet washed and are given clothes. This stopped around the eighteenth century, and was replaced by an allowance to give the poor a chance to buy food and clothing. Today, a selection of elders receive a red and white purse. The red one contains legal currency, while the white one contains special symbolic Maundy coins. The people are selected by the amount of Christian service they have performed. In 2017, the Queen handed out commemorative Maundy coins in a traditional royal service at St. George's Chapel at Windsor Castle. Ninety men and ninety women, representing her 90 years, were presented with the coins in recognition of service to the Church and community. The red purse contained a £5 coin, commemorating the Queen's 90th birthday, and a 50p coin commemorating the 950th anniversary of the Battle of Hastings. The white purse contains one, two, three and four silver penny pieces, which add up to the Queen's age.

Haux Omelets are made every year on Easter Monday, the residents of Haux, France create a large omelet. They can be three yards wide to feed 1,000 people. One year's omelet consisted of 5,211 eggs, 21 quarts of oil, 110 pounds of bacon, onion and garlic.

Every Easter in Bacup, England, The *Britannia Coco-Nut Dancers*, or Nutters, perform a folk dance from one town boundary to the other. What makes these dancers unique is their blackened faces, but no one is sure of their origins. It might be from medieval times to hide the faces of those who participated to stop evil spirits from getting their revenge, or it may have ties to the mining industry. The Nutters blackened faces have no racial aspect.

More Happy Easter - Easter is celebrated on April 16 2017. Put on your Easter bonnet and read some of the traditions around the world.

The Ukrainian Easter tradition of Pysanka Eggs is a special craft. These highly-decorated eggs have been made during Holy Week for generations. While people once made eggs to ensure fertility and avoid fires and nasty spirits, today they take to the art form for the aesthetic allure.

After designing a pattern on an uncooked or empty egg, it is then dipped in a colored dye. Between the dyeing stages, the craftsman draws patterns on the egg with wax, so as to seal the color currently on the egg and create the intricate patterns you see on the final product.

Passion Plays - Villagers take part in an Easter Passion Play re-enacting the crucifixion of Jesus Christ on Good Friday at Gantang Village near Magelang, in the province of Central Java.

One of the longest running traditions of Easter is the Passion Play. Because a lot of people in medieval times could not read, plays were a great way to educate the masses about the story of Jesus' death and resurrection. There are passion plays held all over the world, but one of the most famous is the Oberammergau Passion Play. Its roots began during the black plague, when the residents of Oberammergau were on high alert to keep the disease out. A farmer coming home from a nearby village brought the plague back with him, which killed one-fifth of the town. With the disease ravaging the town, the elders declared that the church would hold a passion play every 10 years in exchange for God's blessing and protection. The play has been performed every 10 years since 1633, with only a ban in 1770, World War I, and World War II stopping three shows.

Don't forget to decorate your Osterbaum - Easter tree with colorful decorated eggs.

International Day of Happiness - The International Day of Happiness is celebrated throughout the world on March 20. It was founded by United Nations during 2012, when all 193 member states of the United Nations General Assembly unanimously adopted the resolution.

The General Assembly,[...] Conscious that the pursuit of happiness is a fundamental human goal. . . Decides to proclaim 20 March the International Day of Happiness, Invites all Member States, organizations of the United Nations system and other international and regional organizations, as well as civil society, including non-governmental organizations and individuals, to observe the International Day of Happiness in an appropriate manner.

World Bipolar Day - I went back and forth as to whether to include this, then decided I should. Seriously, the day, March 30 was chosen, because it is the birthday of Vincent Van Gogh, who is believed to have had bipolar disorder.

World Bipolar Day is a day to remember that those who have bipolar disorder are capable of achieving great things and to remind them that they are not alone. The vision of World Bipolar Day is to bring world awareness to bipolar disorders and to eliminate social stigma.

National Protocol Officer's Week - I hesitated to include this one also, but it seemed like the right thing to do. It is celebrated, the week of March 26-April 1 (last week of month). A Protocol Officer is educated and trained to be a skilled advisor, expert, and leader who plans and orchestrates VIP visits and trips, meetings, ceremonies, and events. Leaders rely on Protocol Officers to guide them in US and foreign order of precedence, customs, and cultural differences. I presume they need a week, because all those protocols difficult to accomplish in a day.

Doctor's Day - March 30 is celebrated in healthcare organizations as a day to recognize the contributions of doctors to individual lives and communities.

The first Doctors Day observance was March 30, 1933 in Winder, Georgia. Eudora Brown Almond, wife of Dr. Charles Almond, decided to set aside a day to honor physicians. This first observance included mailing greeting cards and placing flowers on graves of deceased doctors. The red carnation is commonly used as the symbolic flower for National Doctors Day.

Happy National Tartan Day - The US Senate Resolution on National Tartan Day was passed on March 20, 1998. Tartan Day is a celebration of Scottish heritage on 6 April, the date on which the Declaration of Arbroath was signed in 1320. Thirty four states have their own official tartan. Like official flowers and birds, the patterns in have been adopted by legislators as legitimate state symbols.

It commemorates the Scottish Declaration of Independence, from which the American Declaration of Independence was modeled. It also recognizes achievements of Americans of Scottish descent. National Tartan Day parades occur in major cities on or around April 6. They often feature bag-pipe bands playing Scottish music and people dressed in kilts with tartan patterns that represent their Scottish clans.

Six Interesting April Facts - 1. The Romans called this month Aprilis which may derive from the verb aperire meaning "to open", referring to flowers and fruits opening.

2. April was the 216th most popular name given to a baby girl in England and Wales in 2015 and the 191st most popular in Scotland.

3. Of the eight US presidents who died in office, three died in April.

4. April is the first month of the year with exactly 30 days and the only month with an "i" in its name.

5. In the UK, April is national awareness month for pets, mathematics, stress, irritable bowel syndrome, bowel cancer, and jazz.

6. The Anglo-Saxons called April Eostre-Monadh, possibly named after a pagan goddess.

Cheese Weasel Day - It is the only Internet holiday to say thanks to Techies for all they do. It began in the early 1990s, is celebrated on April 3 or the first Monday after April 3, and has been dishing out great fun ever since then.

Legend has it the Cheese Weasel travels the world, leaving a bit of cheese under keyboards or mouse pads of good techie boys and girls, men and women. Have some fun and surprise your favorite geek with some cheese on that day.

Give your favorite techie a Thank You shout out using #cheeseweaselday on Facebook, Twitter, Google+, or your favorite social site. If you are not close by on that day, send a picture of some cheese. They will understand.

Earth Day - Earth Day observance arose from an interest in gathering national support for environmental issues.

In 1970, San Francisco activist John McConnell and Wisconsin Senator Gaylord Nelson separately asked Americans to join in a grassroots demonstration. McConnell chose the spring equinox, March 21, 1970 and Nelson chose April 22.

National Pig in a Blanket Day - April 24th is National Pig in a Blanket Day. It is a humble dish enjoyed around the world.

National Pretzel Day - April 26 is National Pretzel Day. Eat some pretzels, low in calories and a healthy salty treat. Dunk a pretzel in chocolate. Wrap some pretzels in bacon and add some chocolate. The possibilities are endless. Enjoy!

International Dance Day - It was introduced in 1982 by the International Dance Council, and is celebrated on April 29 each year. The main purpose of Dance Day events is to attract the attention to the art of dance. Every year, the president of the CID sends the official message for Dance Day which circulate in every country of the world.

Tai Chi Day - Last Saturday of April each year we celebrate World Tai Chi and Qigong Day in 80 nations. People come together, to breathe together and provide a healing vision for our world.

Oatmeal and Raisons - April 30 is National Oatmeal Cookie Day and National Raisin Day is celebrated on the same day. *Oatmeal raisin cookies are among my favorite.*

Seven Facts about May - No other month begins or ends on the same day of the week during the year as May.

The Empire State Building opened for all on May 1, 1931. This 443 meter tall building held the honor of being the tallest building of USA until the World Trade Center claimed the glory. However, after the WTC attack on 9/11, this building became the tallest building (including antenna) of New York again.

May celebrates many days, beginning with the May Day on the first day of May. This is also known as international workers' day, a celebration of laborers and the working classes that is promoted by the international labor movement, socialists, communists, or anarchists, and occurs every year on May Day.

Mother's Day is celebrated on the second Sunday in May. Memorial Day is celebrated on the last Monday in May. Armed Forces Day is the third Sunday in May.

Nurses are heavily (and rightfully) honored during the month of May. There is National Nurses Day, May 6, National Student Nurse Day, May 8, and National School Nurse Day, Wednesday of National Nurse Week May 6 - 12. The American Nurses Association has designated 2017 as the "Year of the Healthy Nurse (ANA defines a healthy nurse as someone who actively focuses on creating and maintaining a balance and synergy of physical, intellectual, emotional, social, spiritual, personal, and professional well being.)

Happy Cinco de Mayo - It is celebrated May 5 and is a holiday commemorating the date of the Mexican army's 1862 victory over France at the Battle of Puebla during the Franco-Mexican War (1861-1867). A relatively minor holiday in Mexico, in the United States Cinco de Mayo has evolved into a celebration of Mexican culture and heritage.

Happy Obscura Day - Celebrated May 6, 2017 and is dedicated to the celebration of exploration and discovery. Caution, it can be extremely addictive for the curious. As an example of the types of thing you might find on Atlas Obscura, Molly Lewis whistling Gluck's Melodie "Dance of the Blessed Spirits". The date changes each year.

Celebrate the world's most curious and inspiring places. Explore places like Alexandria, Virginia's Taverns & Women & Chocolate, Bozeman, Montana's Inside the American Computer Museum, Bridgeport, Connecticut's Behind the Scenes with the Barnum Museum and many more fascinating places around the world.

National Limerick Day - It is observed annually on May 12 and celebrates the birthday of English artist, illustrator, author, and poet Edward Lear. He is known mostly for his literary nonsense in poetry, prose, and limericks.

National Limerick Day also celebrates the limerick poem, a very short, humorous, nonsense poem. Within a limerick, there are five lines. The first two lines rhyme with the fifth line and the third and fourth line rhyme together. The first, second, and fifth lines must have seven to ten syllables while rhyming and having the same verbal rhythm. The third and fourth lines only need to have five to seven syllables, and need to rhyme with each other and have the same rhythm. The limerick also has a particular rhythm which is officially described as anapestic trimeter.

A limerick example of a nursery rhyme.
   "Hickory, dickory, dock,
The mouse ran up the clock.
The clock struck one,
And down he run,
Hickory, dickory, dock."

There once was a man named Lodge,
who had seat belts installed in his Dodge.

When his date was strapped in,
He committed a sin,
without ever leaving the garage.

A bather whose clothing was strewed
By winds that left her quite nude
Saw a man come along
And unless I am wrong
You expected this line to be lewd.

Mother's Day - In the US, Mother's Day is celebrated May 14. In the UK, Mothering Day was celebrated March 26, where it is always celebrated on the fourth Sunday of Lent, three weeks before Easter Sunday.

Anna Jarvis had originally conceived of Mother's Day as a day of personal celebration between mothers and families. During 1914, President Woodrow Wilson signed a measure officially establishing the second Sunday in May as Mother's Day in the US. It wasn't to celebrate all mothers. It was to celebrate the best mother you have ever known, your mother.

The day took off in Britain when a vicar's daughter, Constance Smith was inspired by a newspaper report of Jarvis' campaign and began a push for the day to be officially marked in England. Smith founded the Mothering Sunday Movement and even wrote a booklet, "The Revival of Mothering Sunday" in 1920. Interestingly, neither Smith nor Jarvis became mother's themselves.

The French celebrate Mother's Day on the last Sunday in May. Mother's Day in Spain is celebrated on December 8th.

May 7 is World Naked Gardening Day - People are encouraged to tend to the various flora around or outside their home while in the nude. The event is celebrated annually on the first Saturday of May. *Not too much fun in urban Texas where most neighbors have high fences.*

John Wayne Day - A few years ago, Texas declared a statewide John Wayne Day to commemorate the iconic actor's birthday on May 26th for his cinematic contributions to the culture of America.

Texas also named Wayne an honorary Texan, though Wayne, born Marion Mitchell Morrison, was actually born in Iowa. Many films that he starred in were filmed in Texas and for many Texans he has always been an honorary son of the Lone Star State.

Memorial Day, May 29 - Memorial Day is often confused with Veterans Day. Memorial Day is a day of remembering the men and women who died while serving, but Veterans Day celebrates the service of all U.S. military veterans.

Pinch Bum Day, May 29 - I always chuckle when I add this holiday. May 29, also known as Pinch-Bum Day, to commemorate the return of Charles II to London on that date in 1660. Those who did not wear oak leaves could be pinched. Our ancestors were clearly over-fond of this form of retribution, but at least then women could do it to men, also.

Happy National Donut Day - It is celebrated on the first Friday in June. That sweet, doughy goodness that has a day set aside holey in its honor. Go out for some freebies from your favorite donut shop today.

Incidentally, the name was originally hyphenated, as in "balls of sweetened dough, fried in hog's fat, and called dough-nuts, or oly koeks (oily cakes): a delicious kind of cake made by Dutch families." When phonetic-based spelling reform came along, it was changed to donut, which was popularized by Dunkin' Donuts and has become the more popular spelling.

Father's Day - In 2017, Father's Day is June 18. Happy Father's Day to all the fathers in the world. This holiday traces its roots to 1910. However, it took until 1966 for US President Lyndon Johnson to issue a proclamation designating the third Sunday in June to honor fathers. Then, US President Richard Nixon signed a law declaring that Father's Day be celebrated annually on the third Sunday in June. It has been an official, permanent national holiday ever since.

> *"When I was a boy of 14, my father was so ignorant I could hardly stand to have the old man around, but when I got to be 21, I was astonished at how much the old man had learned in seven years."*
> *~Mark Twain*

A bit of history - Mrs. Sonora Smart Dodd thought it might be nice to honor fathers and proposed to the Spokane Ministerial Association and the YMCA that they celebrate a 'father's day'. She chose the 5th of June because it was her father's birthday. The idea received strong support, but the ministers asked that the day be changed to give them extra time to prepare sermons on the subject of fathers. The first Father's Day was observed on June 19, 1910, in Spokane, Washington, and soon other towns had their own celebrations.

Father's Day is celebrated around the world, but many countries celebrate on different days.

Middle Day

July 2, at noon is the
exact middle of the year.
It has 182 days before
and 182 days following.

Canada Day, eh - July 1 is Canada Day. This year, it celebrates Canada's 150th anniversary of Confederation.

Incidentally, The first Saturday in July is also International Cherry Pit Spitting Day. Past year winning spits -
2014   Brian Krause   Dimondale, MI   80' 8"
2015   Kevin Bartz   Niles, MI   48' 8"
2016   Rick Krause   Tuba City, AZ   48' 2 1/4"

2017 Rick Krause Sanders, AZ captured his 17th victory as the 2017 International Cherry Pit Spitting 57' 11"

(Brian Krause is also holder of the US record cherry pit spit of 93' 6 1/2", set during 2003.)

July 4th, Independence Day - Thomas Jefferson, third President of the United States, died the same day in 1826 as John Adams, second president of the United States, on the 50th anniversary of the adoption of the Declaration of Independence. A few years later, fellow founding father, and fifth President of the United States, James Monroe passed away on July 4th, 1831. Interesting that three of the first five American presidents died on the 4th of July.

Incidentally, The people of France offered the Statue of Liberty Enlightening the World to the people of the United States on July 4th, 1884.

Let's remember what Independence Day is really all about, even if they call it just another paid day off in Washington, where they have traded in Free Speech for Cheap Talk.

Hot Dog Day - It is on July 14 and celebrated all over the world. Enjoy some dogs today, especially with bacon and cheese or other toppings of choice.

Bastille Day - The French recognize Bastille Day, July 14, officially National Day or formally La Fête Nationale as the end of the monarchy and beginning of the modern republic. The lasting significance of the storming of the Bastille event was in its recognition that power could be held by ordinary citizens. Today, Parisians celebrate this national holiday with a grand military parade up the Champs Elysées, colorful arts festivals, fireworks, and raucous parties.

World Eskimo-Indian Olympics - July 19 - 22, 2017, the third Wednesday in July, at the Carlson Center in Fairbanks.

WEIO gives people and participants a chance to see supreme feats of endurance and agility and the rare chance to experience a culture alongside those who live within it. WEIO is a time to share stories through dance and display parkas, kuspuks, mukluks, moose hide dresses, vests, and jewelry at the Native Arts & Crafts fair. In additional there is a cultural Miss WEIO pageant to showcase talents and traditional knowledge. Events include: Native Regalia and Baby Regalia contest, Knuckle Hop, Blanket Toss, High Kick, Stick Pull, and more.

Flitch Day - July 19 is Flitch day. The Flitch Trials are held every 4 years in Great Dunmow, Essex, England. The town is located northeast of London, just off the A120 between the M11 at Stansted Airport and Colchester.

4,000 Flitches lined up and ready to go.

Dating back to 1104 in Dunmow Priory, England, monks offered a side of bacon (flitch) to any married couple proving a year and a day after their wedding that they had lived in harmony and fidelity for the past year and had not wished they were single again.

A flitch is a measurement of bacon, now known as a slab.

This tradition was brought to America by English settlers, but did not survive.

Flitch trials are still held in Great Dunmow, England once every leap year. They are organized by the Dunmow Flitch Trials Committee. The jury that reaches a verdict consists of six maidens and six bachelors, even though there is no longer an actual trial. Great Dunmow is believed to be the only location to have preserved the flitch of bacon custom.

National Sleepy Head Day - National Sleepy Head Day (Finnish: Unikeonpäivä) is celebrated in Finland on July 27 every year. Traditionally on this day, the last person in the house (the laziest) to wake up is woken up using water, either by being thrown into a lake or the sea, or by having water thrown on them. Other traditions include shaving the left side of the laziest man's chest. It is based on the story of the Saints of Ephesus who slept in a cave for some 200 years during the Middle Ages whilst hiding from persecution by Decius, the Roman Emperor at the time.

In the city of Naantali, a Finnish celebrity is chosen every year to be thrown in the sea from the city's port at 7 a.m. The identity of the sleeper is kept secret until the event. People who are chosen have usually done something to the benefit of the city. Every city mayor has thus far been thrown to the sea at least once, but other sleepers have included president Tarja Halonen's husband, Dr. Pentti Arajärvi, the CEO of Neste Oil Risto Rinne, along with many writers, artists, and politicians.

Chauvin Day - On the anniversary of Napoleon Bonaparte's birthday August 15, we celebrate the interesting etymological history of the word "chauvinism," which comes from a man named Nicholas Chauvin, who so idealized Napoleon that he became internationally mocked for his blind loyalty to a cause. The term became associated with any misguided or ill-intentioned adherence to a particular cause and the discriminatory mindset it refers to today.

Happy National Aviation Day - During 1939, Franklin D. Roosevelt issued Presidential Proclamation 2343, making August 19, Orville Wright's birthday, National Aviation Day.

Spumoni Day - August 21 is National Spumoni Day in the United States. It is not as popular as it used to be when there were many more Italian ice cream shops around. Spumone (plural spumoni) is a molded Italian ice cream made with layers of different colors and flavors, containing candied fruits and nuts. It is usually three flavors, cherry, pistachio, and either chocolate or vanilla and the fruit/nut layer often contains cherry bits, causing the traditional red/pink, green, and brown color combination. Dreyer's and Edy's still make the delicious mix. My mouth is watering for some with pistachio ice cream. Yum! *Incidentally, November 13 is National Spumoni Day in Canada.*

Mr. Hyde National Burger Day - August 25 was the fourth annual National Burger Day in the UK (celebrated on last Thursday in August). It was launched by Mr. Hyde, a daily email service for men covering style, culture, film and places to eat meat. It began three years ago in a fit of mild indignation that there was not a National Burger Day in the UK, but were two in the US. The event set out to right that wrong.

During 2015 there were 475 restaurants across England, Scotland, and Wales giving 20% discounts for burgers on the day. This year's events were bigger and better. So far over 925 restaurants signed up nationwide to celebrate the big day. *Nice to see our English cousins enjoy a good, wet, juicy burger almost as much as we do.*

Just Because Day - We celebrate the unofficial holiday each year on August 27. You can celebrate this day any way you choose, just because. It started during the 1950s and has been growing in celebrations since then.

Every day we all do things that are expected or required of us. On National Just Because Day, that does not apply. The day is a chance to do something without reason. How about that person you have secretly been wanting to kiss; do it, just because.

Possibly you want to sing really loud while in your car by yourself with your windows rolled down; do it, just because. I may walk around the block backward, just because.

August Fact - In common years no other month starts on the same day of the week as August, except during leap years when February starts on the same day. August ends on the same day of the week as November every year.

September Odd Holidays - Here are a few, just in case you need another reason to celebrate.

National One Hit Wonder Day - September 25
Johnny Appleseed Day - September 26 (1774)
National Pancake Day - September 26
Crush A Can Day - September 27
Gone-ta-pott Day - September 28
Ask a Stupid Question Day--September 28
Confucius Day - September 29
National Mud Pack Day - September 30

International Bacon Day - Well, it is that time of year again when we get to celebrate something we all enjoy - BACON. The Saturday before Labor Day we celebrate International Bacon Day.

Aussie Father's Day - In Australia and New Zealand, Father's Day is celebrated on the first Sunday of September.

Labor Day and Labour Day in Canada - This is observed on the first Monday in September.

National Biscuit Month - September is National Biscuit Month. A biscuit is a kind of small, flat-baked bread product that is usually made with a chemical leavener such as baking powder. The exact meaning varies in different parts of the world. A biscuit can be a hard baked sweet or savory product like a small, flat cake, which in North America may be called a "cookie" or "cracker". The term biscuit also applies to sandwich-type biscuits, where a layer of cream or icing is sandwiched between two biscuits. Some of the original biscuits were British naval hard tack.

In American English, a biscuit is a small bread made with baking powder or baking soda as a leavening agent rather than yeast. This roughly corresponds to a scone in British English usage.

Biscuits have a firm browned crust and a soft interior, similar to bannock from the Shetland Isles. A sweet biscuit layered or topped with fruit, typically strawberries, juice-based syrup, and cream is called shortcake. In Canada, both sweet and savory are referred to as biscuits, baking powder biscuits, or tea biscuits, although scone is now also used.

Biscuits are a common feature of Southern US cuisine and are often made with buttermilk. They are traditionally served as a side dish with a meal. As a breakfast item they are often eaten with butter and a sweet condiment. With other meals they are usually eaten with butter or gravy. However, biscuits covered in country gravy are usually served for breakfast, sometimes as the main course.

Happy Conception Day - September 12 is Conception Day in Russia and couples get the day off specifically to have sex. *Who says Russians have it so bad?*

National Vodka Day - October 4 is the day "The Water of Life" takes center stage. The versatile, once virtually tasteless and odorless tipple accounts for almost 33% of spirits sold today in North America, making it a most popular libation since the 1970s.

German American Day - An annual holiday on October 6th, it marks the day in 1683 when 13 German families arrived in Philadelphia to set up home, although Germans had been in the US since 1608.

Germans make up the largest self-reported ancestry group in the States, their numbers beat Irish, African, English, Mexican, and Italian Americans.

Canada Thanksgiving - Our friends from the great white north celebrate Thanksgiving on the second Monday in October. Interesting to note that although the date is different, the celebration and meals are the same as in the US. It corresponds with the European and English harvest, and a bit different in that it truly is for giving thanks for a bountiful harvest. It has more religious undertones than the US celebrations. Also, in some Provinces, it is an optional holiday.

Columbus Day - Columbus Day is a holiday celebrating the anniversary of Christopher Columbus' arrival in the Americas on October 12, 1492. The event is celebrated in many countries including the United States, Argentina, Venezuela, Colombia, Chile, Mexico, and Spain. Since 1970, the US holiday has been fixed to the second Monday in October. Most States observe the holiday, although 17 states do not.

Incidentally, due to some of his unsavory practices, but still not willing to give up a free day off, some people in the US are trying to change the reason for celebration. Maybe we should join our friends up north, call it Thanksgiving and change that holiday to Pilgrims day.

Celebrate National Emergency Nurses Day - Wednesday, October 12, 2016. They work very hard under difficult conditions. If you know an Emergency nurse, wish him or her well.

Happy World Egg Day - Happy World Egg Day. It was established at the Vienna, 1996 conference, which decided to celebrate World Egg Day on the second Friday in October each year.

Eggs are one of nature's highest quality sources of protein, and indeed contain many of the key ingredients for life. The proteins contained within eggs are highly important in the development of the brain and muscles, have a key role to play in disease prevention, and contribute to general well being.

Failure - *International Day for Failure* is celebrated on October 13th. A holiday intended for people to share stories of failure and learn from them. The goal of the people organizing the event is to have it be an internationally-recognized holiday by 2020. *Maybe next year...*

Halloween - Halloween is October 31. Here is a Halloween Hack - If you want your carved pumpkin to last longer, rub some Vaseline on the cut parts. *Boo!*

Movember - It began in 2003, and the Movember movement has grown to be a global one, inspiring support from over 5 million Mo Bros and Mo Sistas. Men can help by growing a mustache during the month of November, then attending or throwing a party to raise funds for men's health. It is a very worthy cause. My nephew participates each year and has turned his group's costume parties into major events as well as fundraisers.

> The average drinker takes ten sips to finish a pint of beer, of which 0.56 milliliters of Guinness is trapped in the average mustache at every sip.

The Movember foundation says, "We're the only charity tackling men's health on a global scale, year round. We're addressing some of the biggest health issues faced by men: prostate cancer, testicular cancer, and mental health, and suicide prevention. We know what works for men, and how to find and fund the most innovative research to have both a global and local impact. We're independent of government funding, so we can challenge the status quo and invest quicker in what works. In 13 years we've funded more than 1,200 men's health projects around the world."

Happy Veterans Day - This is the day we honor our US veterans. They gave so much. They ask so little. Please honor each of them as best you can.

Love Your Lawyer Day - Love Your Lawyer Day, really! It was created in 2001 by attorney Nader Anise, American Lawyers Public Image Association, to begin a campaign of: "No Lawyer Bashing or Jokes for a day." That's it, just do not tell lawyer jokes on that day. Seems easy enough - Uh, did you hear the one about the lawyer, the donkey and the pig. . .

Happy Birthday Mickey Mouse - Steamboat Willie was first released on November 18, 1928, in New York. It was co-directed by Walt Disney. "I only hope that we never lose sight of one thing – that it was all started by a mouse." ~Walt Disney

----

International Men's Day - International Men's Day that is celebrated every year on November 19. It is dedicated to celebrating men and raising awareness of men's issues and rights.

World Toilet Day - Totally, completely, and absolutely not related to International Men's Day. World Toilet Day is a day to raise awareness and inspire action to tackle the global sanitation crisis.

Happy Thanksgiving - Hope your Holiday is filled with good fun, good family, good friends, good drinks, and good food!

Santa Con and Santa Run - For over 20 years, many groups of people have dressed up like Santa to participate in annual pub crawls. The Santa Con originated in San Francisco in 1994 and has since spread to over 40 countries and 300 cities around the world.

Santa Runs are a bit different, but just as widespread around the world. Groups of people dress up like Santa and do a 2.5k, 5k run/walk to support various, mostly local charities.

Groups sizes of both vary from the hundreds to thousands of revelers. Both are meant to provide good fun for participants and onlookers.

Although many cities have already held their 'runs' and 'cons' there are still a few yet to be enjoyed. Check your local newspapers for details and if you get the chance, join in.

Go ahead get off your butts and have some good clean non-denominational, non-sectarian, non-religious, non racist, non-anti Semitic, non-misogynistic, non-deplorable Holiday fun. Get out there with your friends, make some new friends, get some exercise, and enjoy some fresh air and conversation, away from the TV, Internet, and politics. Wish everyone a Merry Christmas, Happy Hanukah, or Seasons Greetings - with no other agenda than having some fun for a change.

Computer Christmas Songs - "The Christmas tree is filled with flowers. I swear it is Christmas Eve. I hope that is what you say." These are lyrics to a holiday song. You are thinking it is a boy band totally drunk. You assume they are trying to revive a rock band vibe until they fall on their foreheads and their manager rings for a designated driver.

However, the song did not come from a human. The Guardian's Ian Sample, science editor, explained what happened in simple terms. "Scientists fed a Christmasy photograph with a tree and presents into a computer and let it do its thing." Sample said the creators call it "neural karaoke."

The program sang the lyrics to music that it composed along the way. The project is at the University of Toronto. "By feeding the neural network a particular scale, it gives the system a series of notes it can choose from to make a melody." A lab student trained a neural network on 100 hours of online music. Once trained, "the program can take a musical scale and melodic profile and produce a simple 120-beats-per-minute melody. It then adds chords and drums."

The University of Toronto team effort is one example of interest among AI researchers choosing to explore computers and music-making. In September this year it was announced that "At SONY CSL Research Laboratory, we have created two entire pop songs composed with Artificial Intelligence, thanks to Flow Machines." The Flow Machines software learns music styles from a huge database of songs. Then, exploiting unique combinations of style transfer, optimization and interaction techniques, it can compose in any style.

Gingerbread - Christmas time of year we see many confections made with gingerbread. It has long been woven into the fiber of American history. George Washington's mother, Mary Ball Washington, developed a recipe for gingerbread cake in 1784. Gingerbread was Abraham Lincoln's 'biggest treat' and he invoked a gingerbread anecdote in his Lincoln – Douglas debates. Witches used gingerbread men as voodoo dolls in the early 17th century.

During the late Middle Ages, Europeans had their own version of gingerbread. The hard cookies, sometimes gilded with gold leaf and shaped like animals and kings and queens were a staple at Medieval fairs in England, France, Holland and Germany.

Queen Elizabeth I is credited with the idea of decorating the cookies in this fashion, after she had some made to resemble the dignitaries visiting her court. Over time some of these festivals came to be known as Gingerbread Fairs, and the gingerbread cookies served there were known as 'fairings'.

Shapes of the gingerbread changed with the season, including flowers in the spring and birds in the fall. Elaborately decorated gingerbread became synonymous with all things fancy and elegant in England. The gold leaf that was often used to decorate gingerbread cookies led to the popular expression 'to take the gilt off of gingerbread'. The carved, white architectural details found on many colonial American seaside homes is sometimes referred to as 'gingerbread work'.

Gingerbread houses originated in Germany during the 16th century. The elaborate cookie-walled houses, decorated with foil in addition to gold leaf, became associated with Christmas tradition. Their popularity rose when the Brothers Grimm wrote the story of Hansel and Gretel, in which the main characters stumble upon a house made entirely of treats deep in the forest. It is unclear whether gingerbread houses were a result of the popular fairy tale, or vice versa.

Recently the record for world's largest gingerbread house was broken. The previous record was set by the Mall of America in 2006. The new winning gingerbread house, spanning nearly 40,000 cubic feet, was erected at Traditions Golf Club in Bryan, Texas. The house required a building permit and was built much like a traditional house. 4,000 gingerbread bricks were used during its construction. A recipe for a house this size would include 1,800 pounds of butter and 1,080 ounces of ground ginger.

Gingerbread gets its name from the ginger root and its color from molasses. The ginger root has long been associated with many health benefits. It is thought to aid in digestion, be an anti-inflammatory aid, help with menstrual cramps and morning sickness, fend off disease, and even relieve some of the nausea associated with motion sickness. Some folks use it to relieve heartburn as well. It is usually made with a variety of spices, including brown sugar, molasses, granulated sugar, honey, and/or light or dark corn syrup.

Merry Christmas - I wish each of you a sincere Merry Christmas. I hope you get everything you need, all you deserve, and most of which you want.

Eight Other December 25 Events - December 25, 325 is the first date that Christmas was celebrated specifically on December 25.
December 25, 597 England adopted the Julian calendar, now used by most of the world.
December 25, 800 Charlemagne is crowned Holy Roman Emperor by Pope Leo III.
December 25, 1066 William the Conqueror is crowned King of England.
December 25, 1717 the great Christmas Flood ravaged the Netherlands and parts of Germany and Scandinavia.
December 25, 1776 - 11pm, General George Washington, along with 5,400 men, crossed the Delaware River, in order to surprise Hessian troops celebrating the Christmas Holiday.
December 25, 1914 the Christmas Truce. During World War I, the Germans began to sing Christmas Carols, crossed the lines, met with Allies and both shook hands. (The next day they resumed fighting.)
December 25, 2002 University of New Mexico junior place-kicker Katie Hnida attempts to kick an extra point in a game against UCLA in the Las Vegas Bowl. She is first woman to play in Division I football.

Happy Boxing Day - In the UK, Canada, Australia, and New Zealand Boxing Day is celebrated on the first weekday after Christmas.

Incidentally, The day after Christmas, December 26 is celebrated as Saint Stephen's (patron saint of horses) Day. It is one of the reasons Boxing Day has come to be associated with horse racing and fox hunting.

Gemütlichkeit - This word is perhaps best translated as 'coziness', but the one English word can only express one aspect of the German meaning. It is a great word for winter and for the Holidays in particular.

Gemütlichkeit is epitomized by a snug room with a sofa nestled next to a roaring open fire, and the friendly, jovial atmosphere, and the resulting state of mind.

Germans use it to refer to many things from people, to a beer in a warm pub, to evenings watching a film.

The OED defines Gemütlichkeit as, "the quality of being pleasant cheerful; cozy, snug, homely; genial, and good-natured".

Even though it is an accepted word in English, it is yet to find its way into everyday language. *Regardless, my wish to you all for this Holiday Season is Gemütlichkeit!*

What's in a Name, Santa Claus - In the United States and Canada, his name is Santa Claus.

In China, he is called Shengdan Laoren.

In England, his name is Father Christmas.

In France, he is known as Pere Noel.

In Germany, children get presents from Christindl, the Christ Child.

Customs of the Christmas Season in Spanish speaking countries have many similarities and many variations. All of Latin America and Spain are predominantly Catholic. For many of these countries Baby Jesus, el Niño Jesus, brings gifts for children. In Colombia, and parts of Mexico, the gift bearer is el Niño Jesus, "the infant Jesus." In Brazil and Peru, he is called Papai Noel.

> "One of the most glorious messes in the world is the mess created in the living room on Christmas day. Don't clean it up too quickly."
> ~ Andy Rooney

In Puerto Rico, children receive gifts from the Three Kings on January 6, also called the celebration of Epiphany, or Three Kings' Day. Each child puts grass under their bed for the camels. In the morning the grass is replaced with gifts. Also, Puerto Rico has its major gift giving on December 25, with the Christmas Tree and Santa Claus. Epiphany remains a part of the holiday season and is a day off from school.

In Italy Babbo Natale, which means Father Christmas, is Santa. Children put a pair of their shoes by the door on the day before Epiphany and the following morning they find them filled with small gifts and candy. Italy, Spain, Portugal are also mostly Catholic. December 25 is a day of more religious observance, remembering the birth of Christ. The Epiphany, called Little Christmas, is the day for gift giving. However, Babbo Natale does come on Christmas Eve in some parts of Italy.

In Spain children leave their shoes under the Christmas tree the night of January 5th and presents from the Three Kings (Los Reyes Magos) appear the next morning. Santa Claus is called Papa Noel and some children receive presents both days on December 24th from Papa Noel and on January 6th from the Three Kings.

In Japan, Santa Claus is called Santa Claus or just "Santa". Children often call him "Santa no ojisan", which means "Uncle Santa".

In Sweden Jultomten visits the evening before Christmas day, pulling a big bag of julklappar (Christmas presents) in the deep snow.

Pã Norsk (in Norwegian) Julenissen arrives on the evening of December 24.

In the Netherlands, he is called Kerstman.

In Finland, he is called Joulupukki.

Sinter Klaas in Dutch, is much thinner than the American Santa Claus. He rides a white horse and gets help from numerous Zwarte Pieten (Black Petes) handing out gifts and candy. He arrives the first Saturday in November by boat. In the evenings, Dutch Children sing songs in front of the fire place and leave their shoe with a present, such as a drawing for Sinterklaas and Zwarte Piet or a Carrot for Amerigo Sinterklaas' horse. In the mornings they find their shoe filled with candy and small presents. On the fifth of December Dutch households have a "Pakjesavond" (Presents night) and exchange presents.

In Russia, he is called Grandfather Frost. He is also called Kris Kringle - which comes from the German term 'the Christ Child'.

Mummers - The Mummers Parade is held each New Year's Day in Philadelphia, Pennsylvania, US. It is believed to be the oldest folk festival in the United States.

Mummers tradition dates back to 400 BC and the Roman Festival of Saturnalias where Latin laborers marched in masks throughout the day of satire and gift exchange. This included Celtic variations of "trick-or-treat" and Druidic noise-making to drive away demons for the new year. Reports of rowdy groups "parading" on New Year's day in Philadelphia date back before the revolution. Prizes were offered by merchants in the late 1800's. January 1, 1901 was the first "official" parade offered about $1,725 in prize money from the city.

The exact origins of the word "mummer" have become obscure, but they likely had to do with masks or the act of disguise. In England, mummers have dressed up and performed Christmastime plays, which often told the story of St. George and the Dragon and featured themes of winter and rebirth, for many centuries. In some places, mummers' troupes would also go from house to house to raise funds for their celebrations.

Over time, mummering traditions diverged and developed from place to place within the British Isles and spread with British settlers, across the world. Philadelphia's Mummers' Day Parade is derived, in part, from Britain's mummer plays, in combination with Christmastime rituals that other Europeans brought to the city. As mummering has been passed down, it has morphed in each place into an idiosyncratic tradition.

One day each year, in St. John's, Newfoundland, Canada, the streets are filled with misshapen, masked figures wrapped in quilts and oversized jackets, or bright boots and distinctive dresses, with undergarments worn on the outside. Their faces are obscured behind gruesome disguises, lacy veils, giant horse heads, or beneath ghostlike pillow cases. These mummers are the latest iteration of a centuries-old tradition that has its roots in Europe, but is entirely unique to this Canadian island. More than a thousand people come out to the Mummers Parade each year, to feel what it is like to shed their normal identity for at least a few hours.

Happy Bacon Day - Bacon Day is celebrated annually on December 30th.

Bacon is a very popular food and you can find many items also flavored or scented with bacon including popcorn, soap, candles, air fresheners, and more. Do not fill up too much on Christmas. *You need to save room for Bacon Day. It is the second bacon day of the year that we celebrate bacon and its wonderfulness.*

HOROLOGY

The science of timekeeping is known as horology.

Why Clockwise - If you could look directly at the North Pole from space, it would appear to spin counterclockwise. Given that spin, when a stick is placed in the ground parallel to the Earth's axis in Egypt, the shadow cast by the stick as the Sun moves across the sky will move in a clockwise direction and a similarly placed stick in Australia would cast a shadow that moves counterclockwise.

When the ancient Egyptians and Babylonians were fashioning their first shadow clocks (~3,500 BC), the measurement of time moved in a clockwise direction. Even as more precise timekeeping methods came about, sundials (which began in earnest around 1,500 BC) remained popular throughout the middle ages and beyond, given their simplicity of construction and relative reliability. In fact, early mechanical clocks were often regularly calibrated to nearby sundials.

Screws turn clockwise because our ancestors learned that right-handed people (about 80% of people) are stronger when they screw clockwise (righty tighty, lefty loosey).

So, when mechanical clocks were introduced in Europe in the 14th century, their inventors were quite familiar with sundials and the clockwise direction that their shadows moved and marked time. Accordingly, by the end of that century when even cathedral clocks were sporting clock faces, they were made in imitation of their sundial forbears, with hands that moved in a clockwise direction.

The words clockwise and counterclockwise with present meaning did not appear in English until the 1870s.

The use of wise to mean a way of proceeding dates back to Old English. Clock dates to the invention of modern mechanical clocks during the 14th century. It is thought to come from either clokke (Middle Dutch), cloque (Old North French) or clocca (Medieval Latin) which all meant bell. Some of the earliest mechanical clocks were simply designed to strike a bell at set intervals, perhaps to announce prayer times or simply ring on the hour. Many early clocks not have a face. Before they were called clocks, these early mechanical clocks were called horologia, from the Greek for "hour" (ὡρα) and "to tell" (λέγειν).

Leap Second - Twenty-six times since 1972, the world's timekeepers have added a leap second to the clock to make up for time lost to Earth's slowing rotation. The adjustment is necessary because Earth's rotation is not regular. It sometimes speeds up, sometimes slows down, but is gradually slowing overall.

It happened again during 2016. That's right, we received one more second of 2016 added to our lives. The final minute of 2016 had 61 seconds. After all of the political nonsense during the year, it is almost like adding insult to injury to have a leap day and a leap second in the same year. *Oh well, savor the extra second of life. We can never get too many of them.*

Saudi Calendar Change - Saudi Arabia adopted the lunar Islamic calendar when it was founded in 1932. In October 2016, that all changed. Saudi Arabia moved from the lunar based Hijri calendar, which starts with the emigration of Muhammad from Mecca to Medina, and adopted the standard Gregorian calendar as a leap into modernity and as a basis for paying civil servants.

Government employees complained they would have to work an extra 11 days each year, because the Islamic lunar calendar is 11 days shorter than the 365-day solar year.

There are other calendars still in use around the world. It is 1395 in Iran, 2628 in Kurdistan, and 5776 in Israel's Knesset, 2559 in Thailand, and year 28 (of the Heisei era) in Japan.

Political Time - Less than one hundred years ago, the US Congress passed the Standard Time Act in 1918, which established a single, standard system of timekeeping for the entire US and designated its five time zones by reference to the Greenwich meridian. 'An Act to preserve daylight and provide standard time for the United States' was enacted on March 19, 1918. It both established standard time zones and set summer Daylight Saving Time to begin on March 31, 1918. Daylight Saving Time was observed for seven months in 1918 and 1919.

After the War ended, the law proved so unpopular that it was repealed the next year with a Congressional override of President Wilson's veto. Daylight Saving Time became a local option, and was continued in some states and in some cities.

After many changes to the clocks, the Energy Policy Act of 2005 extended Daylight Saving Time in the US. Beginning in 2007, Congress retained the right to revert to the 1986 DST law should "the change prove unpopular or if energy savings are not significant". Going from 2007 forward, Daylight Saving Time in the U.S. begins at 2:00 a.m. on the second Sunday of March and ends at 2:00 a.m. on the first Sunday of November. There are now seven time zones for the United States, EST (Eastern), CST (Central), MST (Mountain), PST (Pacific), AKST (Alaska), and HAST (Hawaii).

The earth is about 4.5 billion years old and finally, nine years ago, US politicians finally agreed to what time it is (unless it proves unpopular). Luckily they have not seen fit to change the calendar and we can still celebrate the New Year on January 1.

These same politicians tell us they can predict the future about many things, including global warming, but they cannot even agree on what time it is or if "energy savings are not significant".

End Thoughts

FINAL ADVICE

Need to Read - World Book Day reminded me of the pleasure of reading. In fact, reading is the cheapest and easiest form of intellectual pleasure. *TV and movies may be fun, but are rarely intellectual.*

There are various ways in which pleasures may be derived. It may be the pleasures of eating delicious food, listening to music, sitting in the cool shade of a tree and enjoying the beauty of nature, inhaling the perfume of flowers, or simply delighting in the soft touch of petals. These, basically, are pleasures of the senses.

Reading, however, is an Intellectual Pleasure and should be nurtured from an early age. Learning the truths of science or philosophy is also a form of intellectual pleasure.

There are various elements that make reading a pleasure. The reader may appreciate the style of the author, the language skills used in expressing ideas, or the arrangement of ideas. Logical sequence of thoughts or the thoughts themselves may also be appealing. The pleasures of reading are truly inexhaustible as there are a variety of books, essays, novels, dramas, sagas, poems, and speeches.

The sages of old recommend that whenever you feel dejected, depressed and under the weather, get into the company of great authors and read their books. Books can be your never failing friends and they can never get you into trouble.

Reading improves your vocabulary and enhances your imagination. The more you read, the more knowledgeable you become. With more knowledge comes more confidence and confidence builds self-esteem.

Reading widens your horizons and exercises your memory muscles.

Index